KOSHER HATE

ALSO BY SHMULEY BOTEACH

Moses of Oxford:
A Jewish Vision of a University and Its Life

The Israel Warrior:
Fighting Back for the Jewish State from Campus to Street Corner

Parenting with Fire:
Lighting Up the Family with Passion and Inspiration

Lust for Love:
Rekindling Intimacy and Passion in Your Relationship

Kosher Emotions:
Understand Your Emotions and Master Your Life

Renewal:
A Guide to the Values-Filled Life

Kosher Sex: A Recipe for Passion and Intimacy

10 Conversations you Need to Have with your Children

The Broken American Male: And How to Fix Him

The Kosher Sutra: Eight Sacred Secrets and for Reigniting Desire
and Restoring Passion for Life

10 Conversations you Need to Have with Yourself:
A Powerful Plan for Spiritual Growth and Self Improvement

Kosher Jesus

Kosher Lust: Love is not the Answer

The Fed-Up Man of Faith:
Challenging G-d in the Face of Suffering and Tragedy

Holocaust Holiday:
One Family's Descent into Genocide Memory Hell

KOSHER HATE:

How to Fight Jew-Hatred, Racism, and Bigotry

BY RABBI SHMULEY BOTEACH

WICKED SON

A WICKED SON BOOK
An Imprint of Post Hill Press
ISBN: 978-1-64293-968-2
ISBN (eBook): 978-1-64293-969-9

Kosher Hate:
How to Fight Jew-Hatred, Racism, and Bigotry
© 2021 by Rabbi Shmuley Boteach
All Rights Reserved

Cover Design by Tiffani Shea

Post Hill Press
New York • Nashville
posthillpress.com

Published in the United States of America
1 2 3 4 5 6 7 8 9 10

To

Miriam Adelson, Global matriarch of the
Jewish people and great Jewish light to the
world, whose generosity lifts the
downtrodden everywhere.

Nily, Simon, and Jana Falic whose love
for Israel, America, and freedom, courses
through their global philanthropy and veins.

David and Mona Sterling, loving friends
who support worthy causes everywhere
and whose wisdom and advice to me is
never-ending.

Without their support and others dedicated
to the triumph of light over darkness, my
lifelong fight against the evils of antisemitism, racism, and bigotry would not
succeed.

TABLE OF CONTENTS

INTRODUCTION:

UN-KOSHER HATRED IN AMERICA TODAY

THIS BOOK DEALS WITH a simple truth: the world will never become a better place until we resolve to fight and resist evil. The globe will never be peaceful until we are inspired to neutralize those who disturb the peace. And social cohesion will never be fully realized until those who seek to tear us apart are stopped.

In order to achieve this goal we must begin by making some very important distinctions. We need to think about these matters in a different way from what we are accustomed to. To this end, traditional Jewish teaching is a better guide than Christianity or modern liberalism.

Our starting point may appear counterintuitive: Love is not always good, while hatred is not always bad. Like many other things in life, it depends on the circumstances. In what follows I will use the terms "kosher" and "un-kosher" to distinguish what is good or bad about these primary human emotions.

There are times when we need kosher love—the kind of love that brings us all together. And there are times when we need Kosher Hate, that is, the kind of revulsion for wickedness that causes us to say, "Enough."

This could not be more true than in the case of Anti-Semitism, the world's oldest hatred, which is out of control and getting worse by the day, in the United States and elsewhere. As I write these words, in the aftermath of the recent eleven-day conflict between Israel and Hamas, Jews are being beaten in the streets of New York, assaulted in Toronto, and terrorized in Los Angeles. Friends have told me that even rabbis of orthodox congregations are advising their communities that they should not wear yarmulkes in the street as they walk to Shul. Others have told me stories of women hiding Magen Davids.

For me, none of this is particularly new. I spent eleven years as Rabbi to the students of Oxford University. I traveled all over Europe, where Jews are becoming a secret society, afraid to display their Jewishness in the open. We just never believed that it could happen here in the United States.

Even less did we believe that a man like Aaron Keyak, who served as President Biden's Jewish liaison during his campaign, could tweet, "…if you fear for your life or physical safety take off your kippa and hide your Magen David." Yes, an adviser to the President is reminding Jews that they are utterly powerless, and that even the most powerful man on earth cannot help them.

I could not disagree with him more. Now more than ever, we need public displays of Jewish identity and pride.

A few years ago I visited Paris with my wife Debbie. As we bought tickets to the Musée d'Orsay, the woman selling us the ticket asked my wife to cover her Magen David. We were aghast. She protested. "No, please, I don't hate Jews. Quite the contrary. I love them, which is why I want to protect you. Please hide it so you don't get hurt."

Here was a woman, working at the second most famous museum in Paris, telling us that Jews were going to be assaulted even in her museum. She may have had the best of intentions, but her words were a searing indictment of modern France. Forget the fact that it spoke to the French Republic's intolerance. More importantly, it spoke to its impotence. It could not even protect people in its capital and cultural epicenter?

Is this also going to happen in the United States? Will the most powerful country in the world succumb to anti-Jewish thuggery? Will the Jewish community surrender to Anti-Semitism? Will we teach our kids to cower in fear?

Not if we learn to practice Kosher Hate, which I define as a firm moral determination to resist and defeat Anti-Semitism, racism, and every other form of bigotry.

I would say to Aaron Keyak, "Would you advise a Muslim woman to take off her hijab to be safe? Would tell a Sikh to take off his turban? Would you have had the nerve to advise an American Christian to hide his cross? If not, why would you tell Jews to hide their yarmulkes?"

Precisely the opposite is true. Now is the time to wear our tzitzis out, to wear our kippas proudly, and to fly American and Israeli flags outside our homes. Now is the time to show courage and fearlessness. Not only so that young Jews can take pride in who they are and in the righteous democracy of Israel, but so America itself can remain the land of the free and the home of the brave. Now is the time to resist and defeat evil by inculcating within our children a moral loathing of wickedness.

My argument in this book is simple, although I also know it will engender strong reactions. There are, in essence, two forms of hate, just as there are two forms of love. There is moral love, like that between a mother and child or husband and wife; and there is immoral love, like that between a man and his mistress. Or, infinitely more odious, like that between the German people and their Fuhrer. Likewise, there are kosher and un-kosher hate. The latter is practiced by the Klan against blacks, by Hamas against the Jews, and by terrorists against democracies. This kind of hate may be described as an irrational loathing of evil against good. But there is also a "kosher" form of hate, which I would characterize as a healthy and supremely moral impulse to prevent those who are evil from harming the righteous. Kosher Hate never allows us to be indifferent in the face of evil. It removes from us the possibility of ever being a neutral bystander.

It speaks volumes that when our African-American brothers and sisters watched a man killed by a bad cop in Minnesota—and for the record, I believe most cops are heroes—they marched through the streets of our nation by the tens of thousands, emboldened by an absolute refusal to put up with ongoing racial discrimination. That's Kosher Hate in action—aimed not against Derek Chauvin himself but against institutionalized racism in our criminal justice system.

In the aftermath of the recent anti-Semitic attacks in New York and elsewhere, Jews rallied as well. But how did we do it? Not by marching bravely in the streets to affirm our identity and rights. Instead our mainstream communal organizations got together at the end of May and staged—get ready for this—an online rally!

Such timid displays of resistance will never defeat the problem of the un-kosher hatred that blames and punishes Jews here in the US for the actions of the Israeli government, which in any event are utterly righteous and just. And unless we begin to show Kosher Hate toward the perpetrators of these attacks, we risk America, in terms of anti-Semitism, becoming like Europe.

In the summer of 2017 I took my kids on a journey to the major Holocaust extermination and concentration sites of

Europe: Poland, Slovakia, Hungary, Italy, France, and more. I chronicled that journey in my recent book *Holocaust Holiday: One Family's Descent into Genocide Memory Hell*. The journey started in Berlin where, as we arrived in Tegel Airport, a security guard walked over to me to plead that I remove my young sons' yarmulkes so that they would not get hurt.

Yes, we had arrived to commemorate the martyrdom of the six million only to be told that in Europe the unkosher hatred of Jews had not abated.

America is different. It was always different. The pilgrims came here to escape Europe's religious persecution and intolerance. Enshrined in our constitution is the freedom to worship as we are and to express ourselves as we please.

We dishonor our Jewishness and commitment to freedom by suppressing that. And we dishonor America by hiding it.

Now is the time for a new generation of Americans to determine that they will no longer tolerate the intolerable or accept the unacceptable. We must resist those whose irrational hatred is tearing our country apart. Beginning with those, from left to right, who are infected with the disease of anti-Semitism, the world's oldest and most malignant prejudice.

Hatred of Jews has been one of the few historical constants of the last 2,500 years. Only one nation has ever been accused of murdering god. The Jews. And our inability to properly respond to so heinous a charge—how can anyone murder an infinitely powerful being?—brought centuries of devastation to our people. Then they accused us of being vampires, of murdering Christian children to suck out their blood. No other nation has faced a similar libel, which led to the spilling of rivers of Jewish blood.

The degree of anti-Semitism ebbs and flows, often according to local conditions and the need for a scapegoat.

When the Black Plague swept across Europe, Jews were often blamed. When the local economy declined, Jews were held responsible. Christians and Muslims alike have accused Jews of using the blood of children to make matzo for Passover. The sinister Russian forgery, *The Protocols of the Elders of Zion*, created the myth of an all-powerful Jewish cabal controlling the world. Hitler's *Mein Kampf* portrayed Jews as "the symbol of all evil" and dehumanized them to the point where "ordinary" people helped him pursue a final solution to the "Jewish problem."

As many others have noted, the establishment of Israel was the catalyst for new outbreaks of anti-Semitism. Jew haters now use "Zionist" as a euphemism for Jews while denying their own bigoted motives. Natan Sharansky suggested a "3-D" test for differentiating legitimate criticism of Israel from anti-Semitism. The first "D" is whether Israel or its leaders are being demonized or their actions blown out of proportion. Equating Israel with Nazi Germany is one example. The second "D" is the test of double standards, as when Israel is singled out for condemnation at the United Nations for alleged human rights abuses while other nations that violate human rights on a massive scale, such as Iran, Syria, and Saudi Arabia, are not even mentioned. The third "D" is delegitimization. One may criticize Israel's actions. But questioning its legitimacy, that is, its right to exist, is always anti-Semitic.[1]

As Sharansky correctly observed, a double standard exists whereby Israel is treated differently from every other country and singled out for criticism and demonization. In the United Nations, the organization established to promote world peace, Israeli actions are routinely condemned and the perpetrators of atrocities against them ignored. According to UN Watch, between 2012 and 2020, the General Assembly voted on 180 resolutions censuring Israel compared to 45 for the rest of the world.[2]

The Orwellian Human Rights Council, composed of some of the world's worst human rights abusers, has a permanent item on the agenda for just one country. Even after terrorist groups like Hamas and Palestinian Islamic Jihad committed war crimes by using civilians as shields and indiscriminately firing rockets at civilian neighborhoods, it was Israel the HRC accused of atrocities. The equally politicized International Criminal Court, which has no jurisdiction over Israeli actions, has likewise given itself a mandate to investigate the only democracy in the Middle East for its alleged crimes. In the midst of the COVID-19 pandemic, the World Health Organization found time to allow twenty-five delegations to accuse Israel of violating the health rights of Palestinians.[3]

The world has settled into a comfortable routine whereby terrorists attack Israel, the Israelis respond, and an outburst of anti-Semitism follows.

Over ten days beginning May 9, 2021, more than 4,000 rockets were fired at Tel Aviv, Sderot, Ashkelon, and other communities within their range. The terrorists know that Israel is expected to fight an antiseptic war that does no damage and kills no civilians. They use civilians as shields while firing rockets from residential neighborhoods, storing weapons in schools and mosques, and building tunnels under apartment buildings, which inevitably results in civilian deaths when Israel legitimately targets them. The result is that more Palestinians die in battles with Israel than Israelis. This imbalance is unfairly described as disproportional.

The publicity of the loss of innocent life predictably sets off new outbursts of anti-Semitism. During and after Israel's operation in Gaza, rallies were held around the world, not to protest the indiscriminate shelling of Israelis, but to condemn Israel for having the chutzpah to fight back.

Even before the war in Gaza, anti-Jewish violence has been rising in the US. There were the horrific attacks on the

Tree of Life synagogue in 2018 and the Poway Chabad in 2019. Vandalism of Jewish institutions has become common. Jews have been attacked on the streets of New York, in Jewish neighborhoods like Crown Heights and the tourist mecca of Times Square in the heart of Manhattan. During the fighting in Gaza in May the ADL reported 131 anti-Semitic incidents. The following week the number grew to 193, including one in which a group of pro-Palestinian men in cars started throwing bottles at Jews dining at a Sushi restaurant in Los Angeles while yelling "dirty Jew" and other slurs. Five people were injured in the attack.[4]

Anti-Semitism is ever-present but has become increasingly overt and tolerated. In Europe, the situation is so bad that serious people question whether Jews have any future there. Jews have felt compelled to hide their Judaism, to remove yarmulkes, Stars of David, or anything that identifies them as Jews for fear of being attacked.

One 2018 survey found that 40 percent of European Jews were considering emigrating, with two-thirds saying they would go to Israel. In Germany, the figure increased from 25 percent to 44 percent in the last five years. The situation was most frightening in France, where 80 percent of Jews said anti-Semitism had "increased a lot." Overall, 28 percent of European Jews (41 percent of Germans) said they had experienced anti-Semitic harassment over the preceding twelve months, including "offensive and threatening comments, offensive gestures or offensive comments on social media." The respondents said 30 percent of the perpetrators were "someone with an extremist Muslim view" and 21 percent were "someone with a leftwing political view."[5]

The growth of anti-Semitism has many causes. In Europe, an uninhibited far right political movement has gained legitimacy and a place in some parliaments. Neo-Nazis remain on the fringe but are increasingly vocal. A few weeks after my family visited Berlin in 2017, 500 neo-Nazis held a march commemorating the death of former Hitler deputy Rudolf Hess.

The large-scale migration of Muslims from the Middle East has also had a deleterious impact. While most European Muslims are inoffensively going about their lives, extremists have proliferated and are responsible for much of the violence directed at Jews.

While there is no talk among American Jews of mass migration, the statistics are equally grim. In a 2021 poll, the ADL found that 63 percent of American Jews either experienced or witnessed some form of anti-Semitism in the last five years, up from 54 percent a year ago. One-fourth said they had been targeted and 9 percent said they had been physically attacked in this period.[6]

Some have blamed former President Donald Trump for fueling this atmosphere through his seeming tolerance for racial bigots, starting with his comment that there were "very fine people" on both sides following a violent rally of far-right extremists in Charlottesville. That event included a march by white supremacists chanting, "Jews will not replace us." He later refused to condemn groups like the Proud Boys and QAnon conspiracists.

Trump may indeed have been too slow to condemn these white nationalists—or his words may have been taken out of context. Yet it is hard to make the charge of anti-Semitism stick. Not only are his son-in-law and grandchildren Jewish, but many American Jews, myself included, have praised him as the most pro-Israel president in American history.

After all, it was Trump who recognized Israeli sovereignty over Jerusalem and the Golan Heights and moved the U.S. Embassy to Israel's capital, overcoming decades of State Department opposition. Trump also pulled out of the catastrophic Iran nuclear deal, which was negotiated by Barack Obama despite Iran's stated intention to annihilate Israel, and took a more confrontational approach to that nation, which has threatened Israel with genocide.

He also took important steps to fight anti-Semitism at home and abroad. He appointed Elan Carr as special envoy to monitor and combat anti-Semitism and he proved to be one of, if not the most effective person to hold the position at the State Department. Under Carr, the Department encouraging other governments and international organizations to use the working definition of anti-Semitism adopted by the International Holocaust Remembrance Alliance (IHRA). A dozen countries adopted or endorsed it on his watch.

Trump also addressed the problem of anti-Semitism on college campuses, and the unwillingness of university administrators to confront the issue, by issuing an executive order to amend Title VI of the 1964 Civil Rights Act, which "prohibits discrimination on the basis of race, color, and national origin in programs and activities receiving Federal financial assistance." The order said, "It shall be the policy of the executive branch to enforce Title VI against prohibited forms of discrimination rooted in anti-Semitism as vigorously as against all other forms of discrimination prohibited by Title VI" and, in seeking evidence of discrimination, agencies enforcing the act should consider the IHRA working definition of anti-Semitism.[7]

Meanwhile, the anti-Semitic attacks we've seen in 2021 are not coming from white racists but from pro-Hamas and pro-Palestinian mobs. Which simply goes to show that Jews are being pincered from two extremes.

One of the most dangerous emerging movements is QAnon. People who support QAnon accept a variety of conspiracy theories, including that a "Deep State" operates a global sex-trafficking ring. According to the ADL, "Several aspects of QAnon lore mirror longstanding anti-Semitic tropes.

The belief that a global 'cabal" is involved in rituals of child sacrifice has its roots in the anti-Semitic trope that Jews murder Christian children for ritualistic purposes. In addition, QAnon has a deep-seated hatred for George Soros, a name that has become synonymous with perceived Jewish meddling in global affairs. And QAnon's ongoing obsession with a global elite of bankers also has deeply anti-Semitic undertones."[8]

A poll by the Public Religion Research Institute (PRRI) found that 15 percent of Americans and 23 percent of Republicans agree with QAnon's contention that "the government, media, and financial worlds in the U.S. are controlled by a group of Satan-worshipping pedophiles who run a global child sex trafficking operation."[9]

Extrapolating from this data, Hannah Sparks noted in the New York Post that "An estimated 30 million Americans are praying at the altar of Q" which means "QAnon has more followers in America than Judaism, Islam, Buddhism and Hinduism combined."[10]

While individuals from the radical right were responsible for some of the most heinous acts of anti-Semitism, such as the gunman who killed 11 people at the Tree of Life Synagogue in Pittsburgh, the extreme left has also become more openly anti-Semitic. Worse, this un-kosher hatred of Jews on the left has been legitimized by mainstream politicians.

The most blatant examples are Democratic congresswomen Rashid Tlaib (D-MI) and Ilhan Omar (D-MN), who have made what many Jewish leaders consider to be anti-Semitic comments but have been shielded by their party. In 2019, after Omar was criticized for making such remarks, the House considered a resolution to condemn anti-Semitism. But after push-back from progressives the resolution that ultimately passed was a catchall rejection of "hateful expressions of intolerance" citing a number of types of bigotry.

After Hamas started a war by launching more than 4,000 rockets at Jerusalem, Tlaib, Omar, and a number of other Democrats called on President Biden to cut off aid to Israel, to stop the transfer of weapons to Israel, and to demand that Israel stop defending its citizens. Omar, for example, tweeted, "Israeli air strikes killing civilians in Gaza is an act of terrorism....It's unconscionable to not condemn these attacks on the week of Eid."[11] She would later accuse Israel and the United States of committing the same human rights abuses as Hamas and the Taliban.

Following her comments during the fighting AIPAC placed an ad for an online petition with a picture of Omar against a backdrop of Hamas rocket fire. I was astonished when AIPAC was attacked by Democratic leaders, though given their prior unwillingness to take action against her I should not have been.[12]

The fact that anti-Semitism is accepted in the halls of Congress has helped normalize Jew-hatred nationwide.

Then there is Hollywood. One would have thought that in this most secular of bastions the Jewish State, with its emphasis on freedom, democracy, religious liberty, women's rights, and LGBTQ rights, it would receive the backing of our culture's most influential personalities. Nothing could be further from the truth.

This past summer Israel fought a genocidal enemy in Hamas, a bloodthirsty death cult with a charter calling for the extermination of Jews wherever they may be found, including in the United States, Europe, and Australia. Hamas aids and abets honor killings of Palestinian women whose only crime is to have a boyfriend. They slaughter LGBT Palestinians. They are ruthless and brutal to the wider Palestinian population, robbing them of the international funds sent to give them a better life and using them instead to fire rockets at Jews in order to murder as many of them as they can.

You would think that the choice between good and evil here would be stark and direct and that the world would stand with Israel. But in Hollywood precisely the opposite is true, as Israel is now portrayed as trying to "erase" the Palestinian people.

Take the example of Mohamed Hadid, the multi-millionaire father of supermodels Bella and Gigi Hadid, all of whom regularly vilify Israel to their tens of millions of followers on Instagram. In May he actually wrote, "No one should be allowed to erase a race... you can't close your eyes... the Pope did in WW1 and WW!! And the rest of the world stood by silently...."

Hadid shockingly compares the holocaust of six million Jews to Israel fighting back, reluctantly and with remarkable restraint, against the Hamas rockets intent on murdering children. It takes incredible audacity to accuse the Jews of genocide for merely defending themselves. This anti-Semitic blood libel should be rejected by all who value truth and human rights. Instead, the blood libel is spreading.

Hadid's daughters, Bella and Gigi, joined by the singer Dua Lipa, who is purportedly dating their brother, have become an unholy trinity of terror-splaining It-girls engaged in outright demonization of Israel and the Jewish people.

Speaking to their nearly one hundred million followers on social media, they have vilified the Jewish State with an all-consuming hatred. They accuse Israel—a nation built in large part by holocaust survivors—of ethnic cleansing, even though millions of Jews in Israel descend from refugees savagely forced out of every Arab land. They condemn Israel for the military checkpoints that were erected only after 700 innocent Israeli Jews and Arabs were blown to bits by suicide bombers on buses and in cafés, many of them sent by Hamas. They call Israel an Apartheid state, even though it is the only country in world history to airlift Africans into freedom and sets the standard for multi-racial and multi-cultural coexistence, with millions of Christians, Muslims, and Jews—black and white—living side by side and working together as doctors, teachers, and soldiers.

If Bella, Gigi, and Dua cared about Palestinians, they'd condemn Hamas, whose brutality toward women and tolerance for honor killings of Palestinian girls is an abomination. They'd demand Hamas stop its use of children as human shields for military stockpiles and rocket launch-pads, cease its regular murders of LGBT Palestinians, and reverse their denial of the Palestinian people's right to elections, after fourteen autocratic years.

Worst of all, they make themselves apologists for the genocidal aspirations of Hamas, which seeks nothing less than a second holocaust: 1,800 shrapnel-packed rockets should be more than enough to prove they mean it.

Americans are used to seeing shallow celebrities embarrass themselves with their political ignorance. But serving as apologists for genocidal terrorists takes celebrity abasement to a whole new level.

One of the driving forces of the new left-wing anti-Semitism, in Hollywood as well as on college campuses, is intersectionality. According to Mitchell Bard, this academic term "refers to the idea that race, class, gender, and other individual characteristics "intersect" with one another and overlap, and that all injustices are interconnected. Women and minorities (theoretically including Jews, but in certain instances excluding them) are seen as victims of white oppression."[13] Supporters of the Palestinians have linked their plight to that of other oppressed groups and succeeded in building anti-Israel coalitions with a range of progressive activist groups, including Jewish ones such as Jewish Voice for Peace and IfNotNow. Ziva Dahl, a fellow with the Haym Salomon Center, noted that, "Today, to the sanctimonious social justice warrior, Jews are part of the oppressor class."[14]

Among the most prominent of the social justice activists are the Black Lives Matter and Women's movements. Both are needed for important social change. Blacks Lives Matter has especially impressed me with its unapologetic demand that African-American lives be treated with the dignity they have always deserved, and rarely received. As a father of six daughters, I also care deeply about women's rights. But as a Rabbi I must ask myself, how is it that both movements have become infected by elements of anti-Semitism?

The Black Lives Matter movement is comprised of many good people seeking to improve the lives of African-Americans and lobby for police reform. Unfortunately, some of its leadership have become virulently anti-Israel. They were behind the platform released in 2016 by the Movement for Black Lives (part of the BLM coalition) that said, "The U.S. justifies and advances the global war on terror via its alliance with Israel and is complicit in the genocide taking place against the Palestinian people." The platform also compared Israel to Afrikaner South Africa, endorsed the BDS movement, and condemned Israeli settlements.[15] Speaking on a panel at Harvard Law School in 2015, Black Lives Matter co-founder Patrisse Cullors said activists should "step up boldly and courageously to end the imperialist project that's called Israel."[16]

I have spent my life working on Black-Jewish brotherhood. So I invited Blacks Lives Matter co-founder Alicia Garza to our annual World Values Network 2021 Gala as an honoree for everything she does to promote racial justice. She accepted but then came under ferocious pressure from virulent Israel haters like Linda Sarsour to cancel. Two weeks before the event she withdrew in a very public way. I thereupon wrote her an open letter thanking her for initially accepting the award and saluting her efforts in fighting racial injustice and prejudice. I noted that I too had been criticized by many of my fellow Jews for hosting the Rev. Al Sharpton on a solidarity mission to Israel, as well as for offering her an award at the gala. Financial funders withdrew support. In both instances, the complaint was about alleged support for anti-Semitism.

I then lamented her cancellation after being "made aware" of our "political positions," a decision I attributed to the direct influence of Sarsour who publicly thanked her for withdrawing. And I expressed my deep concern that Black Lives Matter activists were being influenced by those with an un-kosher hatred of Israel and the Jewish people.

In my letter I explained that I had met Sarsour in 2016 on the Steve Harvey Show, where we had what I called "a warm and extremely civilized dialogue about Jewish and Islamic relations."

I could, therefore, hardly believe how she had no issue becoming quickly radicalized against the Jewish community. In April 2017, Linda spoke alongside Rasmea Odeh at a dinner and told the audience that she was "honored to be on this stage with Rasmea," a member of the PFLP convicted in 1969 for her involvement in the bombing of an Israeli supermarket, an event that took the lives of two young students and maimed nine more. ...

That day Linda also extended her gratitude to her "favorite person in this room, Imam Siraj Wahhaj," a man known for hateful views toward the LGBTQ community, what he calls "a disease of this society." In 1992, Imam Wahhaj expressed his desire to burn down a gay-friendly mosque in Toronto, if only he could. His admonition of "woe to the Muslims who pick kafirs [non-Muslims] for friends" implies that Wahhaj is no fan of peaceful coexistence either, a fact I find surprising considering that Linda holds "radical love" to be a tenet of her faith, which most certainly is in normative Islam.

No wonder that in August 2020, President Biden explicitly condemned Linda Sarsour, stating that as a longtime supporter of Israel "he obviously condemns [her] views and opposes BDS, as does the Democratic platform. She has no role in the Biden campaign whatsoever."

Here is a direct example of a woman and co-founder of Black Lives Matter, fighting for racial justice being influenced by those with an un-kosher agenda to equate the struggle for black civil rights in America—and by extension the terrorists of Hamas—with that of Palestinians who deny Israel's right to exist.

There is, of course, no comparison between the two phenomena. Hamas is a fanatical death cult and terrorist organization that rules Gaza through corruption and fear. BLM is a peaceful and legitimate civil rights movement with broad democratic support. The error of some BLM activists in equating them led to the strange phenomenon of watching BLM fail to condemn the indiscriminate launching of rockets at Israeli towns and villages. Thus, BLM tweeted on May 17, 2021, "Black Lives Matter stands in solidarity with Palestinians. We are a movement committed to ending settler colonialism in all forms and will continue to advocate for Palestinian liberation."[17] The response from the BDS movement was indicative of its intersectional approach: "Thank you for your solidarity. From Ferguson to Palestine, our struggles against racism, white supremacy and for a just world are united!"[18]

It is my hope that members and supporters of BLM will read this book, learn the facts about the Middle East conflict, and understand why Hamas, not Israel or Jews, is the proper object of their Kosher Hate.

Meanwhile, BLM leaders have appeared on podiums with Nation of Islam founder Louis Farrakhan, who continues his unabashed anti-Semitic rants. ADL calls him "quite possibly America's most popular anti-Semite" because of the large crowds he attracts that often include prominent politicians and celebrities. In one speech, Farrakhan denounced

"Satanic Jews" and said, "White folks are going down, and Satan is going down, and Farrakhan by God's grace has pulled the cover off of that Satanic Jew—and I'm here to say, your time is up."[19] BLM leaders have not condemned or distanced themselves from this kind of rhetoric.

Sadly, the women's movement has also in part been hijacked by anti-Semites. In 2017, organizers of Chicago's Dyke March asked three participants carrying LGBT pride flags with a Star of David over the traditional rainbow to leave because the flags "made people feel unsafe" and the march was "anti-Zionist."[20]Two years later, at the DC Dyke March, self-proclaimed anti-Zionists from the radical Jewish organization IfNotNow said they were banning "Israeli flags, as well as flags that resemble Israeli flags, such as a pride flag with a Star of David in the middle."[21]

Three of the leaders of the Women's March movement that emerged after the election of Donald Trump were associated with Farrakhan and had also made anti-Semitic remarks. Two were ultimately forced to leave the board as an apparent result of internal conflicts over the role of Jewish feminists in the movement—Tamika Mallory, an African-American, and the aforementioned Linda Sarsour. The third, Latina activist Carmen Perez-Jordan, remained.[22] It remains to be seen whether the intersectional perspective—with its un-kosher hatred of Jews and "toxic" white males—will ultimately prevail on the left. But at this point it seems likely that it will.

Given the acceptance of anti-Semitism in the progressive movement, it should not be a surprise that many college campuses are hotbeds of Jew-hatred. Though some people think it's new, this has been a problem for decades as university administrations have long been willing to tolerate anti-Semitism under the guise of "academic freedom." This is the only form of bigotry permitted on campus, however, as racism, homophobia, Islamophobia, sexism and every other form of discrimination are considered taboo. As long as you use the word "Israel" instead of "Jew," there are no holds barred.

Growing numbers of Jewish students report having experienced anti-Semitism on campus. It does not always take the form of vandalism or offensive comments; Jewish students now often find themselves ostracized by their peers for the crime of supporting Israel. Many professors also use their classrooms, their departments, and their professional associations to advance anti-Israel agendas.

Professor Cary Nelson, a former president of the American Association of University Professors said, "This national effort to organize an entire academic discipline -- its teaching, research, policies and administration -- around anti-Zionism represents a new and dangerous phase in the politicization of the academy." Anti-Israel group think has become the norm in Middle East Studies departments and many Modern Language, Anthropology, and American Studies programs.

Anti-Israel students who veer into anti-Semitism also appear to be a growing problem. Students for Justice in Palestine (SJP) has become the most ubiquitous group on campus. Though typically small in number, they have been exceptionally successful in building coalitions with other "progressive" groups, including Jewish ones who give a phony kosher stamp of approval to their anti-Israel views.

Jewish students see their Hillels and dorm rooms vandalized, receive phony eviction notices meant to be comparable to what happens to Palestinians, walk through mock checkpoints, and have their speakers shouted down. On more than one hundred campuses each year, Palestinians hold what amounts to Israel Hate Weeks, with speakers, films and other events devoted to demonizing Jews and Israel. Faculty and administrators are typically silent as these events take place.

Perhaps the single most prevalent global manifestation of modern anti-Semitism is the boycott, divestment and sanctions movement (BDS), which is reminiscent of the Nazi boycott of the Jews in the 1930s. Defenders claim it is a nonviolent means of protesting Israel's control of the West Bank, but its founders and most prominent adherents explicitly state that its goal is the destruction of Israel.

Perhaps the greatest difference in the anti-Semitism of today from that of the past is the power of social media to reach tens of millions of people simultaneously with expressions of bigotry. Anti-Semitic web sites, Twitter handles, Facebook pages, and YouTube videos proliferate at an exponential rate, and even as some platforms have taken measures to bar anti-Semitic content, they have done a lousy job and are, in any event, faced with a situation whereby every page they shut down is quickly replaced by another. The ADL reported, for example, that it found 17,000 mentions of the words "Hitler Was Right" on Twitter in the week of May 7 alone.[23]

Sadly, the Jewish community is not doing enough to fight anti-Semitism. Millions of dollars are being donated by philanthropists to organizations that have proved ineffectual in part because of their fear of offending people they see as natural allies, typically liberal Democrats.

While some Jews are willing to stand up to the anti-Semites, the institutions of Jewish communal life have been AWOL. When a rally was organized in NY during the May 2021 war in Gaza, the major Jewish organizations declined to participate. It is all too reminiscent of the 1930s and 40s when some Jews tried to organize a campaign to convince Roosevelt to save European Jewry: the Jewish "establishment" either remained silent, hoped that quiet diplomacy would work, or were afraid to offend the president.

It will take more than words, however, to fight the anti-Semites and racial bigots in our midst. It will take the application of Kosher Hate described in the following pages.

CHAPTER 1:
WHAT IS KOSHER HATE?

IN 1999, I WAS INVITED to address a conference in Cape Town, South Africa, as part of the World Presidents' Organization. One of the sessions was held on Robben Island, where Nelson Mandela and his compatriots were imprisoned for many years. Many of the black prisoners returned to the island with us and recalled what it was like. Then, suddenly, a white man with a goatee and tattoos up and down his arms got up to address the crowd.

What was he doing there?

As I recall, he started his story with this: "In the 1970s, I was a white police officer working for the South African government. I was sent to quiet a black uprising in one of the townships. To teach them a lesson, I ordered my men to torch a home filled with children, killing nine of them. I was arrested, tried, and sentenced to life imprisonment. With the arrival of the black African government, I went before The Truth and Reconciliation Commission, chaired by Archbishop Desmond Tutu, confessed my crimes, and was released. What I did was something that I will regret for the rest of my life." Tears were streaming down his cheeks.

To my amazement, hundreds of people who were in the room with me gave him a standing ovation. I was disgusted. I raised my hand and he called on me.

"I will not rise for you sir," I said, "and I find this standing ovation an insult to decency. You, sir, are a mass murderer and murder is not something you can simply regret, recant, and become a hero for. People regret things in life like the fact that they lost money in the stock market not that they killed nine children. You, sir, are evil, and you deserve our contempt, not our applause."

He was stunned by my words. One of Mandela's closest friends, who had been with him in prison for several years, a relatively young man, rose to his defense. "Your sentiments, Rabbi, are due to the fact that Jews find it difficult to forgive. Indeed, in the entire Hebrew language, there is not a single word for forgiveness."

Whoa, I didn't expect a response that bordered on anti-Semitism.

I rose again. "You are wrong, sir," I replied. "In fact, the Hebrew language has three words for forgiveness: *selicha*, *mechila*, and *kapparah*. The essence of forgiveness is that an individual is so valuable that we allow them the opportunity to start afresh after error. But, since repentance is based on recognizing the infinite value of human life, its premise cannot be simultaneously undermined by offering it to those who have irretrievably debased human life."

I sat down again to hushes and hisses. I had articulated a vision of Kosher Hate, a moral revulsion for evil, and had made myself immensely unpopular by doing so. But what I expressed was not my opinion but Jewish doctrine. There can be no clemency for terrorists, as in this case, or mass murder. Judaism allows no forgiveness for people who murder innocent children. And while some—including the great Nazi hunter, Simon Wiesenthal—would say that it's up to the victim to decide whether to forgive, I believe that life comes from God. It does not belong to man. And it is only for God to decide.

For a murderer to repent in public and achieve instant absolution is an affront to everything forgiveness stands for. That's why we should feel no guilt for our feelings of revulsion toward terrorists. There are some offenses for which there is no forgiveness, some borders whose transgression society cannot tolerate under any circumstances. Mass murder is foremost among them. Hatred has its place.

EVIL TODAY

Indeed, our refusal to hate evil accounts for why it remains so widespread today. The history of the modern world is a history of genocide and the indiscriminate slaughter of innocent men, women, and children. Historian Paul Johnson estimates that at least one hundred million civilians were murdered in the twentieth century alone by murderous tyrants. This is a staggering number. The world could not summon enough hatred of these dictators, or their bloodlust, to stop them and bring them to justice.

Depressingly, the trend has continued into the twenty-first century. Seventy years after Hitler's demise, madmen still run countries, gas their own people; torture men, women, and children; and fill mass graves with the bodies of innocents. Amid the world's protests of "Never Again!" and the ratification of the treaty against genocide that was supposed to commit the great powers to stopping mass murder, no fewer than five genocides have occurred since World War II. Perhaps as many as 5.4 million people were killed in the civil war in the Congo, two million Cambodians were murdered by the Khmer Rouge, 800,000 Tutsis died at the hands of machete-wielding Hutus in Rwanda, tens of thousands of Bosnian Muslims were ethnically cleansed by the Serbs, and at least 400,000 poor, black Africans were slaughtered by the Islamic Janjaweed militias in Sudan.

Now another genocide is taking place before our eyes in Syria. Since 2011, dictator Bashar Assad has murdered more than 600,000 Syrians and notoriously used chemical weapons against his own people. Other than the single missile strike launched by the United States following one of these chemical attacks, the world has been a bystander.

Instead of "Never Again!" the reality has been "Again and Again!"

This is evil on a macro level. But of course, it also flourishes at the micro level. According to the FBI, in 2019, the United States had more than 1.2 million violent crimes—murder, rape, robbery, pedophilia, and aggravated assault. More than 16,000 people were murdered and nearly 140,000 raped.

Could this really be happening in our supposedly advanced societies? How can murder and mayhem continue unabated on this scale in an age of moral progress and technological sophistication? And why does humanity do so little to stop it? We have made great strides in conquering disease, poverty, and even gravity. Yet we have failed to purge the world of awful people who perpetrate the most heinous crimes.

This lack of seriousness about confronting evil was exemplified for me when millions of people, including many who supported the Iraq War, seemed to find the photograph of a captured Saddam Hussein cowering in his skivvies amusing. There was nothing funny about seeing the Butcher of Baghdad, a man who had killed more than a million people— thousands with poison gas—dragged out of a hole in his underwear. Rather than giggles, the mere sight of him should have produced profound revulsion.

Jokes about evil people have become routine and have contributed to a widespread normalization of our feelings toward it. *Saturday Night Live* featured skits with comic conversations between Saddam and bin Laden well after 9/11. The question is not whether such humor is in bad taste, or even whether it is funny. The issue is that we have been programmed to trivialize evil. We laugh because our visceral abhorrence of evil is gone.

We live in a world that idolizes peace and tranquility. Men who are seen as belligerent warmongers, such as former President George W. Bush, are reviled around the world, while ostensible peacemakers, such as the Scandinavians and the UN Secretary-General, are far more popular. After the attacks of 9/11, the United States and its military were scorned for launching a global war on terror while countries known for their amity such as Canada continued to be loved and respected. For example, between 2002 and 2007, positive views of the United States declined in twenty-six of the thirty-three nations surveyed by Pew. In 2006, thirteen of fifteen countries said the U.S. presence in Iraq was an equal or greater danger to stability in the Middle East than the Iranian regime. Majorities in nineteen of twenty-four countries surveyed had little or no confidence in President George W. Bush.[24]

Ronald Reagan was widely ridiculed for calling the Soviet Union an "evil empire." Sophisticated people in Western countries considered this a simplistic view of the world. Nevertheless, he was right. Similarly, George W. Bush was criticized for referring to rogue regimes as "evildoers." He correctly identified Iran, Iraq, and North Korea as an "axis of evil" for their barbaric mistreatment of their own citizens and malevolent activities beyond their borders. Bush, a man of faith who saw the world through the biblical prism of right and wrong, had no qualms about labeling Saddam Hussein evil and battling him to the death.

Secular Europe, along with American "liberal progressives," lacking absolute standards of morality, can only see through the lens of an abstract universalism where no value system is better than another and human rights trumps national interests. At least that is what they profess. In practice they vilify whatever they find personally objectionable, reserving the worst condemnations for their own Western traditions of capitalism, colonialism, and Judeo-Christian faith.

As an American who travels abroad a great deal, I have experienced the widespread disdain for Americans whom many believe are unthinking, uncompassionate bullies. The world loves American culture but dislikes its leaders because they are seen as initiating or escalating violence too often in the name of defending the parochial interests of the United States. America, the warrior nation, is rejected by a world that worships peace.

In ages past, the man who was prepared to face the dangers of the battlefield in the service of his country was considered a glorious hero. The threat of war was constant, and each country valued its strong men—its Hectors and William Wallaces—who they could rely on to defend its vital interests and national freedoms. Nowadays, thanks to increased communication, prosperity, and common understanding of the harms of war, we no longer see the point. Historically, war was seen as an unavoidable part of expanding civilization, today's modern world appears to have become so much safer and more stable, if for no other reason than the proliferation of nuclear weapons, and for the first time in history we can seriously entertain the idea that warfare and large-scale violence may soon be obsolete. Many feel secure enough to push their governments to negotiate away their nuclear arsenals in the hope they will ban war forever. Why, some ask, can't America be like everyone else and just live in peace?

Part of the problem is that Americans still have not recovered from the "Vietnam syndrome" and the sense that we squandered our time, talent, and treasure on a pointless cause that cost more than 58,000 lives and accomplished nothing. Since then, the United States has fought another seemingly meaningless war to remove Saddam Hussein from power in Iraq to prevent his use of what turned out to be non-existent weapons of mass destruction. Now, we are mired in our longest war yet in Afghanistan, nearly twenty years, for the ostensible purpose of preventing terrorism. In each case, we have a good reason to hate our enemy but it is unsatisfying if we fail to vanquish them or if the cost seems to greatly outweigh the benefit.

Is it any wonder that today's heroes are not military leaders but conciliators and pacifists like Pope Francis and the Dalai Lama who represent utopian hopes for a world without war?

People who are backwards enough to remain involved in the activity of war are seen as losers doing an unsavory job—like garbage collectors, only not as necessary—and with any luck, will soon be obsolete. Yes, most Americans still have deep respect for our military. But it's the kind of respect that leads to a detached adulation rather than emulation.

IGNORING HATE

Few people believe the problems of the world can be solved by armed conflict and violence, and fewer still advocate it. Repeatedly, we hear that the trouble with the world today is that there is not enough love when, in reality, we lack sufficient hate.

The problem comes down to our denial that evil exists. Or rather, we have reduced it to a psychological defect. Evil is not seen as an irreducible moral problem that is inseparable from human nature. It is seen as an irrational and unenlightened hatred of the Other. As such, we view it not as something to oppose and defeat but as something to understand and treat with therapy or psychiatric medication. In fact, the truly moral response to the problem of evil is not understanding and treatment. It is hate.

Even as "hate of hatred" achieves a position of bizarre prominence in our political discourse, we must be aware that banishing hate from our vocabulary also means that we are banishing a consciousness of evil. The proper response to evil cannot be indifference. It must be hatred.

Evil currently stalks the earth because we do not hate it enough to fight and eradicate it. People with a commitment to ethics and morality are afraid to hate because they think it is like a poison that will get into their system and corrupt them. They are unaware that their unwillingness to despise those who engage in heinous acts of cruelty and murder renders them indifferent to evil.

What few realize is that the hate of hatred itself is mostly a Christian idea that Judaism would reject. Many Jews have even adopted this secularized Christian idea that hate is not a moral virtue but a defect.

My Christian brothers expect that religion will provide comfort in the face of life's more troublesome metaphysical problems. That is why they are told to exercise love in the face of evil. The tension of perpetual hate—a possible response—is too difficult to live with. Love is a release. It is the great all-curing nostrum of Christianity, the world's religion of salvation and comfort. So the Christian response to evil treatment is to turn the other cheek. The Jewish response to evil is somewhat different: evil is to be hated and fought until it is destroyed.

We do not teach our children to refrain from stealing because they might get caught. Rather, we teach them that theft is fundamentally wrong, even if they can get away with it. Humans, with the exception of psychopaths, have an innate sense of right and wrong, and every human has an inherent feeling for when they are mistreated. Such moral sentiments aren't logical but physical. We feel them in our guts. We should never seek to undermine this natural human revulsion against injustice that is wired into our genes. Upon such feelings are just societies built.

It was the American loathing for taxation without representation—the innate feeling that the colonists were being treated unfairly—that led to the rebellion against Britain. It was a visceral hatred of slavery that drove the abolitionist movement and resulted in a bloody civil war. It was a hatred for the horrors of segregation and apartheid that led Martin Luther King, Jr. and Nelson Mandela to inspire both indignation and action to combat those unjust systems.

Justice is not a cultural construct. Neither is it a human invention imposed upon the members of society so they will treat each other with fairness. Justice was not created by men for some utilitarian end. Rather, justice is essential to human nature.

I am not the one who determines good and evil and I disagree with the teachings of St. Augustine who said that evil was "merely a name for the absence of good." The Ten Commandments explicitly define right and wrong—some as it relates to the relationship between humans and God, and others between humans. These are universal norms that underpin the foundations of America's democracy. It was for this reason that they enshrined their values not in dogma, but in a code of civil law that we call the U.S. Constitution. Every culture, ethnicity, and religion recognize the values expressed in the Ten Commandments that establish which is good and which is sinful. There is not a single culture that believes adultery, murder, or thievery are okay.

Without such absolutes in determining good and evil, everything becomes relative. As a result it is increasingly hard to pass judgment on people's behavior. But modern liberals seemingly prefer this vacuous code of relativity to the "simplicity" of absolutes, which they contend do not consider the possibility that moral questions are not always black and white.

Though the left tends to be more vocal, it is a mistake to believe, however, that liberal thinking dominates the world or even the United States—though it may sometimes seem that way. Gallup polls in early 2020 found that 34 percent of respondents called themselves conservative, 36 percent moderate, and only 26 percent liberal.[25]

America is actually a very religious country. But it is split on the role that the Bible should play in society. A 2020 Pew study found that 49 percent of adults (only 31 percent of Jews) believe it should have "a great deal" or "some" influence, and 28 percent of those think the Bible should take precedence over the will of the people. The other half of the public wants the Bible to have little or no influence on U.S. law. More than 40 percent of Americans (52 percent of Jews) see a conflict between their religious beliefs and American culture.[26] Hence, it is not surprising that it is difficult to get Americans to accept divine guidance for determining good and evil.

The essence of religion is submission to God's will and the practice of ethical norms.

Monotheism is not enough. Ethics are not enough. You need what the noted Jewish thinker, author, and talk show host Dennis Prager refers to as ethical monotheism, which he says means two things:

There is one God from whom emanates one morality for all humanity.

God's primary demand of people is that they act decently toward one another.

An ethical system without moral absolutes based on divine instruction will always be compromised. And a divine system that is not rooted in moral absolutes is compromised. The atheist has no such system and various "isms"—communism, fascism, Nazism—base their morality, or more often immorality, on the dogmatic ideologies of their leaders.

HOW EVIL DOES EVIL NEED TO BE

Don't misunderstand me. I do not believe that all expressions of evil are equal. Adultery, for example, involves moral deception, trickery, the breaking of promises, and is absolutely shattering to the person cheated on. America has a long history of leaders who have been guilty of adultery, either in or out of office, including Eisenhower, JFK, LBJ, Clinton, and Trump. Being an adulterer does not make you a terrible person, it makes you an awful partner. The transgression is between them and their God and their families. Appalling as this behavior is, what a person, even a world leader, does in their personal life is not remotely equivalent to a leader engaged in genocide.

The Bible goes beyond defining what evil is; it commands us to hate it. Indeed, it is the only thing the Bible instructs its followers to hate. In Psalms 5:5 we read, "The foolish shall not stand in thy sight: thou hatest all workers of iniquity." Psalms 97:10 says, "Ye that love the Lord, hate evil." Isaiah 5:20 warns, "Woe unto them that call evil good, and good evil." Similarly, Amos calls on us to "Hate the evil, and love the good." King Solomon says in the Book of Proverbs that hatred of evil is a prerequisite for fearing God and not just loving Him. He says that he hates "pride and arrogance, evil behavior, and perverse speech."

The Bible also teaches us that God is capable of hatred, having destroyed the world in the great flood, the cities of Sodom and Gomorrah, and the army of Pharaoh. In warning the Jews not to worship other gods, Moses explains that by worshipping their gods other nations do all kinds of detestable things the Lord hates. The example he gives is God's hatred of the Canaanites who "even burn their sons and daughters in the fire as sacrifices to their gods."

This Kosher Hate is what I insist is required to rid the world of evil. To be sure there must, first and foremost, be love for the victims of injustice. But without a simultaneous hatred for the perpetrators, we will not be motivated to fight evil until it is eradicated.

Kosher Hate is not an extremist ideology. This is not another name for Manichaeism. The Manicheans believed in absolute dualism between light, which is good, and darkness, which is evil. Kosher Hate is only absolute in its hatred of evil and does not follow the beliefs of an absolute dualism of light and dark. As the Jewish intellectual Todd Gitlin wrote in *Tablet* magazine, the world has suffered, and continues to suffer, from dualism under different guises: "Colonial versus anticolonial; capitalist versus proletarian; Communist versus capitalist; 'Aryan' versus Jew – these lethal polarities of purity against danger, essence against contaminants, retains its temptations."[27]

Whatever group of haters we are talking about, it is important to remember they are comprised of individual human beings. These are not aliens from another planet. They are not monsters; rather, they are people engaged in monstrous activities. As the philosopher Emil Fackenheim observed, "whether it be Hitler or Himmler, Eichmann, Hoess, or the unknown soldier who was an SS murderer," they are all "human beings like ourselves." He adds, "But while this finding chills the marrow and numbs the mind, it must under no circumstances mislead us into the seemingly 'liberal' but in fact trite, cowardly and escapist weakening of the distinction between those who *might have done it* – you, I, the greengrocer next door – and those who *in fact did it*."

Manicheanism as promulgated, for example, by the radical anti-colonialist Frantz Fanon, according to Gitlin, does not recognize the possibility of compromise. "Only violence is 'a cleansing force.'" Unlike Fanon, I do not believe violence is always the answer to injustice. I also do not believe that defeating evil requires an apocalyptic struggle that results in a global conflagration. I would thus amend Edmund Burke's famous dictum to read: The only thing necessary for the triumph of evil is for good men *not to truly hate it.*

Too often these days, people find a moral equivalence between the villains of our time and those who are fighting to defeat them. Israelis are frequently accused of feeding a supposed "cycle of violence" when they respond to acts of terror. This is like equating the firefighter with the arsonist.

The truth is, we know evil when we see it. And our natural inclination is to hate it.

In 2020, many Americans woke up to the continuing evil of racism when they watched video after video of police officers who appeared to use unnecessary force against black citizens. It was nearly as horrifying to see bystanders allowing it to happen. The event that catalyzed nationwide protests was the video of Minneapolis police officer Derek Chauvin with his knee on the neck of George Floyd as he gasped for air and pleaded that he could not breathe. Three other officers, pledged to serve and protect, apparently stood by and did nothing. Chauvin was subsequently charged with second-degree murder and the other officers were charged with aiding and abetting second-degree murder and manslaughter.

The outrage provoked by the killing of Floyd is the response we should always have to evil, whether at home or abroad. The perpetrators of these crimes will only be stopped if they provoke our righteous indignation, which is spurred by our hatred of evil.

When I talk about the application of Kosher Hate as an ideology, however, I am primarily talking about the response to evil on the macro level—that is, within and between nations—where the abuse of human rights and murder typically occur on a mass scale. This is not to say we should not hate individual murderers and rapists. But when caught, these individuals are punished by due legal process. This is not the case when it comes to sovereign nations and their leaders. All too often, the realities of foreign policy preclude us from acting, limiting our response to verbal condemnation or meaningless UN resolutions. Worse, the world has often been too apathetic to act and unwilling to hold bad actors to account. This incapacity for collective moral action shows the weakness of the whole underlying idea that "the world" as such—defined as a community of nations—exists in any meaningful sense.

Not all religions or societies place evil at the center of their worldviews. In Eastern philosophy and religion the highest goal is the attainment of enlightenment (Nirvana), not by combating or hating evil but by effacing the ego. Wickedness and unjust suffering are regarded as a part of life, and it is best to escape life altogether, transcending everyday existence, not morally transform it by our actions.

In much of the Arab and Muslim world, "face," "shame," and "honor" define moral norms, not necessarily standards of good and evil. That is the reason why "honor killings"—the murder of a daughter, sister, or wife who has brought shame to the family through their, usually sexual, actions—are regarded by some Muslims as just rather than criminal. It is also why autocratic leaders, no matter how brutal, are often lionized because of their strength.

Jews are different. Rabbi Shneur Zalman of Liadi published the *Tanya*, a comprehensive review of more than two thousand years of Kabbalistic thoughts, forums, and discussions. Processed in his own special way, Rabbi Shneur Zalman, the founder of the Chabad movement, depicted the *Tanya* as an all-in-one guide to serving God to the tune of Judaism's secret-most wisdom.

Rabbi Shneur Zalman classifies humanity into the wicked, the intermediate, and the righteous. Among the righteous, there are higher and lower levels, one being perfectly righteous, and the other imperfectly so. In describing the difference, he focuses on a single emotion in their hearts: hate.

The perfectly righteous person hates evil with all his heart; the imperfectly righteous never succumbs to evil, but does not completely hate it. Note that the defining attribute of the righteous is not love, as it is in Christianity, but hate.

This is an astonishing revelation, and one we'll explore in more depth later on.

JEWS GETTING IT WRONG

Jews are also sometimes guilty of misinterpreting the Bible and failing to call out evil. Even rabbis—generally among the wisest and most sensible of men—have been known to be myopic when it comes to moral and necessary hatred.

I recall sitting in the back of a synagogue the week after a young yeshiva student was stabbed as he returned from praying at the Western Wall. The rabbi was talking about the murder, which had come just after Israel had evacuated all the Jews from the Gaza Strip. I listened with amazement as he told the congregation that we must not harbor any hatred toward the terrorist. He quoted Rabbi Kook who, at the time of the infamous 1929 Hebron massacre where an Arab mob attacked the Jewish community and murdered sixty-seven people, made a similar stand denouncing hatred. "They are human beings," Kook said, "and we cannot hate them. Only their actions are hateworthy."

I said to the rabbi, "Doesn't it say in the Bible, concerning God, 'And Esau I hated?'" Esau was a savage hunter of beasts and men, as the Rabbinical Midrash declares, and God says, in the book of Malachi, that he hates him. "So, don't we have to do the same?" I asked. "Hate Esau and all his kind?" This would apply to all terrorists and all who prey on the innocent and the weak, including Jewish terrorists like Baruch

Goldstein, who murdered twenty-nine innocent Palestinians in prayer in Hebron.

"No," the rabbi answered. "Only their deeds are hated."

"Are you suggesting," I pressed, "that we shouldn't hate the Nazis, only their deeds? What about Hitler? Are you seriously saying we shouldn't hate Hitler?"

"Even Hitler is a man in the image of God, so we can't hate him." He was quoting from the Bible's very first chapter in Genesis, where it says that God created humanity in his image. I pressed the argument.

"Yes," I said, "but if a man is so utterly evil, he loses his human visage—he obliterates the image of God in which he was formed. He has forfeited the divine countenance and becomes a monster. There is nothing human left about him and he is no longer our brother. At that point it becomes necessary to hate him."

He gave me a puzzled look. I understood why he could not agree with me. The hate of hatred has become in our time its own moral imperative—including for the very religious—even though it has no basis in either logic or the Hebrew Bible.

The implications of the failure to generate sufficient hate to act can be catastrophic. Consider former president Bill Clinton. Clinton is a quintessential liberal—someone who wants to believe in the goodness of people and refuses to hate anyone. His inability to summon a real hatred for evil—a fact demonstrated throughout the morally vacuous years of his presidency—was directly responsible for his culpable inaction in the face of the Rwandan genocide. While helpless African Tutsis were being slaughtered by their Hutu neighbors at a rate of 333 per hour over a three-month period, the most powerful man on earth refused to intervene. As is well documented by Samantha Power in her Pulitzer-prize winning book, *A Problem from Hell*, he never even convened his national security team or met with his senior advisers to discuss the crisis. Apparently, he was afraid that by condemning it he would be obligated to send in American troops. He even refused to block Hutu radio transmissions that orchestrated the massacres.

The Rwandan genocide was unique in the annals of modern mass murder insofar as the world had no excuse not to intervene. The Ottoman Turks' slaughter of 1.5 million Armenians took place during the fog of World War I. Franklin Roosevelt's failure to save six million European Jews was excused by the primary goal of defeating the Nazis. The Khmer Rouge's extermination of one third of Cambodia's seven million citizens was done in a country sealed off from the rest of the world, thus granting the Western powers a plausible excuse for their inaction. Yes, they probably knew. But they pretended not to.

And where was the United Nations, the organization meant to bring about world peace, during these massacres? The UN peace-keeping commander on the ground, Gen. Roméo Dallaire of Canada, one of the few true heroes of this otherwise cowardly tale, informed the world of both the preparations for mass-murder as well as every development once the genocide was in full swing. In Dallaire's extraordinary and haunting book, *Shake Hands with the Devil*, you feel his undisguised hatred for the Hutu killers.

Dallaire is that rare breed of man who is not afraid to hate what is truly evil. He is not afraid to call the murderers "devils," as in the title of his book. But the Kofi Annans and Bill Clintons who brought a professional humanitarian detachment to this obscene crime against humanity sat back and did nothing. Kofi Annan, as global head of the UN peacekeepers, sent two now-infamous cables to Dallaire ordering him to stand down and not interfere. At the Rwandan Genocide museum in Kigali, the telegrams are prominently displayed as you enter the complex, which also houses the graves of more than 200,000 people.

In fact, Clinton obstructed efforts to intervene. His administration robbed Dallaire of any ability to protect the unarmed men, women, and children of Rwanda by demanding the total withdrawal of all 2,500 UN peacekeepers, only later allowing a skeletal force of 270 in response to pressure from African nations. Madeleine Albright, then the American Ambassador to the UN, opposed leaving even this tiny force. She also pressured other countries, according to Philip Gourevitch in *We Wish to Inform You That Tomorrow We Will Be Killed With Our Families*, "to duck, as the death toll leapt from thousands to tens of thousands to hundreds of thousands." He said it "was the absolute low point in her career as a stateswoman."[28] The effect was to signal both the Rwandan people and the Hutu militias that the West cared nothing for African lives.

Truly these so-called humanitarians are people who only love humanity in the abstract. Real flesh and blood human beings are apparently beneath their concern.

Power, who would later succeed Susan Rice as America's UN ambassador, referred to Rice and her Clinton administration colleagues as bystanders to genocide. On an interagency teleconference call in April 1994, Rice was reported to have said, "If we use the word 'genocide' and are seen as doing nothing, what will be the effect on the November [congressional] election?"[29] This was an astonishing statement. Power records the perplexed and embarrassed looks on the faces of her colleagues who heard her make the remark. But Rice did not stop there. She then joined former national security adviser Anthony Lake and former secretaries of state, Madeline Albright and Warren Christopher, in a coordinated effort to impede UN intervention—and minimize public opposition to

American inaction—by removing words like "genocide" and "ethnic cleansing" from all government communications on the subject.

I do not think I'm overstating it when I say that the Clinton administration's response to the Rwandan genocide constitutes one of the most shameful moments in American foreign policy. Not only did the United States refuse to intervene, but to quote *The New York Times*, "It also used its considerable power to discourage other Western powers from intervening. At the height of the carnage, when Belgium lost 10 peacekeepers, the United States demanded a total United Nations withdrawal. Some African countries objected, and eventually Washington settled for a severe cutback in the 2,500-man United Nations force."[30] In the end, eight African nations agreed to send in troops to stop the slaughter, provided the U.S. would lend them fifty armored personnel carriers. The Clinton administration decided it would lease rather than lend the trucks—at a price of $15 million. The carriers sat on a runway in Germany while the UN pleaded for a $5 million reduction as the genocidal inferno raged.

I wish I could say Clinton's response to the Rwandan genocide was his only failure. But he may be the only president in American history who stood on the sidelines of *three* genocides. During the period of ethnic cleansing in Bosnia, his administration again watched from a distance while Bosnian Muslims were slaughtered in Srebrenica. He repeated this mistake when the Serbs cleansed Kosovo Albanians. And to think that the moral failing most people associate with Clinton is having had sex with an intern.

In the case of Bosnia, the U.S. did finally intervene in August 1995 after four years of massacres. As in Rwanda, the failure was not the United States' alone but also, once again, the UN's. What happened?

Unlike the meager UN force sent to Rwanda, the UN Protection Force in Bosnia (UNPROFOR) had a force of 20,000 men. It faced a quandary, one that shouldn't have been a dilemma for an institution committed to stamping out evil. If UNPROFOR intervened to protect the Muslims from the Serbs, it would forfeit the peacekeepers' credibility as impartial observers. But if it remained neutral, the ethnic cleansing would intensify as the Serbs moved into areas the international community had insisted should be "safe."

The United States, which had done nothing for four years, now wanted UNPROFOR to engage the Serbs or at least allow NATO air strikes to protect the "safe" areas. The feckless Europeans, who had sent troops to join UNPROFOR, not surprisingly wanted the force to stick to humanitarian activities. Ivo Daalder, who served on Clinton's National Security Council staff, noted that when nearly 400 peacekeepers were taken hostage following air strikes in May 1995, the UN and troop-contributing countries concluded NATO air strikes did more harm than good and that UNPROFOR should stick to "traditional peacekeeping principles." As in Rwanda, this essentially gave the Serbs the green light to ethnically cleanse "their territory" of Muslims and Croats.[31]

Daalder described what happened next:

> In July, Serb forces turned their focus to Srebrenica, a small village near the eastern border with Serbia swollen with some 60,000 Muslim refugees. It was there that the then-U.N. commander, French General Philippe Morillon, had two years earlier made the U.N.'s final stance, declaring at the time: "You are now under U.N. protection of the United Nations.... I will never abandon you." Despite the U.N. flag flying over the enclave, the Bosnian Serb assault in July 1995 met no U.N. resistance either on the ground or from the air. Within 10 days, tens of thousands of Muslim refugees streamed into the Muslim-controlled city of Tuzla. Missing from the stream of refugees were more than 7,000 men of all

ages, who had been executed in cold blood – mass murder on a scale not witnessed in Europe since the end of World War II.

Belatedly, the allies decided there would be no "pinprick" strikes. It was a recognition of a failed strategy that sadly would be repeated by other presidents who preferred appeasement to stopping atrocities.

Clinton finally decided to intervene in part because of the upcoming election. (As with most politicians, self-interest was a greater motivator than upholding fundamental American and humanitarian values.) The Serbs had to be shown that there would be a high cost if they refused to negotiate an end to the fighting, and that meant the use of military force. Ultimately, it was a prolonged NATO bombing campaign led by the United States that forced the Serbs to the bargaining table where the Dayton Accords were signed. The peace was enforced by 60,000 U.S. and NATO forces.

Three years later, Clinton was faced with the question of whether to respond to ethnic cleansing in Kosovo. The Serbs, led by the war criminal Slobodan Milošević, killed 1,500 Albanians and displaced 230,000–270,000 in a concerted effort to change the ethnic composition of Kosovo through expulsion and mass murder.

On March 24, 1999 NATO began operations to avoid "an even crueler and costlier war;" "to prevent a wider war in Europe;" and to "seriously damage the Serbian military's capacity to harm the people of Kosovo."[32] British Prime Minister Tony Blair said military action was necessary "to save thousands of innocent men, women and children from humanitarian catastrophe, from death, barbarism and ethnic cleansing by a brutal dictatorship." He told Parliament, "the consequences of not acting are more serious still for human life and for peace in the long term."[33] Vaclav Havel, president of the Czech Republic, called Kosovo "the first war for values."[34]

This time, the United States did not allow NATO to be hamstrung by the UN and Secretary-General Kofi Annan's insistence that the Security Council be involved in the decision.

David Clark, who served as an adviser at the British Foreign Office, noted that "about 850,000 people – half Kosovo's Albanian population - were driven out of the country, many with their papers seized to prevent them returning. About 10,000 were murdered by Serbian forces." If not for NATO intervention, supported by the EU and Serbia's neighbors, Milošević would have completed his ethnic cleansing. "Kosovo should be remembered," Clark concluded, "as an example of western nations using their power, however imperfectly, to do something good and necessary."[35]

American intervention went against the grain not only of most liberals but some conservatives. Even champions of democracy who truly hated evil, like the late political columnist Charles Krauthammer, did not see any need to stop the genocide. "Clinton has taken a Balkan conflict that by world standards was relatively minor – three times as many people were killed in the civil war in Sierra Leone as had died in the entire Kosovo war at the time we intervened – and turned it into a world event," he coolly opined. "The Clinton administration, ever seeking to do good, has staked NATO unity and credibility on its ability to pacify the Balkans, a task never accomplished in the century except by Tito."[36]

In Krauthammer's view, the prevention of genocide was not enough of a reason for American intervention. "In war, good intentions are no excuse. They are instead the road to hell."

War is indeed hell. But allowing the devil to have his way is not a viable alternative. Failure to act only emboldens more devilish behavior.

In a trenchant essay, the late critic Susan Sontag— outraged by what she had seen transpiring in Bosnia—explained the all-too-familiar tendency to ignore evil if it does not directly impact us.

> Of course, it is easy to turn your eyes from what is happening if it is not happening to you. Or if you have not put yourself where it is happening. I remember in Sarajevo in the summer of 1993 a Bosnian friend telling me ruefully that in 1991, when she saw on her TV set the footage of Vukovar utterly leveled by the Serbs, she thought to herself, How terrible, but that's in Croatia, that can never happen here in Bosnia…and switched the channel. The following year, when the war started in Bosnia, she learned differently. Then she became part of a story on television that other people saw and said, How terrible…and switched the channel.[37]

This is reminiscent of the answer Martin Niemöeller gave after World War II to a student who asked, "How could it happen?" The process of accommodation to evil was simple to describe:

> First they came for the Communists, but I was not a Communist, so I did not speak out. Then they came for the Socialists and the Trade Unionists, but I was neither, so I did not speak out. Then they came for the Jews, but I was not a Jew, so I did not speak out. And when they came for me, there was no one left to speak out for me.[38]

As Sontag noted, most cases of mass violence are committed by governments against their own people. She rejected the idea, as do I, that we can ignore civil wars.

Sontag also noted the inability to comprehend, even after Auschwitz, that atrocities continue. "And as the horrors multiply, it becomes even more incomprehensible why we should respond to any one of them (since we have not responded to the others). Why this horror and not another? Why Bosnia or Kosovo and not Kurdistan or Rwanda or Tibet?"

This, of course, is an excuse for inaction.

Sontag acknowledged the criticism that there only seems to be interest in saving European lives, or as others would put it, white people. "What's wrong with that," she asked. "If several African states had cared enough about the genocide of the Tutsis in Rwanda (nearly a million people!) to intervene militarily, say, under the leadership of Nelson Mandela, would we have criticized this initiative as being Afrocentric? Would we have asked what right these states have to intervene in Rwanda when they have done nothing on behalf of the Kurds or the Tibetans?" Yet somehow we in the West, by not being universally benevolent, fall short of our humanitarian ideals.

Rather than holding ourselves to an impossibly high standard of moral purity, perhaps we should rethink our ideals.

Sontag also addressed the criticism of the legality of the war in Kosovo. Critics said it was illegal because it was not authorized by the UN Security Council. She asked what would have been the response if Nazi Germany had not been interested in conquest and had only murdered all the German Jews. Actually, we do know, from the lack of international response to the persecution of German Jews and *Kristallnacht.* "Do we think a government has the right to do whatever it wants on its own territory? Maybe the governments of Europe *would* have said that 60 years ago. But would we approve now of their decision?"

For Sontag, NATO intervention came eight years too late. "Milosevic," she says, "should have been stopped when he was shelling Dubrovnik in 1991."

A leader cannot flinch in the presence of evil. Unfortunately, Clinton flinched again when given not one but three opportunities to kill Osama bin Laden prior to 9/11. Clinton told his senior commanders that if there was any risk of civilian casualties, they could not fire on bin Laden's motorcade. Now, I respect Clinton's commitment to preserving innocent human lives. But there are times when lives must be taken *to protect life*. When it comes to taking out the foremost terrorist in the world, our hatred for him and his actions must be part of the calculus.

Clinton knew how to love—the evidence for this is abundant—but where evil is concerned, he never learned to hate. Indeed, he appeased all kinds of evil regimes, only to see them grow stronger as a result. Under Clinton, North Korea became a nuclear power, signifying the ultimate failure of his tolerant approach. His refusal to identify, hate, and fight evil, until belatedly forced to in Kosovo, constitutes the foremost failure of his presidency.

In sum, the inability or unwillingness to hate has had cataclysmic consequences over the last century. Still, most of the world believes despite all evidence that love will somehow conquer all.

Burt Bacharach and The Beatles wrote popular songs in the 1960s that expressed the feeling of that time as well as ours that all the world really needs is love. That's true when it comes to our relations with good and decent people. It's very wrong, however, when it comes to confronting the wicked. Too many well-intentioned people today accept this premise, to the detriment of human values and global peace. I believe a different version of the song should be written, specifically focused on the need to fight genocide and replacing the word "love" with "hate."

CHAPTER 2:

THE IMPOTENCE OF THE WESTERN HEART

MOST OF US REGARD HATRED as some sort of psychological problem—an emotional illness which, if not tempered by love or compassion, can become dangerous and corrosive. Far from seeing it as something useful, we decry hatred as the emotion most likely to tear everything we cherish apart.

We enjoy speaking about how special love is. How God is love. How "all you need is love." Hatred, as the antithesis of love, is identified as negative in every respect.

In reality, love and hate are morally neutral. They are neither good nor bad. The morality of each will be determined by the uses to which they are put and the means by which they are pursued.

Take the idea of conquest. A man's desire to fleetingly conquer a woman, overcoming her resistance, is immoral; but the ambition to fight and conquer a deadly disease is godly. The same is true of hatred. It is demonic when directed at innocent people who happen to have darker skin than you, but it is appropriate when directed at someone whose murderous actions have made the world itself a darker place.

A man who loves God has utilized his love for a moral and holy cause. So, too, the person who loves their spouse and children. But the person who cheats on their spouse has abused love and turned it into a sinister emotion. The man who loves money has done the same, mistaking the means for the end. An exaggerated love of self can turn to narcissism.

When you think about all the stupid and silly things humanity has loved throughout history, it becomes especially puzzling how so many people can see love as an unconditional good.

How many Christian crusaders loved killing infidels? Was that a Godly love? How many men have loved fighting in general, making war a constant throughout history? Was there anything particularly moral about that? Is a person who marries for money—because they're insanely in love with material things—demonstrating a healthy form of love? What about someone who loves doing drugs? These examples show that love is not monolithic.

Yes, we must be careful with hatred. But we must be equally careful with love. Men can fall in love with women who aren't their wives. Wives can fall in love with men who aren't their husbands. Young girls can fall in love with men who appear to love them back, but want only to use and discard them. People can even fall in love with men like Hitler—as many Germans did—who only offer them the means to destroy their own country and those around them.

My point is that if the principal argument against hatred is that it can be misdirected against those who don't deserve it, the same argument can be made about love which, if directed at those who are unworthy, can have similarly devastating consequences.

Indeed, whenever I see silly Hollywood rom-coms like *Pretty Woman* or *Love Actually* or *Crazy Rich Asians* that champion love as the highest ideal, I have to laugh out loud at their absurdity. If love is the highest good, then should a man leave his wife when he falls in love with his mistress, commitment be damned? Have lonely men or women who have never been in love failed at life, even if they do a lot of good for other people? If love is the highest ideal then a man should leave his fortune to his loyal Labrador, as many do, rather than to starving children whom he never met and thus cannot love except in the abstract.

Yes, the idea that love is unconditionally good is ludicrous, born of ignorance and foolhardiness. Yet, it is that silly idea more than any other that is most responsible for the repudiation of hatred. Since love is always good, and hatred is the opposite of love, it stands to reason that hatred must always be bad.

Judaism is clear that nothing in life, except for God, is good or bad in itself. It's all neutral; usage determines righteousness and unholiness. Money is neutral. Used for charity it is Godly. Used to purchase heroin it is of the devil. A doctor who treats a cancer patient with radiation to prolong their life is Godly. A physician who unnecessarily prescribes opioids that create addiction and destroy lives is evil. So love is not always good; indeed, it is sometimes evil.

It is also inaccurate to insist that love and hate are extremes because they are far too similar to be considered opposites. Both are powerful emotions focused on someone or something external and, because of their intensity, they can turn on a dime. Indeed, the more passionately you love something, the more vehemently you will hate if love is lost, as anyone who has ever been through a bitter divorce can attest. Love and hate are not antipodes; their true antithesis, as Nobel Peace Prize Laureate and Holocaust survivor Elie Wiesel observed, is indifference.

When you love someone, you care deeply about their welfare. When you don't love them, you couldn't care less what happens to them. It is a love of humanity that causes us to feed the hungry and house the homeless. That said, our failure to feel a need to act on another's behalf is not—or not typically—driven by hate but by apathy.

Similarly, if we do not hate someone or something, it does not follow that we love it. More likely, we are simply indifferent. When we fail to respond to evil, it is not because we love wickedness, it is because we feel nothing or at least not enough to be moved to action.

Understanding that hate is not the opposite of love is important, because it means there is no need to demonize hate or choose between them. They both define what we feel toward a particular person or thing. With love, we want to draw close, but it does not necessarily follow that hate makes us seek distance. Kosher Hate—the Jewish way of hating—requires us to approach close enough to destroy what we loathe. Just like love, hate cannot be practiced from a distance. Both are up-close-and-personal emotions. And just like love, the greater the distance one puts between oneself and the object of one's hate, the more likely it is to become indifference. As Susan Sontag observed, "it is easy to turn your eyes from what is happening if it is not happening to you."[39]

Just because we are not the victims of hate does not mean we have no role to play. The worst people are bystanders, whether they ignore cries for help from a woman being attacked in an alley or skip over the newspaper article about hundreds of thousands of Africans dying in the Sudan from starvation and war. Feeling indifferent toward our fellow humans is a far greater sin than hating them.

Hatred has become demonized in our culture. If someone opens their newspaper and reads that Bashar Assad has gassed his citizens and calls their member of Congress to demand legislation to sanction this monster, or enlists in the U.S. military because of a desire to punish this miscreant, they are treated as warmongers who want to disturb the peace. If instead that person reads the headline and is disinterested, turning the page to read how the Yankees are doing, they are seen as morally superior because they have refused to hate. If that isn't absurd, I don't know what is.

Sadly, we have become so used to carnage on television, in movies, and on the nightly news that we are rarely moved unless an incident hits home, such as a school shooting or the murder of a well-known figure such as John Lennon. We have become numb and indifferent to much of the violence around us.

Think about this. Why in the Hebrew Bible is the Messiah always referred to as the son of David, the warrior king, rather than the son of Solomon, the wise king who kept the peace?

The reason is that those who do the hard work of fighting evil are those who facilitate peace. I know it sounds paradoxical, but in the confrontation with evil, there can be no peace without war. America eviscerated Hitler and Nazism and have kept the peace in Europe for three generations. The most wicked people cannot be negotiated with. They are unmoved by an offer of carrots, which they interpret as a sign of weakness, and are not chastened by recourse to sticks that fall short of outright war, such as economic sanctions. We see this today in our inability to stop the nuclear programs of North Korea and Iran. Realpolitik is actually an impediment to defeating evil.

It is also easier to advocate military intervention when you have nothing personally at stake. I believe, for example, that Israel should do whatever it takes to wipe out the terrorists of Hamas whose raison d'être is the destruction of the Jewish state. When my son was an Israeli combat soldier, however, I hoped the Israel Defense Forces (IDF) would not have to fight. Of course, one of the strongest arguments against war is that those who are responsible for making the decision should think of every soldier as their own child. That said, most soldiers are patriots who believe in defending their country and are prepared to risk the ultimate sacrifice. It is the obligation of those who send them to war to ensure they will be fighting in a just cause and not for vengeance or to benefit any special interest.

Eternal vigilance is indeed the price of liberty. So long as one's enemies are armed with evil intent, one must forever remain a David. Of the two men, it is the legacy of the father that is greater than the son. Peace will be brought to the world through a son of David rather than of Solomon because war is preferable to a peace where gross injustice persists. I wish it were not so, but the prerequisite to global harmony is the eradication of evil, which unfortunately can sometimes only be accomplished through violent means. That is why we famously refer to World War II as "the good war."

Some readers—especially Jewish ones—may ask: how can this be when the Jewish religion places peace at the head of all godly goals? Consider these examples from Jewish tradition:

"Hate is the product of too much self-love."

- RAV KOOK, *TORAS COHEN*

"Some people who hate others justify their behavior by claiming that they are lovers of truth and the person I hate is false. In fact, a love of truth that manifests itself in hate of others is only imaginary. None of us are completely "true," yet we don't hate ourselves for it. Where is our love of truth when it comes to ourselves?"

- REBBE OF OZOROV IN *AISH DOS*

"If you will notice, most mitzvot depend on love of mankind, i.e., charity, tithes, business ethics, interest and many more. Most of the character traits of God, i.e., mercy, patience, kindness, giving another person the benefit of the doubt, and many others that we must emulate, depend on attitudes and feelings towards another person. That is why loving one's fellow man is an essential rule of the Torah."

- SHNEI LUCHOS HABRIS

"If you are tempted to hate another individual, even if you feel it is a mitzvah to hate a particular person, ask yourself the following question: Are you happy with his downfall? If the answer is yes, then God does not want your hate. In the final analysis, there is almost no justification for hate. The Torah says, "Do not hate your brother in your heart." Those whom it is permissible to hate are almost nonexistent. We should try to replace the emotion of hate with virtue of love, which is a mitzvah of the Torah. There is no difference between the mitzvah of Tefillin or Tzitzit and staying away from non-kosher foods, except that the force of habit which we have acquired from childhood has reinforced these other mitzvot. When it comes to the mitzvah of love, our development has been reversed, as we learn to fight with other children, etc. We need only reverse our habits."

- SEFER HAMIDOS, DUBNOW MAGID

"Learn what is good, not to harbor hatred, rather to help one's enemy, which is only proper according to human values and the principles of the Torah. This is the pride of Israel, that they do not perpetuate hatred. Thus, their characters are upright, that by disposition they will neither hate nor seek revenge."

RABBI YONASAN ELBESHUTZ,
YAROS DEVASH DRUSH 10.

Similarly, in the Torah, God commands the Jews to "love

the Lord your God with all your heart and all of your soul and with all of your might; and may these words that I am commanding you today be on your heart."

These statements elevate love to the highest good and warn against indulging in hate. But these apply only in cases where we are not confronting evil. The murderer in our midst is not our brother. We are therefore obliged not to love him but to hate him in order to stop his bloodthirsty pursuits. Hate as well as love must be contextualized. The Creator is not only a God of peace. As with His decimation of Pharaoh's legions at the Red Sea, He is also "a God of war."

But God, of course, is inanimate. While Christianity assigns godlike divinity to Jesus, Numbers 23:19 declares, "God is not a man, that He should lie. Nor the son of a man, that He should repent." Moreover, in Judaism we do not blame God for evil in the world. We are permitted to rage against God when bad things happen to good people as in the case of the Holocaust. However, humans have free will and whatever wicked deeds they commit are their responsibility alone. When Jews are commanded to love God or hate evil, they are being asked specifically to harness their emotions to feel drawn to—or repelled by—things they might feel indifferently toward.

Solomon makes similar demands regarding wisdom. "Forsake her not," he writes in Proverbs, "and she will preserve thee; love her, and she will keep thee…Extol her, and she will exalt thee; she will bring thee to honor, when thou dost embrace her."

Clearly, Solomon wants wisdom to be not only the object of our pursuit but also that of passionate love and desire. We are meant to lust for knowledge of God and our world the way we do for carnal connection. That's quite a strong force of emotion, but that is why God endowed us with the capacity to love infinitely, so that we could do and be good passionately.

If we love the wicked, however, what is left for the righteous? While a selfish and therefore baseless hatred can destroy cohesion, a healthy revulsion can galvanize us to stop the wicked in their tracks.

To express this point, we'll turn to what might be the most famous tale of the Talmud.

About two thousand years ago, in ancient Israel, a non-Jewish man decided to horse around with some rabbis. What he did not know is that the two rabbis he chose to pick on were respectively the leading voices in the ancient Judean community, each the father of arguably the most celebrated schools of thought ever recorded in the Talmud.

One of these great sages was Hillel; the other was Shammai.

The apostate first approached Shammai.

He asked, "I will convert to Judaism on condition that you stand on one foot and tell me the entirety of your Torah."

Shammai was offended at the assertion that God's own thought could be contained by a human mind, let alone reduced to words, especially words that could be said in the time an elderly man could balance himself on one foot.

Shammai shooed the man away with a measuring stick. The apostate then made his way to Hillel.

He asked, "I will convert to Judaism on condition that while I stand on one foot you tell me the entirety of your Torah."

Here I'll point out one more thing the apostate didn't know, namely that Hillel was going to answer him. Not only would he answer him, but he would do so with words that would define and revolutionize not only all Jewish thought and ethics, but possibly provide much of the bedrock for the ethics of the Western world—something popularly known as the Golden Rule. The words recorded by the Talmud as the original form of the expression, however, might come to some as a surprise.

Hillel, we are told, converted the man to Judaism, and keeping his side of the bargain, raised one of his feet and said the following perfect words:

"That which is hateful to you," Hillel told him, "do not do unto your colleague. That is the entire Torah, and all the rest is commentary. Now go and study."

The Jewish sages have debated this aphorism for thousands of years. Many rabbis angled and elaborated in prolonged tracts, each trying to explain how that sentence could possibly encapsulate the entirety of Judaism without even a mention of God. (Some have pointed out that Judaism inclines us to treat all men as well as we treat God, an inspirational teaching in a world where so many still murder in God's name.)

By far the greatest question asked, however, was why the Golden Rule was delivered in the negative. Why didn't he say, "That which you love, do unto others?" Or better yet, why not just use the Bible's own version from Leviticus: "Love your neighbor as yourself?"

There are scores of fascinating explanations for this story, lining hundreds of pages of Hebrew texts. The simplest explanation, however, is this: Love comes down to preference. In other words, we all love different things.

Some love quiet, some love noise. Some love peace, some love drama. Some love being left alone, while others crave engagement. Making love more divisive is the fact that what we love depends largely on our age, background, values, and environment. What elderly Americans love and enjoy is hardly what the youth do; while one parties, the other will call the police over a noise complaint.

In contrast, we're all very familiar with what it is we find hateful. Being deceived, for example, has a universal distaste. Feeling pain, similarly, is a bad thing to (just about) all. Being rejected, being dismissed, being disrespected, being overlooked: these are all things that we hate and despise. That all would hate being harmed or killed should certainly be clear.

As expressed by Hillel, "That which you hate, don't do unto others"—the Golden Rule—not only holds but is instantly recognizable and understandable to all.

Just as we all stand under the same moon, we all stand united in what we hate. And let me be clear. Here I'm not discussing things like racial hatred, where white supremacists hate blacks and Jews, anarchists hate government, or Islamists hate non-Muslims. That is not hate but prejudice. And it's a bigotry that is almost always learned from something external, like our surroundings. No, I am talking about what we hate *internally*. That which we hate about how others treat us. We all hate rejection. We all hate not being appreciated. We all hate being treated like garbage. What Hillel was trying to convey is that one really big thing you hate, being made to feel like you are worthless, don't ever do that to another person.

Just as God needs to be loved and sought, evil needs to be hated and fought. Thus, if one is finding it hard to keep their eyes open while reports of poison gas attacks in Syria are beamed directly to their TV, you probably need to change the way you feel.

Healthy emotions exist in counterbalance. If you do not hate injustice, can you really love justice? If you do not hate murder, do you truly cherish human life? And we're not talking about killing but rather murder. Killing is sometimes justified if, and only if, it's in defense of human life, or is applied as punishment for having taken human life.

Capital punishment, I believe, is necessary to make clear that the destruction of innocent life cannot be tolerated in a civilized society.

Why is there a resistance to this idea of Kosher Hate?

To determine the starting point of the historical campaign against hate, we must travel back twenty-three centuries to the academies of Athens. There, long after Judaism did, the Greek philosophers began to take notice of the inner workings of the heart, ushering their budding cultures into the complex and undiscovered world of human emotion. While they obviously focused very much on love, hatred was bound to come up.

The cool-headed philosophers of ancient Greece, like the Stoics of Rome, had a notorious distaste for anger. While many confused the two, Aristotle drew a distinction between anger and hatred. Reading his discussion of the difference, one can easily conclude that he saw hatred as being worse than anger.

In *Rhetoric* (Book 2, Chapter 2) Aristotle explains:

> Anger derives from what happens to oneself, whereas hostility arises also without [the offense] being directed at oneself, for if we believe that someone is a certain kind of person, we hate him. Also, anger is always about individuals, for example Callius or Socrates, whereas hatred is also felt toward types: for everyone hates a thief and an informer. Moreover, anger is healed by time, while hatred is incurable. Also, the one is desire to inflict pain, while the other is a desire to inflict harm: for a person who is angry wishes to perceive [the effects of his revenge], but to the one who hates this is a matter of indifference....Also, the angry person might feel pity if enough [misfortunes befall the other], but not one who hates: for the former wishes that the person with whom he is angry should suffer in return, but the other wishes that he should cease to exist.

Let's have a look at Aristotle's claims in this passage.

First, he states that anger stems from an offence to one's own person—which means that the offense can be verified. Hatred, on the other hand, can be due to an offense to another, which means that the offense is not verifiable and may not even have occurred. Germans in the 1930s could not really be angry at Jews, since most Jews had never done anything to them. In their anti-Semitic delirium, they might have been convinced that Jews were responsible for ills in the society, and that would make them angry. But the offense was never real. They could despise them even though their hatred was horrifyingly unjustified and the perceived offenses totally unsubstantiated.

Moreover, Aristotle implies that anger is generally in response to an individual, whereas hatred is felt toward groups of various kinds. This, too, makes hate seem worse than anger. After all, hatred toward an individual may be plausibly justifiable but to harbor resentment against an entire category of people is the essence of bigotry.

Aristotle also implies that while anger has a shelf life, hatred is eternal. This is probably true insofar as irrational hate—as opposed to Kosher Hate—can never be sated.

Finally, Aristotle asserts that while the object of anger is to cause pain to the other, the object of hatred is to inflict harm. In this context, harm is worse than pain. Classics scholar David Konstan understood that this meant "when we are angry, what we desire is that the other person feel hurt in return." Regarding hatred, on the other hand, Konstan says we "may wish that people whom we hate should die." Aristotle seems to agree, asserting that we wish the object of our hatred would "cease to exist."[40]

This useful distinction helps us define Kosher Hate and separates it from garden-variety hate. Kosher Hate is directed at people who deserve extreme punishment.

Up until the end of the Second World War, it was still

fashionable to hate evil. Common sense dictated that one should feel intense revulsion for murderers on the macro and micro level. After Hitler made an overture of peace toward Britain in 1941, Winston Churchill rose before the House of Commons and said that he threw the offer back at the "Fuhrer's rotten, stinking, teeth." His contempt for Hitler galvanized the British public.

Five decades later, President George H. W. Bush was ridiculed for saying he hated Saddam Hussein. Somehow it was considered unseemly for the genteel Bush to hate this manifestly evil man, as though at the level of statecraft and high policy, emotions and moral instincts like love or hate should play no role.

Yet Bush's hatred was not like a cauldron of bile that he simply sat and stewed in. It was put to good practical use. Bush used his hatred of Saddam's evil regime to mobilize an international coalition. He forced Iraq out of Kuwait, demonstrating to the world that it was possible to stand up to a tyrant, punish his aggression, and protect the weak. So his hate had a positive outcome.

Indeed, Bush should have hated him more and sought not just to free Kuwait but to topple his regime. Hundreds of thousands of lives would have been saved, and there would have been no reason for his son George W. Bush to go to war and finish the job a decade later. Bush later admitted his only regret was "thinking that Saddam Hussein would be gone." Still, he believed he made the right decision not to go to Baghdad at the time, because it would have shattered the coalition he had assembled to confer legitimacy on the war.[41]

President George H. W. Bush was right to hate Saddam and go to war against him. While I can understand criticism of the decision, I cannot fathom how anyone could deride his hatred of a mass murderer.

Bush himself was a product of an earlier era. A combat

pilot during World War II, he firmly believed in the imperative to hate evil and oppose and attack it with force. So what
changed between World War II, when Americans had no
trouble expressing their revulsion for genocidal maniacs, and
the Gulf War?

The answer is a misguided cultural liberalism. This is all
the more important to understand, insofar as modern liberals can be profoundly and unnecessarily hypocritical in their
attitude toward hate. When it comes to our foreign enemies,
those who want to kill us just because we are Americans, often liberals will preach love and understanding. But when
it comes to their domestic political foes, those who merely
disagree with them on policy issues like immigration, gun
control, and environmental regulation, they may wallow in
a hatred so intense as to be inexplicable. That doesn't mean
that conservatives can't be hypocritical as well. It does mean,
however, that misguided political hatred on the part of those
preaching love is an all too common sin.

The 1960s gave birth to a modern cult of love. Neither
love nor liberalism were previously unknown, but the '60s
ushered in a new kind of love—unbridled love, a love that
knew no limit and was presented (or rather felt)—as the solution to all conflicts. Of course, like the "summer of love" itself, this feeling could not last. It had to dissipate because
it lacked serious moral grounding. Real love must have an
ethical foundation. But superficial love that embraces form
while overlooking substance cannot last.

Meanwhile, liberalism itself was touted not as a system of carefully circumscribed rights but as a new morality to replace Judeo-Christian ethics. Where Judaism spoke
of anything that was in rebellion against God as being evil,
and Christianity spoke of a duality governed by light and
darkness, this new morally superficial liberalism argued that
everything contained inherent goodness. Indiscriminate tol-

erance thus become axiomatic. In the liberal view, there are no truly evil people. We are told to hate the action, not the person. Murderers should not be harshly punished—let alone put to death—but should be empathized with and treated with compassion. They were probably neglected by their parents or grew up in harsh conditions, leading to their warped personalities and bad character traits. They are thus not ultimately responsible for their actions. Hatred, by contrast, with its absolutist connotations, is treated as the real source of evil rather than as a defense against wickedness.

Hatred of evil implies the right to make judgments and to believe in absolutes, both of which are anathema to contemporary liberalism. I certainly applaud many of liberalism's aims—justice, tolerance, equality—but its fatal flaw is revealed as soon as moral absolutes are removed from the picture.

If there are any grounds at all for the assertion that men are inherently good, it is to be found in our tenacious belief that humans are naturally selfless and cooperative. We obstinately believe that good persists within the breast of even the most wretched of men—despite evidence to the contrary. We desperately want goodness to be real, so it must exist somewhere—inviolably, eternally. And that somewhere is deep within the human soul.

Once upon a time, though, we had God. In those days, God was good, and man not necessarily. To be sure, man wasn't wicked either. Rather, he was born innocent of this distinction, poised between good and evil. And his actions, rather than his birth, would determine his character. God wanted us to be good and empowered us all to be so—if we chose. Good and evil were both within our reach. People knew that good was desirable and would earn the blessings of God and the esteem of their fellow humans. By contrast, going down the path of wickedness would bring curses, vituperation, and hate.

But as the modern age dispensed with God, and thus with any absolute morality including a belief in sin and judgment, we filled the void with a boundless new faith in humanity. This idealistic liberal conviction not only displaced traditional religion but it has also become a secular religion unto itself. This helps explain why those who disagree with it are treated as apostates and heretics who deserve to be hated and expelled from what Rev. Martin Luther King Jr. called the "beloved community." The community of the righteous who are here to bring the dream of perfect justice and equality for all to life on earth. For modern liberals, anyone who stands in the way of this secular project is not just mistaken or wrong but downright evil. Nor can there be any neutrality in the face of this transcendent utopian goal. Hence the expression, common since the 60s, "If you are not part of the solution, you are part of the problem."

All of this paradoxically flows from the liberal error about the fundamental goodness of humanity.

My good friend Dennis Prager, in his book *Think a Second Time,* argues that the belief that people are innately good is a profound mistake. The astonishing horrors of the twentieth century—Auschwitz, the Gulag, Rwanda—should be sufficient to prove this contention. Worse, it is highly destructive, because it allows some people literally to get away with murder. If we are all good at heart, then our crimes must be the fault of some external force—poverty, oppression, lax gun control, abuse as a child, our religious beliefs, or some other cause outside of us that "makes" us who we are. We commonly hear such justifications for terrorists whom we are told are frustrated, desperate, or poor. It is therefore not their fault if they are seduced by violent religious ideas or extreme political ideologies. But none of these things are excuses for acts of violence.

Gideon Hausner, the chief Israeli prosecutor at the trial of Adolf Eichmann, said that the scariest thing about the SS murderer was that he was a normal person who rationalized evil. As Hannah Arendt wrote in *Eichmann in Jerusalem,* the judges had difficulty admitting "that an average, 'normal' person, neither feeble-minded nor indoctrinate nor cynical, could be perfectly incapable of telling right from wrong."[42] Eichmann had no pangs of conscience from his actions; he would order the gassing of thousands of Jews (Zyklon B was a pesticide) as readily as he would spray insecticide on cockroaches. This is what Arendt famously referred to as "the banality of evil."

I agree with Prager and would add that this mistaken belief in an essential human goodness makes it more difficult for us as a society to condemn the actions of wrongdoers and easier to justify their offenses. Too often we label murderers as sick, as if anyone who commits such a heinous crime could be otherwise. By attributing their actions to some form of mental illness, we shift the blame from the person to nature or nurture. Psychopaths cannot be responsible for the harm they do, for example, because they are acting under the compulsion of a diseased mind. The consequence is that we pity those more deserving of a large dose of punishment.

This is not to say that insanity or other forms of mental illness are never an adequate defense for evil deeds. Judges cannot allow hate to cloud their ability to protect the rights of everyone by remaining fair and impartial. But once the determination is made through a system of absolute moral values that a person has committed a heinous crime, the obligation to hate begins.

I'm not saying real psychopaths don't exist—of course they do. I'm only protesting our eagerness to apply labels like "psychopath" to every violent killer in the belief that no person of sound mental health is capable of murder.

The reality is that people do not have to be depraved to be capable of extreme cruelty. Though their actions were vile, Nazi guards were not animals—they were ordinary men who behaved like animals. It has been said that a Nazi camp guard could send Jews to the gas chamber during the day and then go home to their family at night and read Goethe and listen to Mozart. Had the German people learned to recognize and hate evil based on inviolable moral standards, then a man like Hitler might never have risen to power, provoked a war, and exterminated six million Jews.

To the contrary, German children and the Hitler Youth were indoctrinated to see Jews as "the other" and a pestilence in society. I am reminded of the lyrics of the song "You've Got to Be Carefully Taught" from Rodgers and Hammerstein's musical *South Pacific*.

This is not to say there were no good Germans. Think of Hans Scholl and his sister Sophie, graduates of the Hitler Youth who bravely created an organization called "The White Rose" to resist the Nazis—and paid for their efforts with their lives. "The Scholls and their friends," wrote Richard Hanser in *A Noble Treason*, "represented the 'other' Germany, the land of poets and thinkers, in contrast to the Germany that was reverting to barbarism and trying to take the world with it.... What they did transcended the easy division of good-German/bad-German."

There were others like the Scholls. But too few Germans had the moral hatred necessary to confront the Nazi regime.

LIBERAL CONTRADICTIONS

Today's liberals have no difficulty hating perpetrators of violence or other abuse if the victim is a member of a protected class of people and the wrongdoer can be described as a colonialist, capitalist, or racist. Communists, Islamists, and terrorists masquerading as "freedom fighters," on the other hand, are often excused for their crimes.

Consider the story of Matthew Shepard, a gay student at the University of Wyoming who was beaten, tortured, and left to die by two men who hated homosexuals.[43] All but the most extreme homophobes would agree this was unconscionable, despise the perpetrators, and demand justice. Scripture may refer to homosexuality as an abomination, but hatred of gays is not a moral good; it is a disgusting and deep-seated prejudice. Many liberals identified with Shepherd because he was a member of a group who they believe should be protected, along with women, and other minorities. Some are gay or have friends who are gay, and the thought that someone could be murdered because of their sexual orientation is an anathema. Surely hatred for the perpetrator of such a heinous crime is merited.

It should not be difficult to apply the philosophy of Kosher Hate in such a circumstance.

How can anyone retain their humanity, for example, if they do not hate a man like Abu Musab al-Zarqawi—a maniac who shouts "God is great" while sawing off the heads of innocent civilians.[44] You cannot claim to feel compassion for his victims without simultaneously hating this terrorist. Hatred should be a natural response to witnessing the inhumane treatment of a fellow human. Not to feel that is akin to not reacting to hunger by eating or exhaustion by sleeping.

Failure to hate a tormentor shows contempt for their victim. It also proves that declarations of sympathy for victims are phony. You cannot claim to love the innocent without hating their persecutors. Loving the victims might generate compassion for their suffering, but hating the perpetrators will generate action to stop the abuse.

Everyone should be willing to admit that a person who repeatedly and unrepentantly murders innocents in cold blood is evil. Why not hate such a man? What do you lose? Could it possibly be ethically unsound or internally corrupting to be repulsed and enraged by a mass murderer? Or is it possible, to turn it around, that it's ethically unsound and internally corrupting to feel nothing at the thought of a mass murderer?

Those who don't believe that such people are evil are blind. Shepherd's killers deserved to be hated. I am primarily interested in applying Kosher Hate to genocidal maniacs like Hitler, Kim Jung-un, and Bashar Assad, but that does not mean we should not hate an individual killer. It is not the "mass" in mass murderer that distinguishes murder as evil. It is not the scope of an act, but its character that defines evil in this context. The premeditated killing of another person violates the Sixth Commandment and turns a human into a repository of evil.

Yes, the genocidal Hitler can be distinguished from the robber who kills a convenience store clerk, but it's not a numbers game. It all comes down to the crime. I would not limit it to murder, but apply Kosher Hate to the perpetrators of other heinous crimes such as rape and white slavery.

If, for only a moment, you allow yourself to feel enraged by butchers like Bashar Assad—to indulge in a hatred of the evil they represent—then you probably won't fall asleep during that news special about the Syrian civil war. Instead you will be roused from your slumber, angry at the fact that in the twenty-first century such slaughter could still be going on. If you feel deeply enough, you might find out how you can help. At the very least, events in Syria might be an issue you take with you to the ballot box when you contemplate your vote. Then politicians might take notice and be compelled to act.

CHAPTER 3:
COULD JESUS HATE?

IT IS NOT JUST LIBERALS who have forgotten how—or whom—to hate. The other great source of anti-hate sentiment in the West is the great Jewish preacher and rebel, Jesus of Nazareth, a compelling personality to whom I devoted a previous book, *Kosher Jesus.*

According to the New Testament, as Jesus began to gain traction as a renegade religious leader, his followers and others curious to hear his message assembled on a hilltop in the north of Israel, not far from the Sea of Galilee. This is the Mount of Beatitudes, where Jesus looked toward the eager congregants of his new synagogue and delivered one of the most influential speeches in human history, the Sermon on the Mount. You can visit the site today, as I have done several times with my family. There's a small shrine and a church nearby. Tourists mill about taking photos. It's hard to imagine how that small gathering more than two millennia ago could have had such a momentous impact on the world.

Jesus was still quite early in his ministry. According to Matthew, he had just returned from forty days of fasting and contemplation in the solitude of the Judean desert. Upon his arrival at Capernaum in the Galilee region, he began to gather disciples and gain influence as a spiritual leader whose reach extended, according to Christian tradition, across the Jordan River and deep into Syria.

At a certain point, Jesus sees a crowd waiting on a hillside and decides to deliver a sermon—the first and fullest recorded in the New Testament. The Sermon on the Mount takes up three chapters in the book of Matthew, and it contains many, if not most, of Jesus's most celebrated teachings. "Blessed are the meek, for they shall inherit the earth," Jesus says in his opening lines. "Blessed are the peacemakers," he goes on, "for they shall be called the children of God." It is also where he made the famous declaration, "Ask and it will be given to you; seek and you shall find; knock and the door will be opened to you."

The sermon is largely a rendition of Jewish teachings, but one possible departure is this section, taken from the end of the fifth chapter of Matthew:

> You have heard that it was said, 'Love your neighbor and hate your enemy.' But I tell you, love your enemies and pray for those who persecute you, that you may be children of your Father in heaven. He causes his sun to rise on the evil and the good and sends rain on the righteous and the unrighteous. If you love those who love you, what reward will you get? Are not even the tax collectors doing that? And if you greet only your own people, what are you doing more than others? Do not even pagans do that? Be perfect, therefore, as your heavenly Father is perfect.

Luke (6:27-31) gives an account of what appears to be the same sermon, but expresses the concept perhaps even more powerfully:

> But to you who are listening I say: Love your enemies, do good to those who hate you, bless those

who curse you, pray for those who mistreat you. If someone slaps you on one cheek, turn to them the other also. If someone takes your coat, do not withhold your shirt from them. Give to everyone who asks you, and if anyone takes what belongs to you, do not demand it back. Do to others as you would have them do to you.

I describe these words as a "possible departure" because it isn't entirely clear that he really deviates from traditional Jewish teachings. However, from these verses it seems that Jesus wants his followers to love those they would be expected to hate. His words can therefore be understood to demand love even as a response to evil. After all, he says, "He causes the sun to rise on the evil and the good." If emulation is highest form of worship—*imitatio dei*, as this doctrine is called—it follows that Christians must love both the evil and the good.

Consider the sermon's description of the link between anger and murder:

You have heard that it was said to the people long ago, "You shall not murder, and anyone who murders will be subject to judgment." But I tell you that anyone who is angry with a brother or sister will be subject to judgment. Again, anyone who says to a brother or sister, "Raca," is answerable to the court. And anyone who says, "You fool!" will be in danger of the fire of hell.

While the textual similarities can be debated, what is certain is that the Sermon on the Mount provides the fundamental moral teachings of the Christian faith somewhat in the way God's words at Sinai provide those of the Jews.

Thus, when Jesus says one must not hate their enemies—but must love them instead—he seems to be telling his flock to reject hatred as a valid emotion. But did he really mean to advocate passivity in the face of naked cruelty?

That simply cannot be. Rather, he must have meant that if someone offends you in a *personal* way, you should forgive them and transcend the provocation. After all, Jesus said to love *your* enemies, not God's. Your enemy is someone who steals your parking space or the guy who gets your promotion at work. But neo-Nazis marching in Charlottesville chanting, "Jews will not replace us!" or, worse, an actual Nazi working toward the Jews' annihilation are the enemies of humanity. They violate the fundamental tenet of a decent liberal society—the infinite value of every human life. Enemies of humanity are enemies of God.

Indeed, the greatest proof that Jesus never meant to disavow hatred entirely is the fact that perhaps the most influential all the apostles, Paul, makes the same point as David and Solomon in describing how to love God properly. "Love must be sincere," he writes to his growing base of followers in the Imperial capital. "Hate what is evil; cling to what is good."

While the meaning is vague, Jesus seems to support, if not demand, some form of hatred within the hearts of his followers. "If anyone comes to me and does not hate father and mother, wife and children, brothers and sisters, yes, even their own life, such a person cannot be my disciple."

Now, according to one interpretation, "Jesus is not demanding that you literally hate your family. He is using hyperbole to illustrate the steep cost of following him…. Our affections for Christ must be of such an intensity and quality that, by comparison, all other loves seem like hate."[45] Another common interpretation: "Christ is saying that anyone following Him, making a commitment to the Christian way of life, must *love Him more* than family and friends, and even life itself."[46]

These are popular interpretations. And yet, Jesus did not have to use the word hate to make the point. If hate was utterly unkosher in his vocabulary, he would have forbid it entirely.

Jesus is talking about the need to give up everything to be his disciple. Interestingly, one example he gives to illustrate his point in Luke 14:31 seems to also demonstrate a recognition that war may sometimes be necessary:

> Or suppose a king is about to go to war against another king. Won't he first sit down and consider whether he is able with ten thousand men to oppose the one coming against him with twenty thousand? If he is not able, he will send a delegation while the other is still a long way off and will ask for terms of peace.

Jesus seems to be saying that you go to war when you are confident you will win. This reasonable analysis is consistent with a point I will make later about distinguishing our enemies, and how we should confront and defeat them.

Still, it appears those words were too little, too late. The words of the sermon would eclipse the commandments that Jesus himself believed, and hatred would be delivered a near deathblow. On the Mount of Beatitudes, Jesus inspired his followers and laid the groundwork of his nascent church. On that day, Jesus formulated, and essentially gave birth to a concept that would become one of the quintessential tenets of Christianity and western culture—Christian love.

There is another episode in the Gospels where a lawyer asks Jesus to identify the neighbor referred to in the commandment to "love thy neighbor as thyself." Jesus replied with the parable of the Good Samaritan, in which a priest and a Levite ignore a traveler who has been robbed, stripped, and nearly beaten to death. A Samaritan, however, stops to assist him. "The one who showed him mercy," Jesus says, is the good neighbor.

The Samaritan is a kind and ethical human being, but some Christian teachers take this parable to expand the commandment "love your neighbor" to include all people, not just those in need—even the enemies of humanity. For example, in her writing about Christian love, the Bible scholar Jen Wilkin describes the Samaritan as representing the "unlovable." She explains, "If love is an act of the will—not motivated by need, not measuring worth, not requiring reciprocity—then there is no such category as 'unlovable.'"[47]

But it would be foolish to apply this to the category of the truly evil. If the SS is not unlovable then nothing is. And if nothing is unlovable, then everything is lovable, and the categories of good and evil are meaningless. Let's state the most obvious thing ever said. Hitler is absolutely unlovable. Talk about an understatement.

Consider this answer to a question about loving evil people:

> The call to avoid people who can mislead others in the faith is simple prudence. We can still love those people, in the sense that we can pray for them and that we hope they reach heaven someday. For this reason, we shouldn't think of certain people as inherently evil; they too can have a conversion or come to the full knowledge of Jesus' teachings. But loving someone doesn't mean we are obligated to stay close to them and expose our faith to attacks…. Being "nice" to people doesn't mean we go to any extreme to accommodate them. The simple fact is, being Christian means to encounter opposition and at times ridicule. It also entails speaking out at times against the injustice and immorality we see around us. That will make us enemies. It made enemies for Jesus, but he didn't water down his message.[48]

Many of my Christian brothers and sisters mistakenly believe that God loathes hatred. They quote Jesus's instruction to turn the other cheek and his admonishment to love your enemies as proof that we dare never hate.

As one correspondent wrote to me:

> The Christian expects his religion to provide comfort in the face of life's more troublesome metaphysical problems. What else is religion for? That is why he is told to exercise love in the face of evil. The tension of perpetual hate – a possible response – is too difficult to live with. Love is a release.

On the nationally syndicated radio show I used to host, many evangelical Christians called in to tell me that in God's eyes we are all sinners, and thus from a heavenly perspective Osama bin Laden and the average housewife in Kansas are equal. Osama must indeed face justice for his crimes, but we dare not hate him, seeing that Jesus will still love him.

Here is what the U.S. Conference of Catholic Bishops said on the subject:

> It is clear to us today that the only way to peace is by destroying enmity, not the enemy. (Should we destroy half the population of the world dissatisfied with the way things are? And how do we identify the enemy where terrorism is concerned?) Someone once took Abraham Lincoln to task for being too courteous to his enemies and reminded him that his job as president was to destroy them. Lincoln answered, Do I not destroy my enemies when I make them my friends? Enemies are destroyed with armies, but enmity with dialogue. (From the Good Friday 2003 homily by Capuchin Father Raniero Cantalamessa, preacher of the papal household, to Pope John Paul II)[49]

The bishops correctly understand that "turning the other cheek" does not mean succumbing to evil. But they are mistaken in believing, as Pope Benedict apparently did, that violence and injustice can be overcome by more love.

As Benedict succinctly explained, "love of one's enemy constitutes the nucleus of the Christian revolution, a revolution not based on strategies of economic, political or media power: the revolution of love, a love that does not rely ultimately on human resources but is a gift of God which is obtained by trusting solely and unreservedly in his merciful goodness."[50]

Now all of this is true when it applies to *your* enemy, but not when it applies to *God's* enemy. Even while Lincoln said this he still had hundreds of thousands of soldiers in the field to destroy the Confederate armies and the institution of slavery, just as Pope Benedict surely does not mean that he would love the Nazis who had pressed him into being part of the Hitler Youth when he was a boy growing up in Germany.

What we need today is a counterrevolution that rejects this idea that love can defeat evil and acknowledge that only Kosher Hate can rid the world of mass murderers and *genocidaires*.

I would respectfully tell my Christian colleagues that it is a travesty of Jesus's teachings to suggest he would have shown such contempt for the victims as to extend Christian love to their murderers. Jesus advocated turning the other cheek to petty slights and affronts to our sensibilities, not to the perpetrators of genocide. Jesus asks us to find it in our hearts to forgive the kids who bullied us at school, not the tyrants who slaughter children.

My Christian brothers and fellow theologians may sharply disagree with this interpretation. However, I would argue that the only way to comprehend the true Jesus of Nazareth is to understand the Jewish Jesus. As I explained in *Kosher Jesus*, what Jesus taught and preached stemmed from the Torah in which he was immersed, the Judaism he practiced, and the Jewish faith he preached. Divorcing Jesus from his Jewish roots, including the Torah's repeated injunctions to hate evil, cannot but yield fraudulent, even ludicrous interpretations of his words.

Are we really to believe, for example, that Jesus wants to us to love Adolph Hitler? Had he preached as much in 1944, would we not have dismissed him as insane and his teachings as utterly warped? To say that Jesus meant for us to love such monsters as Hitler, Stalin, Pol Pot, and Saddam Hussein makes a mockery of his message and his ministry.

The Bible commands us to "love our neighbor" as ourselves. But the man who kills children is not our neighbor. Having cast off the image of God, he has lost his divine spark, erased the divine countenance from his visage, and is condemned to eternal oblivion from which not even a belief in Salvation will rescue him. He who murders God's children has been lost to God forever and has abandoned all entitlement to love, earning eternal damnation instead.

My Christian brothers and sisters might respond that Jesus did set an example for how to react to evil. The Judeans who viewed Jesus as their savior expected him to lead an army to expel the Romans who persecuted them and occupied their land. He would be like David, the warrior who built a Hebrew kingdom.

But Jesus did not raise an army. Instead, he merely asked his disciples to bring him an ass to ride into Jerusalem. The gospels say that Jesus was fulfilling the prophecy of Zechariah (9:9) who said, "Rejoice greatly, daughter of Zion. Shout for joy, daughter of Jerusalem, for your king is coming, just and victorious, humble, and riding on a donkey."

As retired Auxiliary Bishop of the Archdiocese of Detroit Thomas Gumbleton explains, "the prophet was proclaiming that God overcomes evil and violence, killing and war, not by responding in the same way, but by giving up violence; by not trying to dominate, by loving and only loving in response to your enemy. Love your enemy."[51]

It is unfortunately necessary to point out that over the centuries Christians have been better at preaching brotherly love than practicing it. Jesus did not say anything to suggest he was anti-Jewish; he was Jewish himself after all. It was the writers of the gospels who introduced anti-Semitism—the institutionalized hatred of Jews. Christian love subsequently did not apply to Jews who were victimized by Christians in the Crusades, the Inquisition, and throughout centuries of blood libels and pogroms. Christians also abandoned love of infidels such as Muslims, against whom they crusaded for centuries, and engaged in persecution of heretics and internecine wars against apostates.

Islam can be criticized for having its share of extremists. But there is no Muslim "pope" directing their actions or promulgating a doctrine that calls for the death of non-Muslims. Similarly, it is justified to condemn a Jewish mass murderer like Baruch Goldstein or the Jews who burned and murdered a Palestinian youth, but their actions cannot be attributed to Judaism. No Jewish "pope" promotes a global campaign against the enemies of the Jews. In Christianity, however, there is a pope, one they refer to as the Vicar of Christ, who at different times promoted bigotry and instigated murder. The enemies of the Church they identified were not beneficiaries of Christian love.

If we ignore the perversion of his teachings and go back to the events in Jesus's life, can we find any lessons for our own times?

Some might argue, for example, that our government must use diplomacy to negotiate a nuclear agreement with Iran that will prevent the mullahs from building a bomb and thereby avoid war. Others, however, say this will never work; the only way to stop Iran from starting nuclear war is to destroy the regime or destroy the nuclear sites.

If talks fail, what then? Will we have no choice but to go to war or will it already be too late?

Think about it. What would be the way of Jesus? Would he love his enemies in Tehran and figuratively ride an ass to meet with them to negotiate or would Jesus advocate the use of force?

To this I respond, Jesus understood the brutality of Rome. It's the reason that he asks, on the last night of his life in the Garden of Gethsemane, for swords from his followers. Yes, they were few, but his point was that war must be an option to combat evil. That's why Jesus declared himself to be the King of the Jews. He knew it was a death sentence to do that, to challenge the authority of the Roman Emperor, especially after the Romans had abolished the Jewish monarchy. But he hated Rome for their brutality and their oppression of his people.

Amid my deep and abiding respect for the Christian faith, I state unequivocally that to love or excuse the white supremacist who walks into a synagogue and callously mows down eleven innocent men and women at prayer, as we witnessed at the Tree of Life Synagogue in Pittsburgh, constitutes a passive form of complicity. As Martin Luther King, Jr. said, "he who passively accepts evil is as much involved in it as he who helps to perpetrate it. He who accepts evil without protesting against it is really cooperating with it."[52] Tolerating the intolerable and forgiving the unforgivable is the surest way to empower evil. Hating evil is not a conduit for revenge but the very preservation of justice.

A Christian friend who is an artist showed me a picture he painted of Jesus embracing Hitler. I told him to destroy it because it was obscene. "How can you have Jesus holding Hitler?" I asked. "That's the point," he responded. "That's how far Jesus's love extends."

"That's love?" I asked. "If you love Hitler, then you are showing contempt for the good and decent people who he turned into ash and lampshades. The only response to Hitler is utter contempt and violent hatred. The only way to react to incorrigible evil is to wage an incessant war against it until it is eliminated from the earth."

It boggles the mind to think that someone would believe Jesus could love the man responsible for the murder of 1.5 million children.

One problem with the people who speak of the Holocaust today is that they think only in terms of statistics—the six million—but that gives the cataclysm an antiseptic, abstract, and almost trivial quality. Consider loving the perpetrators of the war crimes committed by ordinary people who behaved monstrously when in a Nazi uniform.

According to war crimes prosecutors, here are some of the methods used to kill Jews at Mauthausen concentration camp: "gassing, hanging, clubbing, heart injections, driving inmates into the electric fence, kicking in genitals, being buried alive, and by putting a red-hot poker down the throat."[53] Elsewhere Jews would be forced to strip naked and dig their own graves before the Nazis lined them up and shot them so their bodies would fall in. If a single shot did not kill a Jew, sometimes they were buried alive in order to save bullets. Groups of Jews were corralled into buildings and locked inside before the buildings were set on fire. In Bialystok, 800–1,000 Jewish men and boys were burned alive in the Great Synagogue on June 27, 1941. My family and I visited the site in the summer of 2017 and prayed where our people were turned into ash in a house of God.

Would Jesus love the "doctors" like Josef Mengele who experimented on Jews, for instance murdering twins and dwarfs as young as two years old so he could compare their internal organs? Or Horst Schumann who sterilized men and women by pointing x-rays at their sexual organs?

Believe it or not, I have spared you from descriptions of even more gruesome acts of murder and genocide committed by the Nazis.

Though it may seem paradoxical to some, any culture that does not hate Hitler and his ilk is a non-compassionate society. The religious response to the evil person is to hate him with every fiber of one's being and to hope he finds no rest in this world or the next. Among Orthodox Jews, there is an oft-used Hebrew phrase whose equivalent I have not found among Christians. The phrase is *yemach shemo*, which means, may his name be erased. This is one way we express our contempt for the evilest people.

One important difference between Christianity and Judaism is that Jews unabashedly celebrate life while Christians venerate the afterlife. It is interesting—remarkable, really—that in the whole of the Jewish Bible there are no passages describing either the joys of heaven or the torments of hell. Discussion of the world to come occurs only in Rabbinic writings like the Talmud, and then only in the most speculative of ways. Christianity, on the other hand, makes much of paradise, purgatory, and hell. The entire religious drama is seen as a struggle to redeem oneself from hellfire and to attain eternal reward. Life as we know it is just a shadow—what really counts is the life to come. Death is the gateway to a more perfect place. It can also be redemptive, as in the case of Jesus.

Jews believe in *tikkun olam*—repairing the world. For the Jew, the goal is to make this world into a better place now and for the future. In the mind, and in the world to come, there is no place for hate, according to many of our Christian brothers. It is true that in the pious mind, the thought of hate is better avoided. But in the real world, hatred is a necessary evil.

How has Christianity come to be so misunderstood? Shouldn't the very first aim of religion be to uphold the moral basis of society by making a clear and unmistakable distinction between proper and improper actions? Indeed, we derive all moral force from religion. The very notions of right and wrong, good and evil, are almost meaningless without a religious basis. Only religion, with its emphasis on a Creator and Lawgiver, has at its foundation the idea of absolute and uncompromising morality as revealed by God.

The secular laws of the United States can only dictate what is lawful and unlawful, not what is inherently good or bad. The underlying ideas of good and evil are ultimately grounded in the Judeo-Christian moral tradition and the Ten Commandments. God is the ultimate arbiter of good and evil, right and wrong. To become all love in response to evil—to come forward and offer forgiveness readily to rapists and child murderers—is to blur those differences and lessen the mighty force that religion exercises over our morals. True, the Jewish sage Moses Ibn Ezra said beautifully, "No sin is so light that it may be overlooked; no sin is so heavy that it may not be repented of." But he was not speaking of the sin of mass murder but of much less serious sins whose consequences are reversible through repentance.

So how has it come to be that so many Christians have become confused and lost sight of religion's most pivotal message for a Godly society, which is a belief in absolute morality and the need to love good and hate evil?

The Christian faith was built up over several generations and by several groups of people: Jesus, St. Paul, the apostles, early church fathers, and preachers of the gospel. And Judaism begins with the immutable code of Mosaic scripture—the written law—followed by prophets, and later the sages of the Talmud who wrote down the oral tradition in order to forever secure the faith.

But there is an important difference. While the Jewish scholars and rabbis of ancient times simply explained the faith to their own—"preaching to the converted" as it were—the first Christian missionaries, such as Paul, were seeking to spread the gospel to a broader public. The apostles and disciples of Jesus and Paul recognized that it would be difficult to pass on the strictures of Judaism to the people they were seeking to convert. So they emphasized, instead, the moral teachings of Jesus and created a set of beliefs more acceptable to the masses. The practicable side of Judaism—the actual observance of the mitzvot—was all but abandoned, surviving only in ecclesiastical rituals, performed only in church, and only by specially trained priests who dedicated their lives to the faith.

God's law came to the Jews all at once when He announced himself from a desert mountaintop to an entire nation of newly freed slaves. Christianity began with Jesus and his select disciples and took several generations to catch on widely. But it worked, and 2000 years later Christianity can claim nearly two billion adherents across the globe, uniting people of every ethnicity. The masses gather for Sunday worship at magnificent cathedrals in Rome, Rheims, Canterbury, Moscow, New York, or Newark, and at village churches in the countryside, all praying for salvation. By emphasizing belief over practice and grace over acts, Christianity became the world's most popular faith.

While some people are busy painting Jesus in pastel colors and proclaiming his everlasting love for all mankind, others have a very different conception of Jesus.

Tim LaHaye's epic *Left Behind* series has now sold more than forty million copies, so a lot of people clearly share his vision. The premise of these novels is that the apocalypse has hit present-day America. Over the course of twelve books, he details the carnage and destruction that he thinks will accompany the end of days. Nuclear bombs are dropped on Manhattan, London, Mexico City, and Montreal and three quarters of the world's population dies in an orgy of war, famine, and disease. Jesus's faithful followers escape, however, having ascended to safety beforehand—"raptured" as he calls it.

Jesus appears from the sky in the post-apocalyptic world, descending on a gigantic horse kitted out like an ancient Viking warrior. This is not the meek Jesus of Renaissance art or Hollywood, dressed in a robe and sandals, but Jesus the avenger overseeing the destruction of the sinful human world.

Did most imagine Jesus to be the hippie from iconography, or from LaHaye's Jesus the Terminator?

The true Jesus must lie somewhere in the middle. La-Haye's view is relevant because it seems to be the Jesus that is depicted in the book of Revelation, Jesus as Lord over Judgment Day. The God of the Old Testament loves the righteous and hates the wicked, but Christians weren't happy with this image; they felt that it was too similar to Judaism. Christianity had to be radically different, so it veered off toward the extremes on both sides of the median. Besides the New Testament writings, the popular iconography has perpetuated the belief in Jesus the pacifist.

It is time for my Christian brethren to take a serious second look at the man who stands at the center of their faith. And it is specifically by learning about the Jewish Jesus that a more authentic Christianity, connected to its Jewish roots, can emerge.

The refusal to hate evil on the part of Christians is puzzling given that exhortations to hate all manner of evil abound in the Bible. But hatred is held in contempt by those who have talked themselves into the belief that God is love and that hate must be of the Devil. Early Christians like the first century theologian Marcion saw a contradiction between the God of the Jewish Bible who felt jealousy and told his followers to feel hate, and the God of the New Testament who is defined by unlimited love and compassion. The inability to reconcile this incongruity is one explanation for the definitive split between Judaism and Christianity.

Before I get into a scriptural refutation of the misconception that Christians seemingly refuse to hate evil, the notion that God is love warrants further scrutiny.

First, God is not love, and this is just one of those shallow and silly sayings that makes people feel warm and giddy. It is sentimental but theologically absurd.

God cannot possibly be love because God is God. God is infinite, which is another way of saying the deity is utterly undefinable and is certainly not an emotion. While God may *express* love and indeed *shows* love, to say that this is the essence of the Almighty is as erroneous as saying that God is a man or a woman. God transcends all description. The Torah attributes human, earthly feelings to God, an ineffable being, as well as anthropomorphic features, like "stretching out his hand to pluck the Jews from Egypt," as a means by which humans can understand God. But the Almighty has no such features.

As the Kabbalists explain, God is manifested in various ways, sometimes as someone who loves but just as often as someone who hates. Sometimes our eyes deceive us. If we put water into a red or blue glass, it appears from the outside to have a color when it has not changed. Similarly, we can be misled when God shows love—as when Manna was sent from heaven to feed the Israelites for forty years in the desert—and believe that God *is* love. If that were the case, then we'd be confounded when God suddenly shows hatred and contempt, as when the chariots of Pharaoh were destroyed in the Red Sea because of the Egyptians' wickedness and their engagement in the genocide of newborn male Hebrew children.

God is never love and God is never hate. Rather, God will manifest love to the righteous, hatred to the wicked, and all the while not become or be limited by either of these emotions. God can express and manifest all emotions, sometimes even contradictory ones, simultaneously, something utterly impossible for a human being to do or contemplate. For instance, God displays anger and fury toward the Egyptians at the Red Sea while simultaneously showing love and benevolence to the Israelites. Humans are limited and governed by their emotions. God is not. So, to say that God is love is both shallow and silly.

Philosophical arguments aside, the whole "God is love" thing is erroneous because it brings us back to the false notion that love is the highest virtue. The idea that God is love is backward. First, people determine that love is the most glorious thing in the world and since God is the greatest being in the universe, it stands to reason that the essence of God is love. But there are many things greater than love, like justice.

Let's say a man is beating his wife and she tells the authorities not to punish him because she loves him. Should we let the guy off because love trumps justice?

Duty is also greater than love. What would we think of a man who refused to fight in the American revolution, even as his country is being invaded by the British, because he loves his homestead so much that he refuses to be parted from it? Or from his sweetheart who lives with him? Would we think him a romantic or a selfish coward? Similarly, would American patriots in 1776 excuse the failure of Tories to participate in the revolution because they sincerely loved their king and sovereign?

What if someone loves money so much that all their decisions are based on how to increase their wealth? Is such selfishness the greatest value? No, such love would be called greed.

Right and wrong, morality, ethics—all these things are greater than love.

KOSHER HATE

The Christian scriptures do recognize evil and frequently say that man will be damned for it. Here are a few examples:

REVELATION 21:8

But the fearful, and unbelieving, and the abominable, and murderers, and whoremongers, and sorcerers, and idolaters, and all liars, shall have their part in the lake which burneth with fire and brimstone: which is the second death. (The second death is referred to as the "spiritual death." These people are no longer man's enemy but God's.)

PETER 3:7

But the heavens and the earth, which are now, by the same word are kept in store, reserved unto fire against the day of judgment and perdition of ungodly men.

REVELATIONS 13:10

He that leadeth into captivity shall go into captivity: he that killeth with the sword must be killed with the sword. Here is the patience and the faith of the saints.

MATTHEW 13:49-50

So, shall it be at the end of the world: the angels shall come forth, and sever the wicked from among the just. And shall cast them into the furnace of fire: there shall be wailing and gnashing of teeth.

JOHN 3:10

By this the children of God are distinguished from the children of the devil: Anyone who does not practice righteousness is not of God, nor is anyone who does not love his brother.

JOHN: 3:19–20

The Light has come into the world, but men loved the darkness rather than the Light, because their deeds were evil. Everyone who does evil hates the Light and does not come into the Light for fear that his deeds will be exposed.

GENESIS 9:6

Whoso sheddeth man's blood, by man shall his blood be shed: for in the image of God made he man.

PSALMS 97:10

Ye that love the Lord, hate evil: he preserveth the souls of his saints; he delivereth them out of the hand of the wicked.

ISAIAH 5:20

Woe unto them that call evil good, and good evil.

ROMANS 12.9

Let love be without dissimulation. Abhor that which is evil; cleave to that which is good.

AMOS 5:15

Hate the evil and love the good.

PROVERBS 3:33

The curse of the Lord is in the house of the wicked: but he blesseth the habitation of the just.

In the Book of Mormon:

ALMA 40:13

And then shall it come to pass, that the spirits of the wicked, yea, who are evil—for behold, they have no part nor portion of the Spirit of the Lord; for behold, they chose evil works rather than good; therefore, the spirit of the devil did enter them, and take possession of their house—and these shall be cast out into outer darkness.

NEPHI 2:5

And men are instructed sufficiently that they know good from evil.

MORONI 7:12

Wherefore, all things which are good cometh of God; and that which is evil cometh of the devil; for the devil is an enemy unto God.

ALMA 61:14

Therefore, my beloved brother, Moroni, let us resist evil, and whatsoever evil we cannot resist with our words, yea, such as rebellions and dissensions, let us resist them with our swords, that we may retain our freedom, that we may rejoice in the great privilege of our church, and in the cause of our Redeemer and our God.

Clearly, Christian theology offers guidance for hate; nevertheless, those passages are superseded in practical belief by those emphasizing love:

JOHN 4:8

Whoever does not love does not know God, because God is love.

JOHN 4:11

Beloved, if God so loved us, we also ought to love one another.

JOHN 4:12

No one has ever seen God; but if we love one another, God remains in us, and His love is perfected in us.

JOHN 4:16:

God is love; whoever abides in love abides in God, and God in him.

JOHN 3:15

Everyone who hates his brother is a murderer, and you know that eternal life does not reside in a murderer.

JOHN 4:18:

There is no fear in love, but perfect love drives out fear, because fear involves punishment. The one who fears has not been perfected in love.

JOHN 4:20–21:

If anyone says, "I love God," but hates his brother, he is a liar. For anyone who does not love his brother, whom he has seen, cannot love God, whom he has not seen.... Whoever loves God must love his brother as well.

And, the most important inspiration for Christian love comes from Luke's recollection of the crucifixion (23:34):

> Then Jesus said, "Father, forgive them, for they know not what they do."

This, of course, ignores those passages of the Bible which reflect not the God of love, but the God of vengeance. For example:

> The Philistines seized [Samson] and gouged out his eyes. They brought him down to Gaza and bound him with bronze shackles.... They put him between the pillars.... Then Samson called to the Lord, "O Lord GOD! Please remember me, and give me strength just this once, O God, to take revenge of the Philistines, if only for one of my two eyes."

> He embraced the two middle pillars that the temple rested upon, one with his right arm and one with his left, and leaned against them; Samson cried, "Let me die with the Philistines!" and he pulled with all his might. The temple came crashing down on the lords and on all the people in it. Those who were slain by him as he died outnumbered those who had been slain by him when he lived. (Judges 21–30)

> Samuel said, "Bring forward to me King Agag of Amalek." Agag approached him with faltering steps; and Agag said, "Ah, bitter death is at hand!" Samuel said: "As your sword has bereaved women, So shall your mother be bereaved among women." And Samuel cut Agag down before the LORD at Gilgal. (I Samuel 32-33)

Consider Deborah's ebullient song:

> Most blessed of women be Jael, the wife of Heber the Kenite

> Of tent–dwelling women most blessed.

She put her hand to the tent peg and her right hand
to the workmen's mallet.

She struck Sisera a blow, she crushed his head, she
shattered and pierced his temple.

He sank, he fell, he lay still at her feet;

At her feet he sank, he fell;

there he sank, there he fell dead.

So perish all your enemies, O Lord!

The Hebrew prophets spoke in the name of a God who,
in Exodus's articulation, may "forgive iniquity and transgression and sin," but who also "by no means exonerates
[the guilty]." Likewise, in refusing to forgive their enemies,
Jewish leaders sought not merely their defeat but their disgrace. When Queen Esther had already visited defeat upon
Haman—the Hitler of his time, attempted exterminator of
the Jewish people—and had killed Haman's supporters, King
Ahasuerus asks what more she could possibly want. Esther
said, "If it pleases the king...let the ten sons of Haman be
hanged on the gallows."

Regarding a *rasha*, a Hebrew term for the hopelessly
wicked, the Talmud clearly states: *mitzvah lisnoso*—one is
obligated to hate him.

There is, in fact, no minimizing the difference between
Judaism and Christianity on whether hate can be virtuous.
Indeed, Christianity's founder acknowledged his break with
Jewish tradition on this matter from the very outset: "You
have heard that it was said, 'You shall love your neighbor and
hate your enemy.' But I say to you, Love your enemies and
pray for those who persecute you, so that you may be children of your Father in heaven; for He makes His sun rise on

the evil and on the good, and sends rain on the righteous and on the unrighteous.... Be perfect, therefore, as your heavenly Father is perfect." God, Jesus argues, loves the wicked, and so must we. In disagreeing, Judaism does not deny the importance of imitating God; Jews hate the wicked because they believe that God despises the wicked as well.

Hate is not absent in Christianity. It is directed at unbelievers and critics. When Jesus did mention hate, it was to define the enemies of his burgeoning church. It is the defining emotion of those opposed to Jesus and his followers.

Take Luke 21:16-17, for example: "But you will be betrayed even by parents and brothers and relatives and friends, and they will put some of you to death, and you will be hated by all because of My name."

Put more simply in the book of John, Jesus asserts that, "All who do evil hate the light..."

Something seems off, doesn't it? The Sermon on the Mount made love the defining emotion of the believing Christian, but anyone who has the chutzpah to question Christianity should be hated.

For centuries, those who hated Christians persecuted them; however, the tables turned as the faith spread across Europe, and the pacifistic religion sought to convert nonbelievers by the sword. For nearly 200 years, Crusaders ruthlessly fought to stop the spread of Islam, regain control of the Holy Land, and punish opponents.

Hatred also applied to those who rejected Catholic orthodoxy, which led to the often-violent conflict between Catholics and Protestants. Christian hatred was extended further to the Jews who, as their original sin, were accused of killing Christ. The consequences were the Inquisition, expulsions, centuries of persecution, and the perpetuation of anti-Semitism to this day.

When scholars trace the roots of thousands of years of Christian anti-Semitism, they pay special attention to the formative years of the early Church when Christianity expanded its reach across the Roman Empire following Constantine's decision to adopt Christianity as the official faith of the empire. As the religion spread, it needed to crystallize its tenets and values and, most important, its identity.

For a faith born out of the Jews, the first order of business was to establish theological independence from Judaism, which, after two failed revolts against Rome, all but disappeared from the empire, and was unpopular with the masses. Three men of note would rise to try and distinguish the God of the Christians from the God of the Jews. In doing so, they argued God's capacity for hatred, recognized in Judaism, was inconsistent with the message Christians wished to promote.

The first theologian to enter the battle between testaments, new and supposedly old, was Valentinus (100–160), who divided God in two. There was the higher God of Christianity, charitable and loving, and the lower God of Judaism who is jealous, hateful, and full of rage.

Saint Justin Martyr (c. 100–165) got his last name after being executed in Rome. He was an anti-Semite from what is present day Nablus who wrote a "Dialogue Against the Jews" and asserted that the Torah's laws were given to the Jews because they were especially hard-hearted and unspiritual, needing more laws to reign them in. It follows, therefore, that the God of the Jews was essentially an angry version of the true loving God tailor-made for the rebellious Israelites. He believed Christians were holier than Jews, who needed to be converted. Even the despised Jews can be redeemed through acceptance of Jesus. If you can avoid the glaring anti-Semitism, you'll notice that once again, the God of the Christians is not a God who hates, unless of course, he hates Jews.

The most infamous of the three is Marcion of Sinope (c. 110–160). Marcion preached that the god who sent Jesus into the world was a different, higher deity than the god of Judaism. More extreme than his peers, though, Marcion believed "the Old Testament was a scandal to the faithful and a stumbling-block to the refined and intellectual gentiles by its crudity and cruelty and the Old Testament had to be set aside," according to the *Catholic Encyclopedia*. Marcion maintained that "Christ was not the Son of the God of the Jews, but the Son of the good God, who was different from the God of the Ancient Covenant."[54]

When these men were writing in the second century, Christianity was still in too formative of a state to adopt any one view. Marcion, for one, is considered a heretic. To understand the early formation of Christian dogma and belief, one must linger over the life, works, and times of the great orator and theologian of Hippo, the church-father St. Augustine (354–430), who, perhaps more than any other man, would lock in the tenets of the Christian faith.

Augustine's influence is due to the scope of his work and its impact on Christian belief, his acceptance by Protestants, and his role in determining Church doctrine pertaining to emotions such as hate. Hence, Augustine was in a unique position to lay much of the groundwork for Western Christianity and Western culture as the slow-burning imperial decay of Rome was finally complete. He was in middle age when Rome was sacked by the Visigoths in 410, and he would die within the walls of his own diocese of Hippo when it too was besieged by another gothic tribe feeding on the corpse of the bygone empire.

From the discarded skin of Rome, a new centralized empire would rise, one that would single-handedly dominate the European mainland for more than a thousand years. The Roman Catholic Church, which remains the single largest religion on earth, would begin to find its bearing during the lifetime of Augustine, due in no small part to the great orator himself.

Early in the fourth century, the pagan beliefs of many Europeans were exchanged for monotheistic Christianity. This transformation existed inside the hearts and minds of the leagues of believers drawn to the newly minted Christian faith. No longer would they partake in the Roman religious rituals, which usually included wine, sacrifice, and extravagant celebration. Christianity taught a new type of worship, one rooted in the Jewish emphasis on personal piety and accountability. Theirs was a God who scoured our hearts and demanded that we purify them of the evil that dwells therein. Salvation, in turn, was no longer the responsibility of a city, nation, or king; it was something personal. Divinity, taught Augustine, did not lie in the hands of powerful nobles and emperors. On the contrary, the greatest spiritual heritage belonged to the simplest *parvili*, as Augustine called them, the "little children" of the church.

According to this new heart-centered Christian worldview emotions were everything, and Augustine singled out love as the ultimate virtue and described hatred as the destroyer of man. He begins his book, *Our Lord's Sermon on the Mount*, by stating, "If any one will piously and soberly consider the sermon which our Lord Jesus Christ spoke on the mount, as we read it in the Gospel according to Matthew, I think that he will find in it, so far as regards the highest morals, a perfect standard of the Christian life."[55] This would include the sermon's injunction to love one's enemies.

Then there are his *Confessions*, a window into his personal attitudes toward God, men, and the world at large. Augustine's emphasis on love is reflected by the word's appearance more than three hundred times throughout the *book*, which is half apology and half love letter. "Lo, I love you," he confesses to his god, "but if my love is too mean, let me love more passionately. I cannot gauge my love, nor know how far it fails, how much more love I need for my life to set its course straight into your arms."[56]

In fact, Augustine aligns his conversion to Christianity with the discovery of his love for God. "Belatedly I loved thee," he laments, touching upon his years of delinquency. "Unlovingly, I rushed heedlessly among the lovely things thou hast made me." Augustine believed his problem was the inability to recognize and not reciprocate God's love and loveliness. Consequently, Augustine insists that people cannot love humankind without loving God. "Anyone who does not love Him who made man has not learned to love man right."

For Augustine, the concept of love between people is unlimited. Harking back to the gospels (Mat. 5:44, Luke 6:27), Augustine posits that one must love even one's enemies, but adds a classic rhetorical glaze: "It's a happy man who loves you, God, and in you loves his friend, and loves his enemy because of you."

Augustine doesn't just characterize love as a divine path or commandment, he portrays it as something that will make a person happy, the emotional imperative for personal well-being. Hatred, it follows, would have the opposite effect.

In his magnum opus *City of God*, Augustine identifies hatred as something literally demonic. The demons are haters of some men and lovers of others, not in consequence of a prudent and calm judgment, but because of what he calls their "passive soul," whereas the true religion commands us to love even our enemies."

More important, Augustine makes an assertion in Book XIV of *City of God* that might be the groundwork justifying the supposedly boundless Christian love for men as evil as Hitler:

And since no one is evil by nature, but whoever is

> evil is evil by vice, he who lives according to God ought to cherish towards evil men a perfect hatred, so that he shall neither hate the man because of his vice, nor love the vice because of the man, but hate the vice and love the man. For the vice being cursed, all that ought to be loved, and nothing that ought to be hated, will remain.[57]

But what Augustine failed to recognize is the principle taught by Aristotle, and elaborated upon by Maimonides. There are two kinds of human nature. There is our natural, inborn nature, and there is habit that becomes a second nature. When you do something repeatedly, it is transformed from something you practice into something you are.

You start off doing something wicked, and through unrelenting repetitive action, you become evil. It becomes impossible to separate the action from the individual and thus, even repentance is impossible, not only because your actions are irreversible but because you and your actions are one and inseparable.

Would we say that a murderous racist like James Earl Ray, who shot Martin Luther King Jr., could be separated from the evil of his actions? When your hatred is so deep-seated that it will cause you to stalk a man across the United States until you cut him down on a motel porch in Memphis, Tennessee, can we say that you and your hatred are separate?

When you are a volunteer member of the SS and *Einsatzgruppen*—the SS was comprised entirely of volunteers—and follow the front-line units of the Wehrmacht into Russia and Ukraine, shoot hundreds of Jews in the head so they fall into ditches they were forced to dig, and burn alive hundreds more you lock in their synagogues, are you someone who practices evil, or have you become evil?

You can only separate a person from their actions if that action has not become their second nature.

Despite this idea of separating the person from their behavior, Christianity sees the person who engages in evil as a sinner who could be condemned to hell. The existence of hell should be a painful proposition for Christians, who profess to believe that Christ died to redeem the world.

But does anyone really deserve to go to hell? Rabbi Soloveichik notes Christian teachings suggest everyone is redeemable. "For just as one man's trespass led to condemnation for all," as we read in Romans, "so one man's act of righteousness leads to justification and life for all." Soloveichik says that Pope John Paul II questioned whether even Judas is in hell.

Forget Judas, a Jew might respond," writes Soloveichik. "What about Hitler?" Soloveichik quotes Richard John Neuhaus, a prominent Christian cleric who edited the *Lutheran Forum*: "'Hitler may have repented, turning to the mercy of God, even as his finger pressed the trigger.' Maybe, Neuhaus suggests, Hitler and Mao spend thousands of years in purgatory or, perhaps, he whimsically says, 'Hitler in heaven will be forever a little dog to whom we will benignly condescend. But he will be grateful for being there, and for not having received what he deserved,' just as 'we will all be grateful for being there and for not having received what we deserve.'"[58] To be sure, its striking to hear a religious leader of renown equate the rest of us with Hitler. But that's his point. Since all are sinners, all are deserving of going to hell, and so our collective guilt differentiating between us is only by matter of degree.

Pope Pius XII was a perfect example of how an inability to hate can aid and abet unspeakable cruelty. During the Second World War, no man was in a better position to alert the world to the evils of Nazism than Pope Pius. As the foremost religious authority, the Pope could have used his pulpit to broadcast to the world the genocide of Jews and Roma being perpetrated by the Nazis. But, inexplicably, Pius did not hate

Hitler. Indeed, he seems to have been incapable of letting go of his considerable admiration for Germany where he had served as Papal nuncio for three years.

When he was appointed Pope, Eugenio Pacelli spoke out against the 1938 Italian racial laws that dealt with mixed marriages and children of mixed marriages, but he was silent following Kristallnacht.

The moral cowardice of Pope Pius XII in the Second World War—having never once summoned the courage to condemn the Holocaust and the persecution and murder of the Jews specifically—is well-established. The Pope knew about the Nazi extermination campaign as early as 1942. Throughout the war, he was asked, sometimes by members of the Church, to help the Jews, or at least condemn the Nazis' persecution, but he refused. When asked by the Assistant Chief of the U.S. delegation to the Vatican to speak out in October 1941, the Pope insisted on remaining "neutral" out of concern for the Catholics in German-occupied lands. The following year he was informed 200,000 Ukrainian Jews had been killed and responded that they should "bear adversity with serene patience."[59] Myron Taylor, U.S. representative to the Vatican, warned the Pope that his silence was endangering his moral prestige. Taylor should have said his failure to speak out was jeopardizing the lives of millions of people.

The Pope did speak generally against the extermination campaign. On January 18, 1940, after the death toll of Polish civilians was estimated at 15,000, the Pope said in a broadcast, "The horror and inexcusable excesses committed on a helpless and a homeless people have been established by the unimpeachable testimony of eye-witnesses."[60] During his Christmas Eve radio broadcast in 1942, he referred to the "hundreds of thousands who, through no fault of their own, and solely because of their nation or race, have been condemned to death or progressive extinction."[61]

In both instances, as he would throughout the war, the pope refused to specifically mention the Jews as victims. Harold Tittman, the Assistant Chief of the U.S. delegation to the Vatican, asked Vatican Secretary of State Luigi Maglione if the pope could issue a proclamation like the one released in October 1942 by U.S. Bishops that said, "We feel a deep sense of revulsion against the cruel indignities heaped upon Jews in conquered countries and upon defenseless peoples not of our faith…. Deeply moved by the arrest and maltreatment of the Jews, we cannot stifle the cry of conscience. In the name of humanity and Christian principles, our voice is raised."[62] Maglione responded that the papacy was "unable to denounce publicly particular atrocities."[63]

When the war started, before the atrocities became known, the pope was already admitting to holding two positions that were in contradiction. In a September 1940 broadcast, the Vatican called its policy "neutrality," but stated in the same speech that where morality was involved, neutrality was impossible.[64]

Indeed, the inability for Pius XII to speak out against the destruction of European Jewry constitutes, arguably, the greatest moral omission by a global religious leader of all time. Books such as *Hitler's Pope* by John Cornwell and *The Battle for Rome* by Robert Katz convincingly demonstrate that Pius's failure, far from being merely a product of a personal prejudice against the Jews, was indicative of his concern for political advantage, papal authority, and the preservation of Church property.

The *Encyclopaedia Judaica* reports that the Vatican received detailed information about the murder of Jews in the concentration camps from 1942 on, but Pius XII restricted all his public utterances to carefully phrased expressions of sympathy for the victims of injustice and to calls for a more humane conduct of hostilities. The pope insisted on, and maintained, a strict policy of neutrality throughout the war.

Imagine for just a moment if Pius, from his window atop St. Peter's Square in the presence of hundreds of thousands of pilgrims, had thundered that he despised and detested the Nazis for their cruelty, their racism, their persecution of the Jews, and their inhumanity. Such a proclamation, using the word hate and acknowledging the threat to the Jewish people, would have proved a serious obstacle to the Nazi's plans for genocide. Righteous souls do not hate, however; it's an un-Godly emotion that must be purged from the human heart.

But what is more wicked: to hate evil or to be the most celebrated religious leader in the world who watched six million Jews being gassed and burned by the Nazi barbarians and say nothing about it?

The pope could have saved countless lives, even if he could not have halted the machinery of destruction altogether. He could have chosen to take a public stand and confront the Germans with the threat of an interdict or with the excommunication of Hitler, Goebbels, and other leading Nazis belonging to the Catholic faith. In Slovakia, Hungary, and Romania, the forceful intervention of papal nuncios who threatened the pro-Nazi governments with public condemnation by the pope were able, albeit temporarily, to halt the deportations. At the very least, a public denunciation of the mass murders by Pius XII broadcasted over the Vatican radio would have revealed to Jews and Christians alike what deportation to the east meant. The reluctance of Pius XII to be drawn into a public protest against the Final Solution stands in contrast to the rescue activities of several of the papal nuncios in Slovakia, Hungary, Rumania, and Turkey. Monsignor Angelo Roncalli, the nuncio in Istanbul who later became Pope John XXIII, helped save many thousands of lives.

To those who would argue that a public pronouncement of abhorrence by Pius XII would not have saved the Jews, I can only offer the example of Pope John Paul II who unhesitatingly stood up to the Kremlin and inspired the Polish people as they demanded independence. After his installation, he conveyed a message to all Catholics, but especially to the Poles: "Do not be afraid. Open wide the doors for Christ. To his saving power open the boundaries of states, economic and political systems, the vast fields of culture, civilization, and development. Do not be afraid." During a visit to his native land, he declared, "There can be no just Europe without the independence of Poland marked on its map!"[65]

Did the pope save Poland?

According to British historian Timothy Garton Ash, "Without the pope, no Solidarity. Without Solidarity, no Gorbachev. Without Gorbachev, no fall of Communism."[66]

There are few religious leaders who did more for Catholic relations with the Jewish people than John Paul II. This great man, who bravely stood up to the Communists, somehow lost his way when it came to his response to terrorism. Although universally admired as a saint, this pope made the tragic mistake of misplaced love for the perpetrators.

When I conjure up an image of the pope, it is invariably in connection with some gesture of warmth and loving kindness to a child, a widow, or the poor. John Paul II's ministry was devoted principally to the suffering third world countries and his dedication to those in pain made him justly famous, inspired our own goodness, and electrified the world. I confess to a considerable sadness at his passing, even as a non-Catholic, attached as I am to the image of an elderly and gentle man, battling illness and weakness while continuing to shower affection on the suffering masses.

In this sense alone the papacy of John Paul II will forever be remembered as an outstanding success because his life and the symbol he came to represent established religion's foremost premise: that leading a righteous life makes one into a Godly individual and that a life of faith transforms its practitioner into an exemplar of compassion.

But for all that, John Paul II's legacy will be mixed, having risen to the challenge of defeating communism early in his pontificate but failing miserably to condemn the terrorist threat at the end of it.

As George Bush prepared the world for an invasion of Iraq to rid that country of one of the world's most brutal tyrants, who had already slaughtered and gassed more than a million of his own people, the Pope saw fit to summon Tariq Aziz, Saddam's diplomatic puppet. He placed his holy hands on Aziz's head, and said, "God bless Iraq." That an American politician could have scoffed at world censure to topple Saddam's evil command while the world's foremost religious authority was mysteriously blinded toward that dictator's murderous regime shall forever remain the moral mystery of an otherwise extraordinary man.

I mentioned earlier that George Bush, Sr. famously remarked that he "hated" Saddam Hussein. He was roundly rebuked for his remark. Hatred is seen as being beneath a president. But is it better for a holy man like the pope to bless the representative of an evil and murderous regime? Is not such an act a betrayal of decency and justice and a grave insult to the memory of the innocent victims?

It was shocking, therefore, when the pope made this jaw-dropping statement after the death of Yasser Arafat: "At this hour of sadness at the passing of President Yasser Arafat, His Holiness Pope John Paul is particularly close to the deceased's family, the Authorities and the Palestinian People. While entrusting his soul into the hands of the Almighty and Merciful God, the Holy Father prays to the Prince of Peace that the star of harmony will soon shine on the Holy Land... "[67] In a second statement, Joaquín Navarro-Valls said in the pope's name that Arafat was "a leader of great charisma who loved his people and sought to lead them towards national independence. May God welcome in His mercy the soul of the illustrious deceased and give peace to the Holy Land."[68]

It is true that politicians such as Tony Blair and Shimon Peres also expressed their condolences, but we justifiably hold religious leaders to higher standards than politicians. That the world's foremost spiritual shepherd could describe himself as being close to Arafat's family, rather than the victims of the terrorism he instigated for over four decades, including wholesale massacres of school children, was an astonishing act of sacrilege. That the most influential religious figure alive could describe the death of a terrorist as "an hour of sadness" and call a mass murderer an "illustrious" soul was obscene. That the Vicar of Christ could say that a man who died a billionaire by stealing from impoverished and desperate Palestinians "loved his people" is an affront to Jesus's teachings about the oppressed, the poor, and the persecuted.

Likewise, the pope never once used his considerable authority to condemn Osama bin Laden, the Al Qaeda network, and the many other terrorist organizations that have made a once-peaceful planet so dangerous to inhabit. The Vatican said the killing of bin Laden, a man who "bore the most serious responsibility for spreading divisions and hatred among populations, causing the deaths of innumerable people, and manipulating religions for this purpose" should prompt Christians to reflect "on the serious responsibilities of each person before God and before men, and hopes and works so that every event may be the occasion for the further growth of peace and not of hatred."[69]

How can we understand this reaction from a man who was devoted to family? How could such a genuinely pious man have preached against the hatred of such unspeakable evil? And how could a leader of such incredible love have shown such callous indifference to victims of torture and murder by blessing and praising their murderers?

John Paul II was one of the greatest men ever produced by the Catholic Church. But the great failing of his life, strangely enough, was that he loved too much. Like a parent who cannot see the failings of a child, John Paul II refused to accept that real evil can lurk in the hearts of humankind. John Paul II so loved God's children so much that he could not see that there were those whose actions had erased the image of God from their own countenance and forever severed themselves from a compassionate Creator. John Paul loved the innocent but never hated the wicked. He loved justice, but one must also condemn injustice. He fought for the poor and the oppressed, but he would not fight their oppressors. Declaring in word and deed that hatred of any sort was an un-Godly emotion that dare not be given sanctuary in the human heart, John Paul II never summoned the faithful to have contempt for the wicked but instead extended them his gentle touch when a strong hand was most needed.

The result of such misguided affection is that while he was loved and admired by the earth's inhabitants, he leaves behind a planet where American soldiers are doing more to create a Godly habitat by fighting the evildoers, like Al Qaeda, ISIS, and the Taliban, than clerics who will not condemn their evil.

As a Jew, I shall forever remain indebted to John Paul II for the respect and affection he extended to the Jewish people. The Pope twice visited the synagogue in Rome, extended diplomatic recognition to the State of Israel, wrote movingly of the wonders of Judaism in his book *Crossing the Threshold of Hope*, visited Israel, and met repeatedly with Jewish leaders through the long years of his reign. As an American, however, I shall remain saddened that as the world chorused condemnation of the American people for fighting the Taliban in Afghanistan and attempting to establish a democracy in Iraq, the Pope did not remind the nations of the earth that the real enemy is not those who fight evil but those who soil God's earth by drenching it in the blood of innocents.

Only recently we learned that John Paul II's myopia extended to the church, ignoring warnings about Cardinal Theodore McCarrick's sexual misconduct and elevating him to archbishop of Washington. "He was unwilling to confront the phenomenon of priests involved in sex crimes. I don't think he thought of it as criminal. He thought of it as a sin, a failing of celibacy," according to investigative journalist Jason Berry.[70]

Pedophile priests who destroy the innocence of children through sexual molestation and rape, leading these youths to lifelong depression and often suicide, are evil. But the Church in general, and John Paul II in particular, could not see that evil. The price paid by trusting children who suffered the world over is staggering. Some within the Church have now said that this is not the behavior of a saint and that his canonization should be reversed. I will not go that far, but I will acknowledge that a truly great man's legacy has been tarnished by such serious moral omissions.

In America, we remember 9/11 as our wakeup call to the danger of Islamic extremists. The English equivalent was 7/7, a reference to a series of coordinated Islamic suicide bombings in London on July 7, 2005, which targeted commuters traveling on the city's public transportation system during morning rush hour. Three bombs were detonated on subway trains and a fourth on a double-decker bus. A total of fifty-two people were killed and more than 700 injured.

This was Pope Benedict XVI's response to the atrocities, "I say to you: God loves life, which is created, not death. Stop in the name of God." Sadly, instead of speaking out against terrorism before the attacks, he only reacted afterward. Worse, after praying for "the people killed, for those wounded and for their loved ones," he added, "But let us also pray for the attackers. May the Lord touch their hearts."[71]

This was astonishing. How could he feel anything but hatred and contempt for men who blew themselves up with the goal of killing as many innocent people as possible so they can go to Paradise? They don't need the Christian Lord to touch their hearts; they believe that by engaging in a holy war against Christians and other infidels their God will reward them with seventy-two virgins in the next world.

Pitying the perpetrators also minimizes the impact of terrorism. The 7/7 bombers, like the 9/11 killers, instilled fear in people beyond the day of their attacks. And they changed our lives. Think about one of the unsuccessful terrorists, Richard Reid, who attempted to detonate a shoe bomb on an airplane. Thankfully, the bomb didn't explode; nevertheless, this one evil man has forced us all to take our shoes off at a security checkpoint before we can board a plane, which of course is nowhere near as serious as if his bomb had detonated but gives us a daily reminder of his sickening evil.

The Vatican newspaper, *L'Osservatore Romano*, acknowledged after 7/7 that terrorism had become "an international plague that does not take account of one's race, religion, social status," and terrorist acts target "the crowd" to "bring about the most injuries possible" and to provoke fear. So, what is the paper's answer to this "plague"? Remain hopeful and don't give in to the "blackmail" of violence.[72]

I disagree. Hope is not a strong enough emotion to combat terror. One must hate the evildoer.

Pope Francis is another great man who suffers from a similar malady. He loves too much. I am gratified that he is a great friend of the Jewish people, but he is compromised because of his incapacity to hate evil. If you love to the point where you cannot oppose wickedness, evil will triumph. It's difficult to get Francis to condemn, for example, the Syrian butcher Bashar Assad. Instead, he stood in front of Israel's security barrier—built to stop suicide bombers from entering

Israel and blowing up buses and cafés—and condemned it. Why didn't he say that he condemns the terrorists who kill children and prays for a day when barriers will not be necessary? Is it so outrageous to expect him to say, "I hate terrorists"? But that's not the way popes are expected to speak. That's why we need Kosher Hate and it's going to come from the Jews.

One might ask, "how is that enough? We're a tiny minority and the pope is the titular head of a church of more than a billion people preaching love." But the Jews are, and always have been, the canaries in the coalmine. We are a people that punch well above our weight and exert global influence. Jewish teachings about hate will slowly percolate through the culture until it will become expected of leaders to stop apologizing for the evil done by evil men and to hate and resist them instead.

Defeating hate sometimes requires violence, but Anabaptist sects like the Amish, Mennonites, and Quakers, the so-called peace churches—disavow war of any kind. But there are gradations even among the pacifists. Some, for example, believe it is permissible to work in hospitals with those wounded in battle. Others, argue that by such actions you are contributing to the war by freeing up other people to do more fighting and helping return soldiers to the fight. The reasoning is that Jesus was a pacifist and wants us all to be peace makers. No one should have to sacrifice life or limb for one's country. A life is God given, they believe, and you cannot give it away, ever.

But war is not always just for a country. It is sometimes, hopefully, for principles—freedom, democracy, and human rights.

It's easy to see how these people, living quiet, pious lives in the countryside of Pennsylvania, would be against war. Their lifestyle, with many of them shunning modern conveniences, is outwardly serene. There is a place for people like this in society—important lessons can be learned, and it's no doubt good for us to hear the voices of conscientious objectors. Hearing from them reminds us that war is terrible.

Even Jesus's love would turn to hate in the face of true evil. When Jesus says, "Love your enemies," he is referring only to *your* personal enemies, people who we don't get along with for any one of a hundred petty reasons. This much is also clear in the Old Testament. We must not bear grudges, act spitefully, or take revenge, but the minute we're dealing with a violent murderer who poses a clear threat to *society*, pity is foolishly naïve. This was so clear to Jesus that he saw no reason to mention it. This radical passivity, stemming from the belief that because Jesus forgave his crucifiers all wrongs can be absolved, was imposed onto his teachings later. We cannot afford docility. If there is a danger to society, we must take preventative action to stop people from being harmed.

Can a Christian really believe Jesus would have said or done nothing to prevent genocide? Would he call on us to love the perpetrators and forgive them?

Fortunately, great leaders recognized that we need more than just love to survive and to defeat evil. The decisions they made may not have always been popular, or reflect the beliefs of the faithful, but they were necessary to ensure those who disagreed with them could continue to enjoy freedom.

When the whole religious experience is based around faith (and finds more particularized definition only in general concepts such as Christian charity) and belief becomes the ultimate goal, it is possible to imagine that faith will solve all the world's problems. If only we believe rightly, we will all be saved. Salvation means everyone deserves our love. If you don't believe the demons of evil can live within the human heart, then those demons will not be there. Like the fairies in Peter Pan, they will disappear and die if no one believes in them.

Judaism has often been criticized for its preoccupation with practice—the letter of the law. Such obsession with trivia is unworthy of an infinite God, they say. But this concern with the mundanities of daily living keeps the religion grounded in the real struggles that we face as human beings, whereas Christianity is more concerned with cosmic issues that transcend our lifetimes and take that as an avenue to ultimate and universal good. Judaism stays behind to try and clear up all the little imperfections.

It is no accident that the Jewish messianic vision involves the participation of all humankind in a utopian transformation as opposed to the Christian expectation of an apocalypse. Jews seek to perfect the world; Christians await Armageddon, the destruction of anyone who failed to join in the earthly celebration of Christ. That is a picture of a messiah imposed from above—or messiah as God. For the Jew, however, the messianic age is the culmination of a process wrought by painstaking, incremental changes over the course of centuries by the entirety of humankind engaging in the redemptive process.

In our brief time on this un-Godly planet, the Christian believes the most we can hope to do is come away without spoiling our souls. If we can learn to love despite ourselves, we will merit eternal love. We certainly should not risk corrupting our souls with anything that even looks like hatred.

I believe, however, that passing through this world without doing something to make it better and, most urgently, to combat the numerous manifestations of evil that are all around us, would be a mistake. It is not just passing up an opportunity—it is shrugging off a task and a duty that God expects from us. Without Kosher Hate, we are limited in that task and evil can persist, if not triumph.

CHAPTER 4:
WHY GREAT MEN HATE EVIL

CONTEMPORARY LIBERALISM VALUES the peacemaker and castigates the warmonger without recognizing that the two are related. Just as there is no love without hate, so there can be no peace without war to enable it.

The greatest leaders in history have understood this and consequently were willing to fight to defeat the greatest evils: Fascism, Hitlerism, communism, Islamism and slavery.

Clear-eyed leaders, for example, saw the Soviet Union as an enemy of the United States, of freedom, and of humanity itself. Nixon believed the world was divided between the wicked Soviet Union and the good United States; Reagan saw the distinction as the free versus the "evil empire;" and George W. Bush identified a broader "axis of evil."

The late *New York Times* columnist William Safire once quoted a correspondent who captured the liberal mindset: "Accusing a politician of harboring a Manichaean view of the world is a shorthand way of saying this poor chucklehead lacks sophistication, is ignorant of nuances and doesn't know – yokel that he is – that there is no black or white, but only shades of gray."[73]

There are two kinds of warriors. The first, like Alexander, Caesar, Napoleon, and Hitler, fight not to protect life but to win glory. They create conflict not out of the need to protect their people's security but out of their deeply ingrained insecurities; not for universal values but for corrupt personal beliefs; not to uplift the downtrodden but to diminish those viewed as impure; and not for the betterment of humanity but for its enslavement for their benefit.

In contrast, the virtuous warrior fights to preserve life, defeat evil, and ensure the welfare of innocents. They make peace possible by ridding the world of terror. They understand that wickedness must be uprooted entirely before peace can flourish.

The virtuous warrior desperately wants peace and will compromise when possible but recognizes that sometimes the only alternative is to defend oneself even if that requires aggressive action. This is the situation Israel has found itself in since its founding. As Israeli Prime Minister Golda Meir explained:

> We're not the only people in the world who've had difficulties with neighbors; that has happened to many. We are the only country in the world whose neighbors do not say, "We are going to war because we want a certain piece of land from Israel," or waterways or anything of that kind. We're the only people in the world where our neighbors openly announce they just won't have us here. And they will not give up fighting and they will not give up war as long as we remain alive…. Therefore, there can be no compromise. They say we must be dead. And we say we want to be alive. Between life and death, I don't know of a compromise.

The most celebrated people in history are those who opposed and defeated wickedness. However, their decisions were not always popular and they frequently required great sacrifice that cost lives and imposed hardship on their people.

Abraham Lincoln is considered one of America's greatest presidents because he fought to preserve the Union and end the immoral practice of slavery. He had many opportunities to make peace with the South and let them go their own way. He never considered it and was prepared, if need be, to see the tragic loss of hundreds of thousands of American lives rather than allow the country to be disunited and lose its moral compass. This type of epic choice I refer to as a "Lincoln moment." Certainly, the end of slavery did not eliminate racial injustice. But it was an indispensable first step toward forming a more perfect union.

Winston Churchill is Britain's greatest statesman because he battled the demonic forces of Nazism and communism, strengthening a free, prosperous, and peaceful Western Europe. Many people may not be aware, however, of how long he spent whistling in the dark. As early as 1930, he expressed the belief that Hitler would waste no time resorting to the use of force.[74] In 1931, he told the House of Commons, "England's hour of weakness is Europe's hour of danger."[75]

In 1932, he warned of the danger of German rearmament and, two years later, predicted that Germany's new air force would soon be more powerful than Britain's.[76] Nevertheless, in 1932, he met a German in a Munich hotel who tried to arrange a meeting with Hitler; but the Nazi leader did not show up. Churchill told the German, "Tell your boss from me that anti-Semitism may be a good starter, but it is a bad sticker."[77]

Britain had its own problems at the time, however, and some people were sympathetic to Germany's grievances. They admired how Hitler had restored the economy and hoped that a strong Germany could counter Russian expansionism. In 1937, a year before Britain's appeasement of Hitler at Munich, Churchill wrote in the *Evening Standard*:

> My only regret is that I was not believed. I can quite understand that this action of mine would not be

popular in Germany. Indeed, it was not popular anywhere. I was told I was making ill will between the two countries.[78]

Churchill recognized the intolerance of the Nazi regime. "We cannot say that we admire your treatment of the Jew or of the Protestants and Catholics of Germany," he said. "We even think our methods of dealing with Communism are better than yours. But after all, these matters, so long as they are confined inside Germany, are not our business." So he said the British would "grasp the extended friendly hand of Germany" (emphasis added).[79]

Even Churchill was unwilling to intervene in Germany's domestic matters—abusers always warn outsiders to stay out of their internal affairs. However, he also said that Britain would not pay any cost for friendship with Germany. Presciently, he stated:

> We should be very wrong if we were to give Germany a guarantee that so long as she left Britain and France alone in the West, she could do what she likes to the peoples of the center and southeast of Europe. To give such an assurance at other people's expense would not only be callous and cynical, but it might actually lead to a war the end of which no man can foresee.[80]

He ended the article with what sounded like his own bit of naïve optimism, suggesting, "the Fuhrer of Germany should now become the Hitler of peace." Writing decades later about the origins of World War II, American political commentator Pat Buchanan ignored Churchill's criticism of the Nazi regime and suggested he was naïve and had failed to act on his convictions:

> Thus did even the Great Man believe about Hitler, a year after he reentered the Rhineland, and years after Dachau was established, Versailles overthrown, Roehm and the SA leaders murdered on Hitler's

orders and with his personal complicity, and the anti-Semitic laws enacted.[81]

Churchill was not naïve, however; in March 1936, he had said, "Germany...fears no one. She is arming in a manner which has never been seen in German history. She is led by a handful of triumphant desperadoes.... Therefore, it seems to me that all the old conditions present themselves again, and that our national salvation depends upon our gathering once again all the forces of Europe to contain, to restrain and if necessary, to frustrate German domination."[82]

Following Germany's absorption of Austria in March 1938, Churchill said, "Europe is confronted with a programme of aggression, nicely calculated and timed, unfolding stage by stage, and there is only one choice open...either to submit, like Austria, or else to take effective measures while time remains to ward off danger." He believed it was not too late. "If a number of States were assembled around Great Britain and France in solemn treaty for mutual defense against aggression," he said, "and if it were done in the year 1938...then I say that you might even now arrest this approaching war."[83]

At the time, Churchill was ignored and ridiculed. The *BBC* supported appeasement and censored Churchill's criticisms and *The Times of London* limited his exposure. Even many in his own Conservative Party believed he was a dangerous troublemaker. Churchill's biographer Sir Martin Gilbert found a letter written in 1937 by the editor of *The Times* that captures his attitude toward Hitler: "I simply cannot understand why they [the Germans] should apparently be so much annoyed with *The Times* at this moment. I spend my nights in taking out anything which I think will hurt their susceptibilities and in dropping in little things which are intended to soothe them."[84]

Churchill was treated as a Chicken Little by many of his countrymen, warning about impending doom, which "provoked only mocking laughter in some quarters, even among his own party." Undaunted, Churchill told the House of Commons on March 14, 1938, "Laugh but listen."[85]

The British people, however, were in no mood for another war so soon after World War I. Hence, it is understandable that Prime Minister Neville Chamberlain would seek to avoid conflict with Germany, although it remains shocking to consider the lengths to which he would go.

Chamberlain faced his "Lincoln moment" when he had to choose between appeasement and the horror of war to defend Europe. In a broadcast to the British public on September 27, 1938, he rightly said, "War is a fearful thing."[86] But he naïvely believed that Hitler had no imperial or genocidal intent and signed the Munich Pact in September 1938, which ceded parts of Czechoslovakia to Germany. Chamberlain declared, "My good friends, for the second time in our history, a British Prime Minister has returned from Germany bringing peace with honour. I believe it is peace for our time… Go home and get a nice quiet sleep."[87]

Like other appeasers of evil, Chamberlain is remembered in infamy. His willingness to treat with evil and his incapacity for hatred of tyranny led to his historical undoing and to five unspeakable years of total world war.

Churchill believed the agreement represented "the complete surrender of the Western Democracies to the Nazi threat of force." He presciently warned, "Many people at the time of the [Munich] crisis thought they were only giving away the interests of Czechoslovakia, but with every month that passes you will see that they were also giving away the interests of Britain, and the interests of peace and justice."[88]

In March 1939, Hitler violated the Munich Pact by invading Czechoslovakia. Churchill anticipated the likelihood that Germany would next invade Poland and form an alliance with Russia. Britain and France agreed later that month to protect Poland, but Chamberlain did not declare war on Germany until after Hitler's forces invaded Poland that September. "This is not a question of fighting for Danzig or fighting for Poland," Churchill declared, "We are fighting to save the whole world from the pestilence of Nazi tyranny and in defense of all that is most sacred to man."[89]

The situation, of course, got worse. Churchill proposed that Britain occupy Norwegian iron mines and seaports, but Chamberlain rejected the advice. In April 1940, Germany invaded and occupied Norway.

Churchill called the subsequent conflict "The Unnecessary War" because he believed that it could have been prevented if German aggression had been opposed and resisted more forcefully. Even Roosevelt hesitated prior to the attack on Pearl Harbor, leaving Britain to fight alone through what would be called the Battle of Britain.

Hitler gave Churchill an opportunity for a peace agreement after he became Prime Minister in 1940. As a sign of his good intentions, Hitler allowed the British to evacuate their stranded invasion force from the beaches of Dunkirk. This was Churchill's "Lincoln moment." Historian David Pyne argues that, ironically, Hitler's gesture led Churchill to reject his 1940 peace offer, which Pyne says he was considering. Had he accepted, it might have allowed Germany to win the war.[90]

A year later, the British received the first reports of the massacres of Jews. Churchill believed Hitler was the "mainspring of evil" and, in 1942, told his cabinet that if Hitler were captured, he would be put to death in the electric chair like a "gangster" without trial.[91]

Dangerously, the appeasement of tyrants is not dead. The West, led by Barack Obama during his presidency, did nothing to stop Russia from gobbling up Crimea, nor did it strongly confront the bloody regime of Bashar Assad in

Syria. Rather than risk a confrontation with Iran over its pursuit of nuclear weapons, Obama, negotiating from a position of weakness after demonstrating his unwillingness to use force, capitulated on nearly every demand he originally made.[92] Even after negotiating the fundamentally flawed deal, he refused to submit it for Senate approval as a treaty, knowing it would be defeated because it would have required support from two-thirds of the Senate and Obama knew he had only forty-two votes. Nevertheless, that was enough to prevent opponents from getting the sixty votes they needed to bring a resolution of disapproval to the floor.[93] Each time Obama was challenged by a "Lincoln moment," he chose the path of least resistance.

Obama was not alone in his misunderstanding of Iran. Britain, France, and Germany all pushed for the agreement. Even after it became clear that the Iranians were flouting the terms, and Donald Trump withdrew from the deal, the Europeans continued to adhere to it and did everything possible to circumvent U.S. sanctions, which interfered with their commercial interests in Iran. Saving the world from a nuclear Iran was not as important as supporting their economies.

The Palestinians have also repeatedly failed to meet their "Lincoln moments." When Fatah's Mahmoud Abbas became prime minister of the Palestinian Authority, he pledged he would not risk a civil war by confronting his rivals in Hamas, the radical Islamist terror group that runs the Gaza Strip. As Mitchell Bard, an American foreign policy analyst, expressed it at the time, "The Palestinians have repeatedly faced their Lincoln moment when they must choose between a more perfect Palestinian union living in peace beside Israel or some fractured people condemned to statelessness by the terrorists in their midst."[94]

After Israel withdrew from Gaza, Abbas was faced with a coup by Hamas and was unwilling to use force to stop it.

Consequently, Hamas took control in Gaza and created a split between Palestinians who gave lip service to peace and those who vowed to wage a holy war against Israel.

History has shown us that it is not the liberal desperately craving peace who achieves their objective. More often it is the person regarded as a right-wing hardliner who can drive a hard bargain and who the public believes will prioritize their security over the desire for a deal. Thus, we hear the expression that "only Nixon could go to China." The American public did not object to his visit to China and the establishment of relations because of his anti-Communist credentials. He could not be accused of being soft on communism or sacrificing American values.

Similarly, Israel's Menachem Begin was the first prime minister from the right-wing Likud Party. No one doubted his commitment to Israel's security. So when his "Lincoln moment" came this commitment allowed him to decide that peace with Egypt was worth the sacrifice of the strategic depth of the Sinai desert, the Israeli communities there, and the oil reserves that could have made the country energy independent. It is unlikely the Israeli public would have supported any other leader in taking such a risk—and Begin's judgement was even questioned by members of his own party, several of whom voted against the Camp David Accords.[95]

I personally applaud Begin's courage in making peace. But it was a cold peace that he made and Israel's relationship with Egypt has not warmed in four decades, leading me to question the wisdom of sacrificing Sinai for a freezing-cold peace. Indeed, Israel's surrender of the Sinai Peninsula is what led to global pressure for Israel to surrender even more land. This then followed with the catastrophic Oslo Accords that costs thousands of Israeli citizens their lives in terror attacks, and the Israeli withdrawal from Gaza which established a Hamas terror state on Israel's border. Still, Begin's intentions were always noble, if not carried out in actuality.

Sure, the warrior still has a place in the world, but this is not an intrinsic but a transitory position. Indeed, the world most respects the soldier who ultimately hangs up his gun and makes peace with his enemies. Military men like Eisenhower, who enter government to keep the peace, are heroes both in life and death, which explains why so many warriors trade in their general's stars for the opportunity to make peace.

That is, after all, the goal of Kosher Hate. It is not a formula for glory or conquest. It is a recipe for ridding the world of evil with peace as the outcome. Complete victory is necessary or evil can easily return. We have seen it time and again. For example, Israel's failure to achieve total victory, at least in the eyes of the Arabs seeking its destruction, led to wars in 1956, 1967, 1969, 1973, 1982, and 2006. And it continues today with the ongoing conflicts between the Palestinians and the Iran-backed Hezbollah terrorists in Lebanon.

Middle East scholar Daniel Pipes, President of the Middle East Forum, has long argued that the Palestinian issue can only be resolved with Israel's total victory. The Forum's "Israel Victory Project" is inspired by the words of Aristotle, "Victory is the end of generalship" and of Eisenhower: "In war, there is no substitute for victory." Pipes explains:

> Victory consists of imposing one's will on the enemy, which typically means compelling him to give up his war goals. Conflicts usually end with one side's will being crushed…. Ironically, Israeli success in crushing the Palestinian war morale would be the best thing that ever happened to the Palestinians. It would mean their finally giving up their foul dream of eliminating their neighbor and offer a chance, instead, to focus on their own polity, economy, society and culture.[96]

The project's premise is that "Israeli concessions have inflamed Palestinian hostility. The Israeli effort to 'make peace' was received as a sign of demoralization and weakness."

To win, Israel does not have to annihilate the Palestinian population (God forbid, nor would Israel ever countenance even the thought of such horror) but it does need to "convince" the Palestinians—and other Arab states—that Israel "will endure and that dreams of its elimination must collapse."[97]

Seeking peace with an enemy may be ill-advised and even dangerous—but it is not treasonous. This is why the people of Israel were rightly shocked and enraged when a deranged individual named Yigal Amir assassinated Yitzhak Rabin in 1995 at a rally in support of the Oslo Accords. A supposedly devout Jew, Amir nonetheless misdirected his hate, deciding to play God and take Rabin's life for his supposed betrayal of the Jews. Hence his hatred was anything but Kosher.

The doctrine of total victory is certainly appealing and has ample historical precedent. Germany did not surrender until it was defeated on every battlefield and Berlin was in ruins. Likewise, Japan only gave up after losing the territories it had conquered and faced annihilation from atomic bombs.

The Israeli case is different. First, Israel has long engaged in many of the actions Pipes advocates. The problem is that unlike the Allies in World War II, Israel cannot defeat the Palestinians in the decisive way required because the Jewish people are not ruthless. We are a humane and Godly people with infinite reservoirs of heart. Israelis have ample Kosher Hate for Palestinian leaders and the terrorists they incite, but victory would require the application of the so-called Powell Doctrine—the use of decisive force to compel the enemy to capitulate. That would mean unending misery for the Palestinian people. In order to implement this strategy, Israel would have to be willing to bomb targets in the West Bank and Gaza with little regard for collateral damage. Israel's limited retaliatory strikes that destroy buildings but kill few if any terrorists are not sufficient to break the will of the Palestinians.

The United States did not flinch from killing tens of thousands of Iraqis to defeat Saddam Hussein and was unapologetic afterward. And this, of course, was child's play compared to the unbridled bombing of German and Japanese cities carried through by Roosevelt and Churchill throughout World War II. Israel would have to be equally callous to "defeat" the Palestinians. Israel is not the United States during the war, however, and cannot act with the same impunity. Much of the Israeli public and the international community would see Israel's behavior as disproportionate and immoral. Israel would attract international condemnation and the United States would inevitably intervene, forcing Israel to cease military operations before total victory. But that's not even the main issue. It's the people of Israel itself, as well as its military, which would never countenance such a strategy. Hence Bard, the American foreign policy analyst, maintains that Israel "does not have the same freedom as a superpower to use decisive force and therefore cannot militarily defeat the Palestinians."[98]

Stinging accusations of butchery in the civil war leveled against Ulysses S. Grant led him, in his first run for president, to campaign under the slogan, "Let us have peace." Grant saved the Union with his military genius, but he wanted to be remembered not as a warrior but a peacemaker. In his desire to be forgiving and accommodating, Grant pursued moderate policies in the reconstruction of the South that backfired and led to the rise of the Ku Klux Klan, which in turn terrorized and murdered blacks and whites alike. Although Grant approved the Enforcement Force Acts of 1870 and 1871 to curb the Klan's violence and was authorized to declare martial law, he did so only once, in South Carolina. The result was that blacks could not enjoy a measure of equality in the South until the Civil Rights Act was signed nearly a century later.

In a similar way, near the end of his life, General Douglas MacArthur suggested that America and other great powers adopt laws that would forever ban all war. The catastrophic consequences had the United States embraced the doctrine of the old warhorse are scarcely imaginable. Such self-imposed restraint would have allowed communism to take over Southeast Asia and much of Europe with scarcely a hint of resistance. Meanwhile, Islamic terrorists would have taken over the Middle East.

Nuclear physicists like Robert Oppenheimer, Joseph Rotblatt, and other architects of the Manhattan Project spent the rest of their lives campaigning for the abolition of the very weapons they had created. They were following the famous example of Alfred Nobel, the inventor of dynamite, who sought to find redemption through the establishment of the Nobel Prizes.

In the United States, there has long been an extreme liberal faction that had an affinity for communism and glorified Cuba and the Soviet Union. More broadly, liberals rejected the idea that the United States should act as the world's policeman to combat evil. Had it not been for the Japanese attack on Pearl Harbor, it is conceivable America would have sat out World War II and we would be living in a dystopian world like the one Philip K. Dick imagined in his novel *The Man in the High Castle*, where the West coast is ruled by Japan and the East coast by Germany.

We don't need a novelist, however, to imagine what happens when evil triumphs; we need only recall the history of the Soviet Union. In World War II, Roosevelt and Churchill felt the need to ally with Stalin, who then was the lesser evil, in order to defeat Hitler. Afterward, however, Stalin murdered his own people and enslaved much of Europe. Just ask those Germans who ended up on the wrong side of the Berlin Wall how their lives differed from those on the other side.

The liberal resistance to using war as a tool in the fight against evil was reinforced by the Vietnam debacle, which was widely viewed as an unjust war, even as we sought to protect the people of Southeast Asia from the tyranny of communism. The fact that we lost the war at the cost of 58,220 lives has led to a fear of being stuck in a similar quagmire should we choose to intervene in a far-off war that does not directly impact Americans.

To forestall going to war, liberals conflate malevolent actors with those dedicated to their destruction. The media, for example, often repeats liberal talking points about a "cycle of violence" in the Middle East whenever Israel responds to a terror attack. There would be no need for an Israeli response if the terror ceased, but the perpetrators themselves are rarely blamed. Instead their crimes are excused as justified resistance. Again, it is like the analogy of the arsonist and the firefighter. We don't equate the two. We understand that the firefighter would not be needed if the arsonist did not first set the fire.

Most Americans accepted the idea that President George H. W. Bush was responding to the fire Saddam Hussein started by invading Kuwait in August 1990. In that case, opposition to the war was somewhat muted by Bush's ability to build a global "coalition of the willing" composed of forty-nine countries who shared his belief that Saddam Hussein's aggression must not be allowed to stand.

Instead of being viewed as a fireman responding to a blaze, President George W. Bush is portrayed as the arsonist who took America into an unjustifiable war against Saddam. He failed to build a coalition like his father, preferring instead to act peremptorily. He also did not convince the American people of the need to remove Saddam from power following the 9/11 attacks. Most Americans, and certainly Europeans (with the notable exception of British Prime Minister Tony Blair), did not care that Saddam was murdering his own people. The impression was that the world was at peace and this

American warmonger came along and plunged them into conflict. Of course, the thousands of people whom Saddam were murdering were not at peace, just as the region he plunged into conflict was not.

George W. Bush easily persuaded the American people that it was necessary to invade Afghanistan and overthrow the Taliban, who had sheltered Al Qaeda's training camps and had given sanctuary to Osama bin Laden. But when it came to invading Iraq, they were reluctant to support another war. Many, including some Democrats in Congress, accepted the administration's insistence that Iraq had weapons of mass destruction (WMDs), and some believed the administration's claim that Saddam had supported Al Qaeda. After an exhaustive search, when no WMDs were ultimately found and doubt was raised about the Al Qaeda connection, much of America, certainly progressives, concluded that we had been hoodwinked into an unnecessary war and occupation, which reinforced resistance to fighting the so-called "axis of evil" or other malevolent regimes.

The feeling was further exacerbated when Bush sent troops to Afghanistan on the grounds that we needed to go where the terrorists lived to kill them before they could come to our shores. Though still unpopular with liberals, the case that Osama bin Laden and other terrorists were plotting from inside caves in the mountains of Afghanistan was more convincing at least.

Still, there was a backlash reflected in President Obama's election and his promise to withdraw U.S. troops from Iraq and Afghanistan. Initially he drew down our forces in Afghanistan and ultimately he withdrew some troops from Iraq, which only strengthened Iran (and allowed the rise of ISIS). Even Obama was convinced, however, of the need to continue the fight against terrorists in Afghanistan and approved a surge of 30,000 forces in 2009. According to *The New York*

Times he was, "betting that a quick jolt of extra forces could knock the enemy back on its heels enough for the Afghans to take over the fight."[99]

U.S. troops are still in Afghanistan, even after Trump also promised to bring them home. After nearly two decades, the longest war in U.S. history with its inability to either defeat the Taliban, negotiate peace, or abandon the fight is reinforcing the "Vietnam syndrome." Once again, many Americans feel it is a mistake to send troops to a distant land that seems to present no threat to the homeland, become embroiled in a civil war which we cannot stop, and results only in needless losses of American lives. President Biden has now pledged to bring all American troops back from Afghanistan before the end of 2021. But many are concerned that this will just give the terrorist Taliban free rein to take the country back.

As president, Trump too discovered how difficult it is to extricate the United States from such a quagmire. More than three years into his term, he struggled to fulfil his promise to bring U.S. troops home. Meanwhile, in other areas where he did withdraw troops, he was forced to at least partially reverse course because of the consequences. For example, in Iraq, he withdrew some forces only to see Iran fill the vacuum. Similarly, when he pulled troops from Syria, Turkey invaded with the intent of slaughtering our Kurdish allies.

Obama made a similar mistake, which played a key role in Iran's willingness to sign a nuclear agreement that would prevent them from obtaining nuclear weapons. George W. Bush had scared the Iranians. They did not know if he would attack them next and had to worry so long as American troops were next door in Iraq. When Obama withdrew troops and the Iranians listened to the antiwar rhetoric coming from the White House and Obama's supporters, they did not take seriously his "all options are on the table" threats during negotiations. Confident that Obama would not resort to war to stop their nuclear program, the Iranians used their bazaar bargaining skills to negotiate a beneficial deal. It omitted any requirement that they end their global sponsorship of terror, their development of ballistic missiles, and their campaign to destabilize the region and to threaten their neighbors—including Israel to whom they swore annihilation. The agreement itself was so full of loopholes they could continue their pursuit of a bomb while reaping the benefits of the cessation of sanctions and a $150 billion windfall in unfrozen assets.

Now President Biden, with his Secretary of State Tony Blinken, seem all too eager to coax Iran back to the negotiating table. As of this writing, they have not yet made the mistake of lifting economic sanctions in order to bring Iran back. But I fear they may do so, given the administration's constant rhetoric about how passionate they are to strike a deal with the rogue Iranian regime. Will Biden overlook Iran's vile human rights record for the sake of an uncertain deal, like President Obama? Will he too send billions of dollars to the Iranians while they continue to hang gays from cranes and stone women to death? Or will he be guided by a dose of Kosher Hate and first demand that Iran cease their barbaric practices and embrace civilized norms of behavior?

The problem is not that Americans don't care about the human rights of others; they do. Rather, there is something more deeply ingrained, namely, a belief that peace is always better than war. That war is wrong. That evil, if it exists at all, can be ignored because fighting would upset our inner state of tranquility and outer state of civility. It is only when evil is directed at us that we feel moved to act and, even then, we prefer to minimize the cost. Thus, for example, most Americans are content with the use of drones to fight terrorism. It seems as harmless as a video game. Many probably are not even aware that hundreds of our enemies—along with many unfortunate civilians—are being killed.

Whenever the threat of war arises, inevitably someone misstates the famous quote of Winston Churchill. Usually, it is cited as "Jaw-jaw is better than war-war." But this is not what Churchill said. What he actually said was, "Meeting jaw to jaw is better than war." The meaning is the same, that it is always better to negotiate than to fight. When it came to resisting evil, however, Churchill did not believe this was always the case. Churchill conveys this viscerally with the vivid phrase "meeting jaw to jaw," conjuring an image not of empty diplomatic jawboning but of a tense confrontation between belligerent adversaries who are ready to go to war at any moment. In short, for Churchill, war was always on the table.

To put it bluntly, Churchill was not Chamberlain. He did not seek talks with Hitler for their own sake; Churchill was implacably committed to Hilter's destruction and he made that clear consistently in every word and deed.

Ronald Reagan also did not believe we must "turn the other cheek" and allow the Soviets to engage in malevolent activity with impunity. Despite being widely ridiculed, he did not hesitate to call the Soviet Union an "evil empire." He understood that the United States could not go to war, given the Soviets' nuclear arsenal. But it was his commitment to defeat that empire by any means short of war that ultimately brought down the Berlin Wall and triggered the collapse of the Soviet Union.

Contrast Reagan's policy with that of Obama who was unwilling to acknowledge the evil of the radical Muslims controlling Iran even as they pursued a nuclear weapon and threatened Israel with genocide. In his desperation to reach an agreement and notch a major foreign policy accomplishment, he was out negotiated by the Iranians and signed a deal so full of loopholes that it had no chance of deterring Iran's nuclear ambitions. Worse, he gave them $150 billion in unfrozen assets that they could use to continue to sponsor global terror, develop ballistic missiles, and destabilize the region; activities he failed to include in the agreement. In trying to sell this catastrophic deal, Obama naïvely told the American people the Iranians would miraculously turn over a new leaf.

Now, fifteen years later, we know Iran did not moderate its behavior becoming, if anything, more hostile toward the United States. It exploited the loopholes in the nuclear deal to secretly continue its pursuit of a nuclear bomb and now openly flouts the agreement by violating its restrictions on uranium enrichment, the size of its stockpile, and Obama's requirement that there would be "anytime, anywhere inspections." Iran has also continued its ballistic missile program, expanded its terrorist activities (assisting Hamas in Gaza and Hezbollah in Lebanon), involved itself in civil wars in Syria and Yemen, supported attacks on American troops in Iraq while attempting to destabilize that country, attacked our Saudi allies, and built up a presence in Syria aimed at targeting Israel.

President Donald Trump came into office promising to end the nuclear deal, which he called "defective at its core," and fulfilled that promise in 2018. He subsequently imposed sanctions that have crippled the Iranian economy and forced the country to reduce its financial support for terrorist organizations. While sending a message that the U.S. will not stand by idly while Iran continues to threaten its own people and the world, Trump's actions did not prevent its malign activities or force the Iranians to return to the bargaining table to sign a new, stricter nuclear agreement.

Whatever criticism one may have of U.S. policy, however, it pales in comparison to the spinelessness of the Europeans, who prefer commerce to confrontation. Even after Iran openly began to defy them and ignore the terms of the nuclear agreement, the Europeans refused to take the measures Obama had promised—snapback sanctions—and instead continued to seek ways to expand their business relationships and circumvent U.S. sanctions.

I am critical of my own country's failure to stop genocides in Cambodia, Rwanda, and Bosnia. But that does not absolve the Europeans who were also nowhere to be found during those months and years of wanton slaughter. European amorality and refusal to hate anyone, except perhaps Jews, has allowed basic justice to be subverted.

This is nothing new, of course. At the time of the Gulf War, it seemed the French and Germans hated George W. Bush more than they did Saddam Hussein. In fact they clearly did. Their efforts to prevent the United States from invading Iraq and their treatment of Saddam as little more than a nuisance, spoke volumes about their indifference to bloodshed and their troubling neutrality on the subject of evil. To the contrary, they regarded Bush's desire to solve the festering problem of Hussein as more of a threat—more objectively evil—than Hussein himself. The same unwillingness to act characterized the European non-response to the Bosnian genocide, and it persists today as the preventable slaughter of innocents continues in Syria.

To be sure, policies of deterrence or containment can be employed effectively in the fight against evil. Kosher Hate does not require that countries always go to war. In fact it regards war as always a last resort. But as with Churchill, it must be credibly on the table.

I do not believe that the United States should have attacked the Soviet Union during the Cold War, unleashing a nuclear war of mutual annihilation. The half-century policy of containment was as effective as it could be. But it needed to be accompanied by Ronald Reagan's open declaration that the Soviet Union is indeed an "evil empire." And he openly called for its destruction, even as he engaged in high-stakes nuclear arms reduction talks with Mikhail Gorbachev.

Likewise, our policy of deterrence against North Korea is about as effective as any policy can currently be, given that the regime is now nuclear. But a clear statement about the wickedness of a government that will starve to death hundreds of thousands of people—including children—is critical to sustaining economic sanctions that might ultimately lead to its demise.

What about the liberal's alternative to war through peaceful protest and passive resistance as exemplified by Mahatma Gandhi and Martin Luther King Jr.? Gandhi's success in getting the British to leave India through a campaign of national strikes and civil disobedience inspired King to do likewise in the civil rights era. Both men are rightly admired and loved—and not just by liberals—for their conviction, courage, leadership, and vision.

To be sure, Gandhi was not the absolute pacifist those unfamiliar with his background imagine him to be. He supported the British in the Boer War, for example, at the end of the nineteenth century. He recruited roughly one million Indians to join the British army in World War I. When criticized by real pacifists, of whom there were many in India and Britain itself, Gandhi said, "it would be madness for me to sever my connection with the society to which I belong."[100] He was also motivated by a British promise to support self-government for Indians after the war.

In 1920, Gandhi wrote, "where there is only a choice between cowardice and violence, I would advise violence."[101] When the British were attacked by the Nazis, however, Gandhi opposed Indian involvement believing, paradoxically, that doing so would weaken imperialism. His subsequent contribution to history was his philosophy of passive non-violent resistance.

In 1938, just a few weeks after the horror of *Kristallnacht,* an event that shocked the world, Gandhi stated that his "sympathies are all with the Jews. I have known them intimately in South Africa. Some of them became life-long companions." Nevertheless, he said, "The cry for the national home for the Jews does not make much appeal to me.... Why should they not, like other peoples of the earth, make that country their home where they are born and where they earn their livelihood?" He added, "This cry for the national home affords a colourable justification for the German expulsion of the Jews."[102]

Interestingly, the pacifistic Gandhi adds, "the German persecution of the Jews seems to have no parallel in history.... If there ever could be a justifiable war in the name of and for humanity, a war against Germany, to prevent the wanton persecution of a whole race, would be completely justified."

But in the next sentence he says, "But I do not believe in any war." He is only willing to say there should be no alliance with Germany. Here he appears to be referring to Britain after the Munich Pact. He goes on to recommend that Jews engage in passive resistance because, even if they are massacred, it will somehow bring them "joy."

> Can the Jews resist this organized and shameless persecution? Is there a way to preserve their self-respect, and not to feel helpless, neglected and forlorn? I submit there is.... If I were a Jew and were born in Germany and earned my livelihood there, I would claim Germany as my home even as the tallest gentile German may, and challenge him to shoot me or cast me in the dungeon; I would refuse to be expelled or to submit to discriminating treatment.... If one Jew or all the Jews were to accept the prescription here offered, he or they cannot be worse off than now. And suffering voluntarily undergone will bring them an inner strength and joy

which no number of resolutions of sympathy passed in the world outside Germany can. Indeed, even if Britain, France and America were to declare hostilities against Germany, they can bring no inner joy, no inner strength. The calculated violence of Hitler may even result in a general massacre of the Jews by way of his first answer to the declaration of such hostilities. But if the Jewish mind could be prepared for voluntary suffering, even the massacre I have imagined could be turned into a day of thanksgiving and joy that Jehovah had wrought deliverance of the race even at the hands of the tyrant. For to the god fearing, death has no terror. It is a joyful sleep to be followed by a waking that would be all the more refreshing for the long sleep.[103]

Gandhi paradoxically believed that Jews should be thankful if they are massacred because it will bring them "inner joy." I beg to differ. This line of coldly detached moral reasoning is actually quite chilling.

In another example of selective pacifism, Gandhi goes on to justify Arab violence directed at Jews in Palestine: "I am not defending the Arab excesses. I wish they had chosen the way of non-violence in resisting what they rightly regarded as an unwarrantable encroachment upon their country. But according to the accepted canons of right and wrong, nothing can be said against the Arab resistance in the face of overwhelming odds."[104]

A year later, philosopher Martin Buber wrote an open letter to Gandhi debunking his views on Palestine and briefly addressing his views on German Jews. Buber rejects the analogy Gandhi made to Indians living in South Africa, noting "they were not deprived of rights, they were not outlawed, they were not hostages to a hoped-for change in the behavior of foreign Powers." As for following Gandhi's guidance, Buber says, "do you think perhaps that a Jew in Germany could pronounce in public one single sentence of a speech such as yours without being knocked down?" He adds, "An effective stand in the form of non-violence may be taken against unfeeling human beings in the hope of gradually bringing them to their senses; but a diabolic universal steamroller cannot thus be withstood."[105]

In February 1939, a few days before Buber wrote his letter, Gandhi had criticized German Jews. "The Jews are not angels," he said. "My point was they were not non-violent in the sense meant by me. Their non-violence had and has no love in it. It is passive. They do not resist because they know that they cannot resist with any degree of success."[106]

On July 23, 1939, Gandhi wrote a two-paragraph letter to Hitler in which he says he had been urged to write "for the sake of humanity" but resisted because of the feeling that "any letter from me would be an impertinence."[107] He somewhat obliquely calls on Hitler not to go to war and bizarrely concludes by asking for Hitler's forgiveness "if I have erred in writing to you."

On September 1, 1939, the day Germany invaded Poland to start World War II, Gandhi wrote a Jewish New Year greeting to the head of the Bombay Zionist Association, Avraham Shohet: "How I wish the new year may mean an era of peace for your afflicted people."[108]

By September 1940, the war in Europe was going badly for the Allies and the British were at the beginning of what would be a seven month German bombing campaign—"the Blitz." At that bleak time, pacifistic Gandhi offered the following helpful advice to the British Government: "I would like you to lay down the arms you have as being useless for saving you or humanity. You will invite Herr Hitler and Signor Mussolini to take what they want of the countries you call your possessions. Let them take possession…If these gentlemen choose to occupy your homes, you will vacate them. If they do not give you free passage out, you will allow yourselves, man woman and child to be slaughtered, but you will refuse to owe allegiance to them."[109]

We can only shudder to imagine what would have happened if the British had taken any notice of Gandhi's delusions about Nazism, not to mention how Gandhi and his people would have been treated by the Axis powers.

As George Orwell noted, Gandhi's belief that his approach would make "political opponents simply disappear" would never work with a ruthless totalitarian regime like the Third Reich.[110] Gandhi's naïveté was apparent before the war when he publicized the following announcement to the Jewish community:

> Sufferings of the non-violent have been known to melt the stoniest hearts. I make bold to say that if the Jews can summon to their aid the soul power that comes only from non-violence, Herr Hitler will bow before the courage which he has never yet experienced in any large measure in his dealings with men, and which, when it is exhibited, he will own is infinitely superior to that shown by his best storm troopers. The exhibition of such courage is only possible for those who have a living faith in the God of Truth and Non-violence, i.e., Love.

He admits that his philosophy has not been accepted "in toto" in India but says he is so sure of its efficacy that he felt compelled to "draw attention to it when I saw cases where it could be effectively applied."[111]

Indians did not follow this prescription during the war and, of course, non-violence didn't work in India when it came to relations between Hindus and Muslims, which led to the 1948 partition of their country at the cost of hundreds of thousands of lives. Apparently non-violence only works when the adversary has some sense of shame or inner moral compunction to which the weak and persecuted victim can appeal.

Non-violence could also work in the United States, which despite its flaws is a law-abiding democracy where the courts have the final say. Martin Luther King Jr. was therefore wise to embrace Gandhi's example, leading mass strikes, protests, and disruptive campaigns of civil disobedience to great effect, especially in the age of network television. The sight of hoses being turned on peaceful and dignified demonstrators by thuggish cops like Bull Connor shamed the nation and inspired a wave of support for serious civil rights legislation. That is a testament to the civility and decency of Americans themselves.

But to believe that such methods could work in a dictatorship like Nazi Germany is a tragic delusion. Gandhi, for all his incomparable greatness, was blind to this and refused to invoke or adopt the moral power of Kosher Hate.

In December 1940, Gandhi wrote a second letter to Hitler, which he addressed, "Dear friend," and said he used the word "friend" because "I own no foes." He goes on, "We have no doubt about your bravery or devotion to your fatherland, nor do we believe that you are the monster described by your opponents. But your own writings and pronouncements and those of your friends and admirers leave no room for doubt that many of your acts are monstrous and unbecoming of human dignity, especially in the estimation of men like me who believe in universal friendliness."[112]

Most of the letter explains the Indian position regarding British rule and Gandhi says he doesn't want German help. He then appeals to Hitler to stop the war because, "You are leaving no legacy to your people of which they would feel proud." His only mention of Hitler's actions is the "humiliation of Czechoslovakia, the rape of Poland and the swallowing of Denmark."

He concludes by suggesting that Hitler share his sentiments with "Signor Mussolini, whom I had the privilege of meeting" and signs the letter "Your sincere friend."

Gandhi was well aware that Jews were being murdered and persecuted by the Germans, having mentioned it in his remarks before the war, but he probably could not yet have known about the Final Solution. After the war, however, where he of course did know all the facts of the genocide, he made this shocking statement about the Holocaust: "Hitler killed five million Jews. It is the greatest crime of our time. But the Jews should have offered themselves to the butcher's knife. They should have thrown themselves into the sea from the cliffs.... It would have aroused the world and the people of Germany.... As it is, they succumbed anyway in their millions."[113]

Louis Fisher, Gandhi's official biographer, wanted clarification and asked: "You mean the Jews should have committed collective suicide?"

"Yes," he responded, "That would have been heroism."[114]

I have no idea what Gandhi meant by this. Was he perhaps referring to the mass suicide at Masada in the year 74, when approximately 700 Jewish fighters took their lives rather than be conquered by the Romans? If so, was he seriously suggesting that Jews all over Europe do the same? True, in May 1943 the fighters of the Warsaw Ghetto uprising blew themselves up with grenades rather than suffer torture at the hands of the SS. But at the risk of stating the painfully obvious, there is a vast difference between a few hundred fighters taking their own lives—and those of their families—to avoid barbaric torture and telling the entire Jewish population of Europe to march off a cliff for no good reason. That is not heroism but an abomination, an act of mass suicide unprecedented in human history.

Heroism is not sitting back passively and doing nothing in the face of evil. Heroism does not require millions of people to offer themselves as human sacrifices to the evilest regime the world has ever known. How can the spectacle which

Gandhi so vividly paints of millions of human beings hurling themselves into the sea—apparently dragging their children with them—be considered heroism by any sane person? What kind of mind could even imagine such a thing?

One of the most odious myths about the Holocaust is that the Jews went like lambs to the slaughter. They did not. There were countless armed rebellions by Jews against the Nazis, with the Warsaw Ghetto being the best known. But Gandhi thought they should not have resisted at all but rather killed themselves, to somehow to maintain their moral purity.

I fully realize that Gandhi was a visionary leader and the father of the Indian nation. He led his people to independence from foreign rule and set a unique standard for revolutionary politics that has been a powerful inspiration to the whole world. His ideals are admirable and the restraint he demonstrated and preached can serve as an example to oppressed people everywhere. His tactics only worked, however, because the British were a decent, law-abiding democratic people who eventually realized that colonial rule was unsustainable, and even unjust, in the emerging postwar world. Thus Britain in the end, after a period of grudging and sometimes violent resistance, willingly disbanded its empire.

However, to suppose that the nonviolent approach would work against the likes of Hitler, Stalin, Pol Pot, Saddam Hussein, Bashar Assad, and other genocidal maniacs is frankly delusional.

Remember the Chinese man who bravely stood blocking the advance of a tank in Beijing's Tiananmen Square. How many people know what happened to him?

The answer is no one. Despite years of efforts to identify him, he remains unknown, referred to as "Tank Man." Former Chinese President Jiang Zemin suggested in an interview in 1990 that he had not been killed.[115] The Chinese government, after allowing people to view the video of his protest to show their magnanimity in not killing him on the spot, later censored online images of him and prosecuted those who talked about him. Today, few Chinese know about Tank Man.

But as iconic as his action was, he failed to stop the army from crushing the protests. While he was praised worldwide for *his* action, *no country* was willing to take any serious measures to punish China for its crackdown. The French Foreign Minister, Roland Dumas, said he was "dismayed by the bloody repression" of "an unarmed crowd of demonstrators." The West German Foreign Ministry urged China "to return to its universally welcomed policies of reform and openness." Pope John Paul II expressed hope that the events in China would bring change. British Prime Minister Margaret Thatcher expressed "utter revulsion and outrage" and said she was "appalled by the indiscriminate shooting of unarmed people."

President George H. W. Bush suspended military sales and visits to that country, but in a bid to improve relations, vetoed legislation permitting Chinese exchange students to remain in the U.S. until the Chinese government improved its human rights record. In exchange the Chinese made minor concessions such as releasing a small number of detainees and accrediting a *Voice of America* correspondent.[116]

The idea at the heart of all this was not that Americans don't care about the human rights of others. They clearly do. Rather, there is something much more deeply ingrained, namely, a belief that to be at peace is always better than to be at war because war is inherently wrong. That evil, if it exists at all, should be ignored rather than fought because fighting it would upset our inner state of tranquility and outer desire for civility.

CHAPTER 5:

KOSHER HATE APPLIED TO TERRORISTS

WHERE IN THE WORLD today is Kosher Hate an appropriate response? This question is where religiously observant Jews and modern liberals often part company. It is a particular challenge for liberal Jews, who by and large have embraced a version of Judaism that is heavily imbued with liberal politics.

The most serious global threat today requiring the application of Kosher Hate is terrorism in general and radical Islam in particular. The Russians and the Chinese peddle their ideology around the world, but communism has lost its allure and few people fear its spread anymore. Radical Islam and its call to jihad and violence is a different story, however, because it has tens if not hundreds of millions of adherents who do not answer to a temporary terrestrial leader but believe they are following the instructions of Allah.

Let me be clear. I believe Islam to be a great world religion. For at least two centuries during the "Golden Age" science, math, and culture flourished in the Muslim world. In fact, we would not have some of the most important philosophical and scientific works of the ancient world if they had not been translated by Muslim scholars. Avicenna, Averroes and other philosophers influenced psychology, metaphysics, logic, and ethics. Omar Khayyam and other mathematicians played important roles in the development of algebra and geometry. In the ninth century Al-Mamun, a caliph of the Abbasid dynasty, established state-funded places of study, focusing on translations of Greek and other works of antiquity that predated the first European universities by more than 300 years.

The Abbasid Muslim Empire had an agricultural revolution in the eighth century that produced technological innovations the likes of which wouldn't been seen in the West until at least 1180.

In the tenth century Al-Razi of Baghdad wrote numerous medical books which western medicine could not match until the eighteenth century. Sultan Akbar of India was known for enactment of laws embracing religious toleration and protection of women and children well before such advances were known in Christian Europe. In the Golden Age of Muslim Spain during the sixteenth and seventeenth centuries, scholars made important contributions in physics, chemistry, and biology.

Today, Islam continues to be a great world religion, but it is facing a serious challenge from Islamists who would defile their faith with violence in the name of God. Sadly, the fanaticism of Muslims who oppose modernity, such as the mullahs in Iran, have prevented their societies from keeping pace with the innovations of Western countries.

The overwhelming majority of Muslims are good people who simply want to raise their children and worship their God in peace without threatening others. The Islamists, however, have their own Manichean view of good versus evil, them versus us. They see Western culture as permissive, indulgent, devoid of visible morals, and weak whereas Islamic culture is dignified, hierarchic, austere, and pietistic. We have no common ground and Muslims fear their society will be corrupted by Western decadence. They do not want to be seduced by a hedonistic culture that is more alluring than a traditionalist culture of restraint and moderation. The Islamists don't see, or choose to ignore, how religious most Americans really are. They don't see our churches and synagogues, our charities, and our devotion to social welfare. Their principal exposure to American life is produced by Hollywood.

The response of some Muslims—a relatively small but highly destructive number—is to strike out against us while others stand on the sidelines and cheer.

Most moral human beings, including most Muslims, understand that killing people is wrong and do not commit murder. Muslims who are radicalized, however, are convinced that killing infidels, including apostate Muslims, is Allah's will and that their acts will be rewarded in the afterlife.

How many radicals are there?

The number of extremists may be much larger than many people would like to believe. In the book, *Who Speaks for Islam?: What a Billion Muslims Really Think*, John Esposito and Dalia Mogahed argue that most Muslims are just like ordinary Americans and that only 7 percent are radicals. The West, they concluded, has nothing to fear from the overwhelming majority of Muslims.[117] Consider, however, that 7 percent represents roughly *91 million* Muslims.[118]

Moreover, when Robert Satloff, the Executive Director of the Washington Institute for Near East Policy, took a closer look at the responses to the survey cited in the book, he found that the authors vastly underestimated the number of Muslims with extremist views. If you consider those radical who believe the 9/11 attacks were somewhat or completely justified and hold unfavorable opinions of the United States, more than one-third of Muslims—nearly 470 million(!)—are "radical." Satloff concluded that "according to Esposito and Mogahed, the proper term for a Muslim who hates America, wants to impose Sharia law, supports suicide bombing, and opposes equal rights for women but does not 'completely' justify 9/11 is…'moderate.'"[119]

The problem is not the *faith* but the *silence* of hundreds of millions of Muslims when murderers invoke their religion and their God to maim and kill. The problem lies in radicals being allowed to slowly take over the faith.

We cannot hide our heads in the sand, however, and ignore that Muslim extremists have declared a holy war. They have carried on a decades-long campaign of terror against the "decadent infidels" of the West, the "apostates" in Muslim countries, and the Jews and their homeland. Presenting such evidence, or quoting passages from the Koran and Muslim scriptures expressing intolerance toward gays, Christians, and Jews (who are compared to pigs and monkeys) in this era of political correctness provokes cries of "Islamophobia."

That term has become a weapon used to silence truth-tellers. Muslims believe Jews use the word "anti-Semitism" to silence critics of Israel and despite the endless attacks on Israel, think it is a successful strategy. Many throw out the charge of "Islamophobia" in the hope of muzzling people who speak about Islamists. A phobia is an irrational fear, and yes, there are bigots who may see a woman in a hijab and unreasonably associate them with terrorism. Those people are indeed bigots. But it is not irrational to believe there are radical Islamists who do want to kill us because they have done so in the past and continue to do so. Calling out those who justify murdering in the name of Islam is not Islamophobia.

Too often sage moral guardians are dismissed because of fear that their words are offensive. Out of deference to Muslim sensibilities, the Obama administration went so far as to create its own nomenclature for the extremists to avoid saying Muslim or Islamic terror. President Obama meant well. But he failed the test of Kosher Hate by insisting on calling them "violent extremists" rather than Islamic terrorists.[120]

Donald Trump criticized Obama's timidity and abandoned the pretense during his administration soon after his inauguration. In his first speech to a joint session of Congress, he vowed to protect the nation from "radical Islamic terrorism."[121]

Much of our attention during Donald Trump's term as president was focused on ISIS, which hoped to restore the caliphate that dominated the Middle East and beyond for more than a thousand years. For a brief period, ISIS succeeded in declaring a caliphate in roughly a third of Syria and 40 percent of Iraq, but the United States and its allies dismantled the unrecognized entity and have decimated the organization.

What makes Islamic extremism so insidious is that it does not require government sanction, though governments often provide support such as in Qatar, providing a haven and funding for Hamas and the Muslim Brotherhood, and Iran backing Hezbollah. There are "lone wolves," as well as cells of terrorists who are motivated by their distorted interpretation of Islam. More dangerous, of course, are Islamist organizations such as ISIS and Al Qaeda that seek to spread Islam through terror.

A far more serious threat, however, are Islamist governments. The most dangerous is Iran where the mullahs hope to restore the former glory of the Persian Empire and spread their radical version of Islam around the globe. While they make genocidal threats against Israel, which should generate Kosher Hate from all corners of the globe, they see the Jewish state as just a speedbump to be removed on the way to refighting, and winning, the war to take over Europe.

In the meantime, the Iranian mullahs are busy oppressing their own people, destabilizing their neighbors, threatening Sunni Muslims, sponsoring global terror; intervening in civil wars in Syria, Yemen, and Libya; ruining Lebanon, and trying to establish a beachhead in Syria from which to attack Israel. Oh, and they are seeking a nuclear capability to insulate the regime from attack and escalate its threats.

Any of these activities should be grounds for marshaling our resources and allies to encourage and support the Iranian people to revolt and, if necessary, directly engage in military action to destroy the regime.

Iran is not alone in its dream of placing the world's population under the umbrella of Islam. Turkey has increasingly become a threat as Recep Tayyip Erdogan has turned the once proud secular democratic nation into an Islamist state that seeks to spread its influence and challenge Iran for regional hegemony. President Trump viewed Erdogan as a friend, but he did cancel a planned sale of F-35 fighter jets to Turkey after they bought an anti-missile defense system from Russia over U.S. objections. Erdogan has been unmoved, however, and has tightened his tyrannical control over his people and become increasingly aggressive, sending troops to fight in Syria and Libya, and threatening Cyprus over its collaboration with Israel in the exploration and export of natural gas.

Once a close ally of Israel, Turkey under Erdogan has become one of its most vociferous critics. Though Turkey is a NATO member with an important base and strategic location, it may be time to consider booting the country out of the alliance if it does not dramatically change its policy. Better still would be a revolution to restore democracy. An earlier coup attempt failed but the United States and its allies might direct some Kosher Hate toward Erdogan and support his opponents. It would be welcome to see President Biden taking a strong approach against Erdogan, warning him sharply against further erasing democracy in Turkey and inciting hatred against Israel.

Saudi Arabia has become much more moderate under Crown Prince Mohammed bin Salman (usually referred to as MBS). Before him, it exported its extreme brand of Wahhabi Islam around the world through the mosques and madrasas it funds. For years, the Saudis promised the United States they would revise their textbooks that teach intolerance toward non-Muslims and are littered with anti-Semitic references. In 2020, changes were finally made to remove some of the more problematic passages but maps still do not show Israel and texts contain language demonizing Jews and Israel.[122]

Media reports maintain that Saudi Arabia has taken steps to develop a nuclear capability, though like Iran it claims to only be interested in peaceful uses. A Saudi defense official noted in January 2012, "We cannot live in a situation where Iran has nuclear weapons and we don't... If Iran develops a nuclear weapon, that will be unacceptable to us and we will have to follow suit."[123] The fact the Saudis are pursuing a nuclear capability is a direct consequence of the failure of Obama's nuclear deal, which has dangerously increased the threat of nuclear proliferation in the Middle East.

There are signs of reform under MBS. There even exists the possibility that he might join the Abraham Accords and make peace with Israel. Yet the Saudi education system continues to teach intolerance towards Jews, Christians, and secular Westerners.[124]

It is not difficult to feel Kosher Hate for the terrorists that directly threaten and attack us. Americans also have largely cheered their government's efforts to destroy Al Qaeda, although liberals have taken issue with some of the methods used (torture, drone strikes, indefinite incarceration at Guantanamo Bay). Hopefully the Biden administration will not back away from our commitment to confront and oppose evil and will continue to deploy troops where needed, order drone strikes, and take whatever other measures are required to keep American citizens safe at home and abroad.

In the case of ISIS, which grew partially out of President Obama's ill-considered decision to withdraw troops from Iraq (which also contributed to a resurgence of Al Qaeda) the U.S. successfully assembled a coalition of fourteen countries to destroy the "caliphate." In that case, there was little objection to our use of force, less because of the understanding of the danger of militant Islam, and more because it required a limited number of troops and there were few casualties.

Europeans have been resistant to openly speaking about the threat of radical Islam and have mocked the United States for declaring a war on terrorism. America is denigrated as a crude neighborhood bully in the international village as the memory of 9/11 recedes. Quietly, other nations have recognized the threat to themselves but most leaders, like Obama, are afraid to refer to the danger as Islamic radicalism. Nevertheless, even the intelligence agencies of some of the "peace loving nations" such as those in Scandinavia, have described Islamism as a threat. The civil war in Syria escalated the threat to Europeans who feared the flood of refugees from the Middle East would facilitate the infiltration of terrorists among the refugees and magnify the danger of the growing Muslim populations within their countries that resist assimilation.

This is especially true in France, which has the largest Muslim population in Western Europe and has been the site of multiple terror attacks. As I was writing this section, a Pakistan-born teenager stabbed two people with a meat cleaver in Paris in what French Interior Minister Gérald Darmanin said was "clearly an act of Islamist terrorism."[125] The eighteen-year-old said he wanted to avenge the republication of cartoons of the Prophet Mohammad by the satirical *Charlie Hebdo* newspaper.

After three attacks in one month at the end of 2020, including the beheading of a teacher who showed cartoons of the Prophet Muhammad during a class discussion, President Emmanuel Macron sought to impose several restrictions on Muslims in France. Macron asked Muslim leaders to agree on a "charter of republican values" that called for "the rejection of political Islam and any foreign interference."[126]

Such restrictions would be impossible in the United States. President Trump tried to prevent the infiltration of Islamists by instituting a ban on immigration to the United States from several Muslim countries. The decision, however, was very controversial and seen by many as racist.

I understood the president's motivation but still opposed the so-called Muslim ban. I argued that he had every right to introduce new vetting procedures for immigrants to this country, but he should have established safe zones, primarily in Syria, where people facing brutality could be protected. This way the president could have protected these immigrants at their origin. He also should have said the ban did not apply to those brave souls who worked with American forces in Iraq, and to those who have already obtained a green card and been properly vetted.

The application of Kosher Hate to Islamic terrorism is anathema to liberals who cannot accept that people are different or that a religion (other than Christianity of course) could be a source of brutal violence. During the Cold War, they heard the pop musician Sting naïvely suggest that we should not fear the Soviet Union because, like us, they love their children.

This is undoubtedly true. However, it does not mean that we all treat our children the same way. Why do Muslim mothers allow their children to become suicide bombers and praise their actions after they die during an attack that kills the children of other mothers?

To be sure, religion has been abused for millennia and many have preached hatred in its name. Jews especially have been the targets of hatred in the name of God. But this religiously inspired hatred of Jews should not be confused with Kosher Hate. The former involves an irrational loathing of a designated "other," an infidel, and is motivated by corrupt and fraudulent spiritual teachings. The latter is a moral response to the encounter with evil and is designed to combat evil so that destructive bigotries will not rule the earth.

The Islamic terrorist typically comes from a different educational background than you or me. They are indoctrinated with a particular interpretation of Islam that emphasizes the danger of the infidels and glorifies martyrdom. They believe that Allah has instructed them to pursue a holy war against the infidels, to subjugate *Dar al-Harb*, the House of War to *Dar al-Islam*, the House of Islam. As the Middle East scholar Bernard Lewis explained, the law of Islam "divides unbelievers theologically into those who have a book and profess what Islam recognizes as a divine religion and those who do not; politically into *dhimmis*, those who have accepted the supremacy of the Muslim state and the primacy of the Muslims, and *harbis*, the denizens of the Dar al-harb, the House of War, who remain outside the Islamic frontier, and with whom therefore there is in principle, a canonically obligatory perpetual state of war until the whole world is either converted or subjugated."[127]

Those who employ this outlook to massacre innocents whom they consider infidels must be confronted with the kind of conviction that only comes from Kosher Hate.

The media contributes to the problem of refusing to hate terrorists as they deserve because they frequently refuse to label them as such, preferring euphemisms such as "militants," "gunmen," or "armed attackers."[128] But when Americans are victims, they are less reticent. As foreign policy expert

Clifford May observed, "No newspaper would write, 'Militants struck the World Trade Center yesterday.'"[129]

Many liberals are ignorant of history and prefer to believe the myth of Islam—or any religion for that matter—as a religion of peace. The truth, of course, is that whether or not a religion is peaceful will come down to its practitioners, preachers, and adherents. And that can change in any given era. For many centuries Christianity was a religion at war, while today it is a religion that practices and advocates peace.

There have been long periods when Islam was at peace and long periods when it was at war. To assert that Islam in its essence is a religion of peace would be specious and completely unhistorical.

Sheikh Ahmed al-Tayeb, the grand imam of Al-Azhar, the Islamic world's most prestigious university, Al-Azhar in Cairo, declared that "Islam doesn't seek war or bloodshed, and Muslims only fight back to defend themselves." Historian Raymond Ibrahim noted that "such claims fly in the face of more than a millennium of well documented Islamic teachings and Islamic history.... One need only look at a map of the Muslim world today and realize that the vast majority of it—all of the Middle East, North Africa, Turkey, Central Asia, as far east as Pakistan, and farther—was taken by violent conquest in the name of jihad."[130]

Ibrahim points out that Muslims believe *they* are the good guys fighting evil. Hence, "the historic Islamic conquests are never referred to as 'conquests' in Arabic and other Muslim languages; rather, they are *futuhat*—literally, 'openings' for the light of Islam to enter (or *fatah* in the singular, as the Palestinian group tellingly calls itself). In this context, every land ever invaded or seized by Muslims was done 'altruistically' to bring Islam to wayward infidels, who are seen as the aggressors for unjustly resisting Islam."

Ibrahim quotes an American historian of Islam who explains how Muslims rationalize their history:

> [T]he conquests were seen from the beginning as one of the incontrovertible proofs of Islam. To disavow them or to examine them critically—which has yet to happen in the Muslim world—will be very painful for Muslims especially Arabic-speaking Muslims. At every point ... when Muslims have tried to abandon militant jihad for the internal, spiritual jihad ... the memory of the conquests and the need to rationalize them have defeated this effort. The problem may lie in the unwillingness to confront the fact that the conquests were basically unjustified. They were not a "liberation" and they were not desired by the non-Muslim peoples; they were endured and finally accepted[.]

Strangely, much of the secular left has bought into the "religion of peace" mantra even though Muslim countries are extremely illiberal when it comes to issues such as women's rights, gay rights, and other civil and human rights we take for granted. In truth, of course, whether or not any religion is one of war and peace will come down to how its leaders interpret its texts and core beliefs in each epoch. I believe Islam can, of course, be a religion of peace. It has been in the past. But it has also been, like Christianity, a religion of war. Many "progressives" turn their own fashionable post-colonialist theory on its head, portraying Muslims as victims of Western colonialism (which at times they were) when they were often colonialists and slave traders themselves.

I agree with my liberal friends that we must fight the abuse of human rights. In some cases, this involves confronting allies such as Turkey, Qatar, Saudi Arabia, and Egypt. Kosher Hate can certainly be directed at regimes that abuse their people. But the internal affairs of countries, absent mass slaughter, is insufficient justification for using force. Every country in the world, including the United States, fails at some level to achieve its stated ideals. Democracies, however, cannot compare to other forms of government. Western countries have a system of justice with an independent judiciary, a free press, and governmental checks and balances to hold their leaders accountable. That is not the case in the countries with the worst human rights records. And we are not powerless to effect change in them. American determination to fight Soviet communism led to the dissolution of the Soviet Union and increased freedom for peoples in Eastern Europe. Military force was also not required to bring about the collapse of apartheid in South Africa. We have tools such as moral suasion, sanctions, boycotts, and repeatedly calling out abuses.

What we cannot do is allow good and evil to be dependent on the eye of the beholder, with every religion believing it is acting in the interest of its god. Rather, every religion must adhere to their own version of the Ten Commandments, which is a universally accepted code of moral conduct.

In the struggle against radical Islamic violence, directional hatred has a very important part to play. This frightening phenomenon is at root a product of the mind. Ideologues formed it, teachers and propagandists spread it. When I say it begins in the mind, I mean that except for women or others who are coerced, a person must be in a certain mental state and hold certain ideological opinions in order to be willing to murder innocents by blowing themselves up. Terrorist attacks, especially suicide attacks, are not done impulsively. They require planning and total commitment. Therefore, I believe that positive, oppositional propaganda is vitally important in the fight against it. Part of that effort has to be a public acknowledgment that their actions are hateful and that rather than seeking to understand and forgive what they do in the name of the God, we should robustly hate and oppose them.

Kosher Hate requires us to fight till the end those who believe in the mass murder of innocents for political or religious purposes. We should have no interest in their justifications; what they are doing is always wrong and there is no excuse for it. They must have no confusion or doubt that our response will be not just disapproval but hatred. By their actions, they have ceased to behave as human beings and have therefore forfeited the right to be treated as such. They should be neutralized because they have shown themselves to revel in horrific violence.

When Donald Trump ordered the killing of Qassem Soleimani, the head of the Iranian Al Quds Revolutionary Guard and one of the world's most evil terrorists, it was easily justifiable on these grounds. The man was an unrepentant murderer who disabused himself of any spark of the divine. Letting him live would simply have meant more innocent people dying.

It is not solely up to non-Muslims, however. Muslims must also hate terrorists. The only way to change the culture is to reform Islam and that must be done within the Muslim community. It cannot be imposed by outsiders. Jews can no more tell Muslims what to believe and how to behave according to their faith than Muslims can tell Jews.

Kosher Hate is therefore necessary but not sufficient to end Islamic terror. A condemnation of all violence in the name of religion, and a feeling of Kosher Hate for those who practice it, must be internalized by Muslims so they will feel the same revulsion as non-Muslims toward those who kill in the name of Islam. Ultimately, it will take a reformation of Islam by Muslims to root out extremism. I feel increasingly confident that we will witness more and more mainstream Islamic leaders condemning those who tarnish a great world religion with their un-Kosher Hate.

CHAPTER 6:

RIGHTEOUS INDIGNATION

I HAVE HEARD THE ARGUMENTS against hatred. It is the cause of all wars. It consumes the soul of he who hates. If you learn to hate, you'll end up part of the problem. You will be like Anakin Skywalker in *Star Wars*—remember those episodes?—going over to the "dark side" and becoming Darth Vader. Anakin did not go over to the dark side because he hated evil; he went over because he didn't hate evil enough.

OK, I know, I know. Seriously, Rabbi Shmuley? You're going to use *Star Wars* to make a moral argument for Kosher Hate? But why not. Kosher Hate needs all the reinforcement it can get! And since the time of Homer, popular culture has been the greatest moral teacher of the common folk.

So let's get back to Anakin Skywalker. First, he devoted his life to serving the Jedi council and what they stood for. He was obedient to their every request and supported killing the Sith Lord, the evilest presence in the galaxy. In his eyes, the Jedi council represented what was good and just and were looked upon as defenders of freedom. Like prophets and God-fearing leaders in our world, Jedi leaders embodied the virtuous life, and their knights were looked up to as heroes.

Even though they were righteous, they still absolutely hated wickedness. The Jedi knew evil had to be eradicated to keep balance in the galaxy. This was their greatest task and sworn duty.

At one point in the series, Anakin discovers who the Sith Lord is and has the chance to kill him. The Sith Lord pleads for mercy and tells him he can help him gain special powers. Anakin chooses not to kill him. For me this was the turning point of the story and the seminal moment of the new trilogy. This choice created inevitable consequences not only for Anakin, but the future of the galaxy as well. Anakin did not have enough hateful emotions to kill the Sith Lord, even when he had the power to do so. He was unsure of where he stood and truly thought he was doing the right thing by showing—should we call it Christian love?—and giving him another chance. Forgiveness triumphed over Kosher Hate with terrible consequences for the galaxy (of course, it worked great for the series).

Because of the murder of Anakin's mother in childhood, he let fate rule his life. His nightmares convinced him that his true love's death was imminent and the thought of losing his beloved wife was unbearable. He was willing to sacrifice everything for her love and for power, not realizing the long-term consequences. He couldn't know the future, but he knew the consequences of betraying the Jedi and then willingly set about to destroy them. Because he did not deliberately choose good, he became susceptible to evil.

Like Anakin, many Americans today are allowing fate to rule their future.

Anakin believed he knew better than his fellow Jedi and did not need them. He decided to give up his Jedi principles "temporarily" to obtain greater power, which he believed would thwart the fate he feared and allow him to rule the galaxy. But he did not understand that giving up his principles cost him his integrity and soul. He became compartmental-ized and therefore would never experience true happiness. Anakin can be compared to people who mistakenly fear that they will be devoured by hate if they set aside compassion and choose to hate evil.

Today, we must be as heroic as the Jedi, prepared to give our lives to preserve mankind's liberty. We must be guided by a force—the force that comes from the divine inspiration for freedom and justice—to avoid a fate like the Galactic Empire in Star Wars.

Of course, one does not have to look to the movies for examples of the power of un-Kosher Hate. The evilest men have been the most effective in using hate for their own ends. Hitler's power was driven largely by un-Kosher Hate, which he skillfully directed at the countries that sought to perma-nently weaken Germany at Versailles, along with political rivals, communists, Jews, Roma, homosexuals, non-Aryans, and the mentally ill. The list is long and yet Hitler managed to convince the German people and his allies to hate them with sufficient passion that it was possible to convince even "ordinary" men and women to collaborate in mass murder or to silently stand by.

Hate has been used effectively by dictators throughout history, which understandably makes people fearful of what that emotion can lead to. This again confuses the sentiment, which is neutral, with the person. It is like saying that be-cause haters go to war, we should oppose all war and become pacifists; but such a response is precisely what allows the purveyors of hate to succeed. It produces people like Charles Lindbergh, an isolationist who opposed fighting the Nazis. In fact, he wrote a secret memo to the British saying that a mil-itary response to Hitler's violation of the Munich Pact would be a grave error.

Like Gandhi, Lindbergh was selective in his pacifism. In 1941, he testified in Congress that the United States should sign a neutrality pact with Hitler.[131] While blaming Jews and others for advocating war, he himself advocated a German attack on Russia, which he saw as the greatest threat to Western civilization. He believed, much like Hitler, "We can have peace and security only so long as we band together to preserve that most priceless possession, our inheritance of European blood, only so long as we guard ourselves against attack by foreign armies and dilution by foreign races."[132] About six months later, however, he gave a radio address on May 19, 1940, in which he said the country only faced internal threats so long as the United States did not interfere in the affairs of other countries. The Germans had just invaded France, but Lindbergh said, "Regardless of which side wins this war, there is no reason…to prevent a continuation of peaceful relationships between America and the countries of Europe." Roosevelt said the speech could not have been "better put if it had been written by Goebbels himself."[133] Lindbergh would later support the war effort, but only after Pearl Harbor and Germany's declaration of war. I have twice visited Lindbergh's gravesite on the island of Maui in Hawaii. As burial real estate, he has one of the finest views of any person buried anywhere in the world. And I felt a darkness visiting the site, even as it is perched right outside a beautiful church. Lindbergh was an American hero and one of the most famous men of the twentieth century. He showed vast courage flying across the Atlantic on his own from New York to Paris. But while he was an aviation giant, he was a moral pigmy, a bigot and anti-Semite whose admiration for Hitler and the Nazis will forever tarnish his dark legacy and soul.

Rabbi Meir Soloveichik, one of the eminent scholars of the Jewish world, wrote an important scholarly piece on the virtues of hatred. He also succinctly addressed the associated dangers:

The danger inherent in hatred is that it must be very limited, directed only at the most evil and unrepentant. According to the Talmud, the angels began singing a song of triumph upon the deliverance of the Israelites from Egypt until God interrupted them: "My creatures are drowning, and you wish to sing a song?" Yet the rabbis also state that God wreaked further vengeance upon Pharaoh himself, ordering the sea to spit him out, so that he could return to Egypt alone, without his army. Apparently one must cross some terrible moral boundary to be a justified target of God's hatred—and of ours. An Israeli mother is right to raise her child to hate Saddam Hussein, but she would fail as a parent if she taught him to despise every Arab. We who hate must be wary lest we, like [Baruch] Goldstein [a Jew who killed twenty-nine Muslims and wounded another 125 while they were praying in Hebron in 1994], become like those we are taught to despise.[134]

Amidst an otherwise persuasive article, Soloveichik makes the mistake of exerting every effort to minimize the power of kosher hatred. He accuses many Jews of harboring a hatred of Christianity because of past sins committed by its followers against Jews: "Burning hatred, once kindled, is difficult to extinguish; but that is precisely what Jews must do when reassessing our relationship with contemporary Christianity. The crimes of popes of the past do not negate the fact that John Paul II is one of the righteous men of our generation. If Christians no longer hold us accountable for the crime of deicide, we cannot remain indifferent to such changes. Christians have every right to assert the truth of their beliefs. Modern anti-Christianity is no more excusable than ancient anti–Semitism."[135]

Soloveichik believes that because Jews followed the moral imperative of abhorring evil and allowed themselves to detest Christians when they were viciously oppressing Jews, many now unjustly retain a hatred for Christianity, ignoring the changes made by the Church and the good relations between most Jews and Christians today. I believe he is being far too hard on his coreligionists, and that the comparison between "modern anti-Christianity" on the part of Jews, and "ancient anti-Semitism" on the part of Christians is unfair and inaccurate.

Christians had no reason to hate Jews. It was unjustifiable. But even in modern times when, admittedly, Christianity is overall very friendly to Judaism and evangelical Christians are Israel's most staunch allies and supporters, Jews have good cause to be suspicious of certain denominations who have not yet come in from the cold. Some Christian denominations continue to spend tens of millions of dollars per year trying to convert Jews to Christianity. Some evangelical Christians believe the conflict in the Middle East will lead to Armageddon and insist that Jews will go to hell when they die because they don't believe in Jesus. This, admittedly, does not affect their strong support of Israel, for which the Jewish community remains justly grateful. But it's a troubling religious doctrine to say the least. I, for one, am a great admirer of Christian evangelicals and remain deeply grateful for their unfailing support for Israel and Jewish interests. But I also believe that it's time that my Christian brothers and sisters began to discover the Jewishness of Jesus and his practice of the Jewish faith as a Pharisaic Rabbi, which is why I wrote my book *Kosher Jesus*.

Some other Christian denominations and organizations—usually the ones that aren't Catholic or evangelical, including the World Council of Churches, the Quakers, and many Presbyterians—are among the most vitriolic critics of Israel. You also have the disturbing practice of Mormons posthumously baptizing Jewish victims of the Holocaust (Elie Wiesel was reportedly on the list while he was still alive).[136] And I say this even as I have a deep-seated affection for the Mormon religion and community, where I have spent considerable time and study.

Soloveichik, who defends the virtue of hatred, uses the Jewish people as an example of how hate can get out of control. I know and respect Soloveitchik for his fertile mind, inspired leadership, and deeply felt humanity. But in using the Jewish suspicion of modern Christianity as an example, he goes too far. Jews are immensely grateful to Christians in general and evangelical Christians in particular, for their extraordinary friendship, support of Israel, and contribution to combatting anti-Semitism. That does not mean, however, that we are blind to the painful 2000-year history of Christian anti-Semitism or its modern manifestations.

Jewish philosopher Martin Buber is another brilliant person who had lifelong difficulty with the recognition of evil. Religiously, he was predisposed to hold "no one to be 'absolutely' unredeemable."[137] Philosophically his basic framework, the celebrated "I-Thou" dynamic, leaves room for decay and dehumanization but not fear for an evil that is truly heinous. His thinking might be summed up in his statement that "evil cannot be done with the whole soul; good can only be done with the whole soul."[138] In a moving passage, Buber applies this doctrine to an "important poet" who grieved to his death for having allowed himself to accept a high Nazi honor. It is inconceivable, however, that Hoess, Eichmann, Himmler, or Hitler would have ever felt repentant.

Alas, even scholars and rabbis can be confused about the meaning and utility of hate.

No less a personality than Holocaust survivor, Nobel Peace Laureate, and humanitarian Elie Wiesel, who served as a mentor to me and whom I respect as one of the modern world's greatest heroes, disagreed with me and argued that it is wrong to hate. It is a very dangerous emotion, he told me. You don't know when you will lose control over it, when you will no longer be able to direct it at the right targets. It can consume you.

It is heady stuff disagreeing with a man who experienced firsthand the evil of the Holocaust. But here I have no choice because of the unassailable conviction that Kosher Hate must be employed to fight evil.

Hatred is only harmful when it is directed at the good and the innocent, as with Hitler's loathing of Jews. It is Godly, however, when it is directed at cold-blooded killers and mass murderers, motivating us to fight and destroy them before more blameless people die.

If we must fear hatred lest it become all-consuming, then we ought to take the same attitude toward love. After all, love can also engulf us completely. But do we tell wives not to love their husbands, lest they be so overcome by this powerful emotion that they fall in love with total strangers? We don't teach our children not to love for fear that their love will be directed to the wrong people. On the contrary, we believe in their powers of discernment. We try and instill within them a guidance mechanism so they will love decent, kind, and honest people, even though love is just as powerful as hate.

Emotions play a nuanced role in Jewish mystical thought. First, they are never given control of the mind; to the contrary, passions are meant to be hand-selected and monitored by a thoughtful, practical intellect. Simultaneously, Jewish thought, especially as expressed in Kabbalah, recognizes that feeling alone can fuel effective action. The result is a combinative approach whereby the mind guides and selects our emotions, which in turn can be used to fuel effective, energetic action. Thus, whereas evil hatred is rooted in the loose soil of human instincts, righteous hatred is rooted in the bedrock of rational conviction.

Hatred should, of course, never be the foremost emotion of our lives. It cannot be allowed to consume us. That would be a recipe for disaster. We would create a world of pure darkness.

We need to learn to harness hatred and distinguish acts that warrant Kosher Hate rather than simply indulging in anger. We may, for example, rightly feel different levels of anger toward someone stealing our parking space, our wallet, or our identity. Kosher Hate, however, like chemotherapy, should only be introduced when the patient, in this case society, requires treatment with extreme measures. It must be applied only in the face of raging injustice on a national or international scale. It has no other valid application. By dealing with hatred honestly and according it a rightful place in our hearts, we learn never to abuse it. "We learn never to demonize the partner we had a financial falling out with. Even if he stole from us, he is not evil, but he hasn't killed anyone. Rather, he's a thief and the proper legal remedies need to be pursued until justice is done."

There is always a risk of becoming consumed by hate and ending up bitter, angry, and cynical about the world, which is exactly Wiesel's point. That is why I have devoted this book, above all else, to making hatred directional. We must have a laser-like focus on the truly evil. I am never suggesting that someone be consumed by hate, just as I would never suggest they be consumed by another negative emotion, like bitterness or feelings of betrayal. Rather, hatred of evil must be commensurate with that evil and inspire us to combat and negate that evil.

Why shouldn't decent people everywhere feel a hatred for terrorists? And what's wrong with it becoming obsessional for the Western powers until the terrorists are defeated? Is it better that they slowly forget the events of 9/11 or the rise of ISIS and return to a complacent existence of binging Netflix while killers continue to plot the destruction of innocent life? Why shouldn't decent Americans hate Al Qaida, ISIS, and Hamas for their destruction of human life? Is it better for this country to pursue a policy of business as usual with a corrupt regime that is guilty of the most horrendous human rights abuses, so long as we continue to get enough oil to power our SUVs?

Hatred can sometimes be misplaced. Take the case of Cindy Sheehan who became famous as an anti-war protestor during the George W. Bush administration. Her son Casey, a twenty-four-year-old soldier from Vacaville, California, tragically died in Iraq on April 4, 2004, when his unit was attacked with rocket-propelled grenades and small arms fire. When President Bush prepared to honor her son's sacrifice, Cindy decided to direct her hate toward Bush rather than the Iraqis who had murdered her son.

In a documentary made a year later by Truthout, an on-line group opposed to the Iraq war, she criticized the Bush administration: "They send them out to die for a lie. They don't give them enough food, water, armor, supplies. It's just hypocrisy – it's evil."

Casey Sheehan was an altar boy, an Eagle Scout, and church youth group leader. He had a gentle but firm commitment to family, church, and country. He even reenlisted after the war started and volunteered for the rescue mission that cost him his life. As one friend Steve Tholcke said, "If something needed to be done, Casey was there to do it."[139] Tholcke knew this side of Casey because of the Catholic youth camp he directed while Casey worked as a counselor and helped organize youth retreats.

Another friend of the family, Stefanie Fereday-Mannel, also shared her feelings about Casey's character, saying he shared his mother's faith and commitment to the church. Casey helped found the church's youth group and remained active even after graduating from high school. "He didn't really care what people said or thought. He had very strong values about his family and church."[140]

Later, Sheehan created a media spectacle by camping out in front of President Bush's Prairie Chapel Ranch in Crawford, Texas, with supporters holding signs and chanting, "No more blood for oil," "Support our troops, bring them home now," "Iraq is Arabic for Vietnam," "Frodo failed. Bush has the ring," and "W. Killed her son. W. Killed her son."

Sheehan's protest was in response to President Bush's remarks one week prior, when he said, "Our men and women who have lost their lives in Iraq and Afghanistan and in this war on terror have died in a noble cause, in a selfless cause."[141]

Sheehan was quoted saying, "We all know by now that that's not true, and I want to ask George Bush, 'Why did my son die? What was the noble cause that he died for? I don't want [President Bush] to use my son's name or my family's name to justify anymore killing or to exploit my son's name, my son's sacrifice, or my sons honor to justify more killing. As a mother, why would I want one more mother to go through what I'm going through, Iraqi or American? I want to tell him that the only way to honor my son's sacrifices is to bring the troops home now.'"[142]

Later, she added, "Make my son's death count for peace and love, and not war and hatred."

Everyone can understand the anguish of a Gold Star mother who lost her son in battle. Her sacrifice and patriotism are greater than we can imagine. We have no right to judge her; we can only offer comfort to a bereaved and grieving parent.

But the American government did not kill Casey Sheehan. The terrorists did. Nor did President Bush send Casey to Iraq. He volunteered out of a sense of patriotic duty. This is why, despite his mother's understandable and unspeakable pain, the young man's life and death did count for something: a willingness to sacrifice in order to defeat evil. And if a man—Saddam—who killed 800,000 Arabs and 300,000 Kurds is not evil, then the word has no meaning.

Most Americans today believe that the war in Iraq was a mistake, brought about by a fallacious emphasis on finding weapons of mass destruction, which it appears Saddam Hussein did not possess. I respect this opinion. It may indeed, in hindsight, be correct. But there is no denying that Saddam was one of the greatest mass murderers in the history of the world, and arguably, along with Bashar Assad of Syria, took more Muslim lives than any man in history. If that doesn't merit Kosher Hate, then nothing does. George W. Bush should not be the target of our hatred but rather Saddam Hussein.

Peace and love do not eradicate evil; only hatred will. Cindy Sheehan's pain must be validated and the hate she carries is needed to fight a just cause. But such hate must be directed toward the terrorists. Thus her hatred of Bush was not kosher. It is another instance of confusing the arsonist with the firefighter. Saddam set the Middle East ablaze and George W. Bush attempted to put it out, however flawed his methods may have been.

The American government is directed by flawed humans, but let's not confuse their behavior, even when they make significant mistakes, with that of terrorists and genocidal maniacs. Unlike Cindy Sheehan, the terrorists feel no pain, no moral qualms, or remorse after they commit murder. Their goal is not to bring about a better world but to gain power through intimidation and fear.

Our government's objective is not mass murder. We believe in freedom and democracy and the price is sometimes excruciatingly high with young men and women making the ultimate sacrifice. Disagreeing with policy is one thing, but hating our government—the firefighters—only encourages the arsonists to set more fires.

Many Americans are like Cindy Sheehan, who champion all that is good and just. Casey Sheehan carried wisdom beyond his years; he knew his cause was right, even without WMD's in Iraq, because he knew the savagery and butchery of Saddam Hussein. Casey hated evil enough to fight it, and so must we all if we are to thwart it. We mourn his loss every day.

CHAPTER 7:
DOES KOSHER HATE HAVE A PLACE FOR FORGIVENESS?

I HAVE ARGUED THAT Kosher Hate is righteous, which raises the question whether it is equally moral to absolve those we hate for their actions. Some may say that by promoting hatred of evil I am trampling on the ideas of atonement and forgiveness. I disagree. Repentance is based on recognizing the infinite value of human life. Because God loves humanity, God provides a point of return so that the individual might find their way back to the light. Repentance, however, is not available to those who inhumanly debase life.

Certain offenses are unforgiveable. Mass murder is foremost among them. For a murderer of even one person to lament his actions in public and achieve instant absolution is an affront to everything forgiveness stands for. God may forgive, but it is our duty to mete out punishment. Judaism says that we may not forgive certain sins, so while you cannot compare a mass murderer with someone who has killed a single person, taking any innocent life is evil. You can never bring back that life.

Murder is murder, but we do distinguish between a bank robber killing a guard and a *genocidaire* such as Cambodian dictator Pol Pot. It is the difference between a crime against an individual where the perpetrator is held responsible by the state, and a crime against humanity where the offender can be held accountable by the international community. The latter involves specific crimes committed in the context of a large-scale attack targeting civilians, regardless of their nationality. These crimes include murder, torture, sexual violence, enslavement, persecution, and enforced disappearance "committed as part of a widespread or systematic attack directed against any civilian population."[143]

Katie and Emily Benton were victims of the horrific 7/7 bombing in London. A terrorist's bomb blew apart the subway car they were riding in and killed fifty-six people. The siblings from Tennessee were on a sightseeing trip when the attack occurred and left Emily with broken bones in her left foot and right hand and Katie with shrapnel wounds in her right foot. Both suffered hearing loss.

I cannot imagine how frightening that experience must have been or how difficult it was to recover from their injuries and try to live a normal life. I also can't understand their response. They told a reporter they considered their injuries "souvenirs" and said the experience strengthened their Christian faith. "There's no better way to fight terrorism than to turn what they meant for evil into good and the Lord is certainly capable of that," Katie said.[144]

Good of course can be the by-product of evil. But it never stems directly from evil. Rather, if we choose to do good or embrace life, after an evil occurrence, it is not because of the evil we experienced but despite it. Emily refused to be cowed by her encounter with terrorism and channeled her Kosher Hate for the perpetrator into the fight against such senseless violence, a positive outcome that is attributable to her fortitude.

Emily said she believed God had "given us this opportunity I think to just reach out to others and to encourage others who are sick or hurt and just to make a stand against terrorism."

This raises the age-old question: Why didn't the Almighty *prevent* evil? Should we question why God did not? Setting God aside, wouldn't it be infinitely better that such evil didn't exist to maim and kill people than to see it as a motivator to fight evil?

Katie at least sounded as though she was not going to let the terrorists win by making her too scared to return to her regular routine. She said she wouldn't hesitate to ride the subway in London in the future. By contrast, her sister Emily, the one who said God inspired her to fight terrorism, said, "I don't think I'll ever ride a subway again."

Their attitudes must, of course, be understood from the perspective of their youth and traumatic experience, but it is also a function of their generation and upbringing. Contemplating what it means to be evil is to be avoided, for all people are susceptible to a few bad choices, so who are we to judge them? Murder, however, is not simply a misunderstanding where we don't appreciate the killer's motivations. Generations X, Y, Z and whatever comes next are expected to tolerate everyone and everything. Few are taught to eschew such moral relativism and recognize that there is such a thing as objective right and wrong.

Liberals want to understand the motives of the killers; I don't care. They must be hated. But too many people are influenced by a secularized ideal of Christian love and want to show compassion. Books and theses have been written about the mind of killers. This may help us prevent future killings, which is what criminal profiling is all about. But it should never be used to excuse their actions.

When I was on the *BBC* discussing the horrific bombing of a gay pub by homophobic murderers that left three people dead, I referred to the bomber as an abomination, to which Pastor Tony Campolo, President Clinton's spiritual advisor replied, we had to love the bomber in the spirit of compassion and forgiveness. Similarly, in my years in Britain I was accustomed to hearing victims of IRA terrorist attacks, after having lost fathers, brothers, or sons, immediately announce to the world their forgiveness for the killers. Such misguided nonsense allows murderers to flourish.

One of the most interesting explorations of the bounds of hate and forgiveness can be found in Simon Wiesenthal's book, *The Sunflower: On the Possibilities and Limits of Forgiveness*. The world's most famous Nazi hunter describes his own conundrum of whether a Nazi should be forgiven for his crimes and then offers the responses of fifty-three other people to the same question.

Wiesenthal was in the Lemberg concentration camp in 1943. He was sent to an army hospital for a work detail and was ordered to attend to Karl Seidl, a dying Nazi soldier who said he wanted a Jew's forgiveness for what he had done as a member of the SS. In his bedside confession, Seidl tells Wiesenthal his life story and admits that he participated in an attack on a house that had been set ablaze with 300 Jews inside. He and other soldiers shot Jews who tried to escape the burning building.

Seidl then asks Wiesenthal to forgive him. Wiesenthal gives no answer and leaves. The next day he learned that Seidl has died and has left his belongings to Wiesenthal, but he refuses to accept them.

"Today the world demands that we forgive and forget the heinous crimes committed against us," Wiesenthal wrote. "It urges that we draw a line, and close the account as if nothing had ever happened."[145] Wiesenthal refused to do that, but he also doesn't explain his decision and challenges his readers to answer the question of whether he did the right thing. The responses published in the book come from theologians, politicians, human rights activists, writers, psychiatrists, Holocaust survivors, former Nazis, and victims of attempted genocides in Bosnia, Cambodia, China, and Tibet. Only ten of the fifty-three (19 percent) believed the evildoers should be forgiven, thirty-four (64 percent) disagreed, and nine (17 percent) said they were uncertain.

In a Wikipedia breakdown of the responses, there are twenty-two Jews, nineteen non-Jews (sixteen Christians, two Buddhists and a Muslim) and twelve with no religion. It is not surprising that nine of the ten forgivers were non-Jews (seven Christians and two Buddhists, including the Dalai Lama). The only Muslim was one of the five non-Jews who were uncertain. Two of the five Christians who said they would *not forgive* the Nazi were Holocaust scholars. By comparison, nineteen of the twenty-two Jews would not forgive the Nazis, the other three were uncertain.[146]

Of the twelve whose religion is not identified (including Nazi Albert Speer and one man who survived nineteen years in a Chinese labor camp), only one person was willing to forgive, Dith Pran, the photojournalist who survived the Cambodian genocide and was the subject of the film *The Killing Fields*. One Holocaust scholar was uncertain.

Archbishop Desmond Tutu recalled that after all the suffering Nelson Mandela endured, he "invited his white jailer to his inauguration as South Africa's first democratically elected president." Tutu noted that many Christians were also willing to forgive the Afrikaners who had tormented South African blacks based on their belief in "the Jewish rabbi who, when he was crucified, said, 'Father, forgive them, for they know not what they do.'" Tutu himself never really answers the question about the Nazi and reduces forgiveness to "practical politics." Perhaps he meant only in the context of the Truth and Reconciliation Commission in South Africa because he concluded, "Without forgiveness, there is no future."[147]

One Christian who was not quoted in the book, Father Edward Flannery, said, "I can well understand Simon's refusal [to forgive], but I find it impossible to defend it."[148]

Rabbi Meir Soloveitchik writes, "The Jewish writer Cynthia Ozick, reflecting on how Wiesenthal, in a moment of mercy, brushed a fly away from the Nazi's broken body, concludes her response in Deborah's blunt but poetic manner:

Let the SS man die unshriven.

Let him go to hell.

Sooner the fly to God than he."[149]

Eva Mozes Kor was also a survivor. She was only ten when her family was sent to Auschwitz where Josef Mengele experimented on her and her twin sister. Both were liberated in January 1945, two of only 180 children who survived. Their parents and two older sisters perished. In 1995 she founded a Holocaust museum in Indiana: CANDLES—Children of Auschwitz Nazi Deadly Lab Experiments Survivors. The same year, the fiftieth anniversary of her liberation, she visited Auschwitz with one of the doctors who worked with Mengele. She wrote a "Declaration of Amnesty" while they stood together in the spot where the gas chambers had poisoned tens of thousands of Jews. Remarkably, she granted amnesty to "all Nazis who participated directly or indirectly in the murder of my family and millions of others" and "to all governments who protected Nazi criminals for fifty years, then covered up their acts, and covered up their cover up."

In an interview with My Jewish Learning she later said, "What I discovered was life changing—that I, a survivor of Mengele experiments, had the power to forgive."[150]

Many Jews and Holocaust survivors were angry with her, but she was unbowed: "Do I remain a victim for the rest of my life? It gives the perpetrator power and I have no power over my life. That is absurd. I decide when I forgive. Maybe this Jewish tradition should be changed. We should never wait for the perpetrator to ask for forgiveness. It is the victim's right to forgive whenever they want."

Some might say she has a point. What's the harm in forgiveness? Isn't it meant to help the victim not the perpetrator? Isn't there a difference between a sin against God and a sin against man? This is also a case of the victim unilaterally forgiving, not responding to a request from the perpetrator. Doesn't that make a difference?

Was she wrong?

Wiesenthal said something similar. At the end of *The Sunflower* he wrote, "Forgetting is something that time alone takes care of, but forgiveness is an act of volition, and only the sufferer is qualified to make the decision."[151]

I believe forgiveness is a fundamental act of separation between the sinner and the sin. And you forgive the sins. So, if someone repents, you forgive them, or if the sin they commit is not fundamentally part of their makeup, you can forgive them. But let's say the sin is recurring or that the perpetrator has no remorse. Then it is ingested and becomes part of their character. It is the Aristotelian-Maimonidean idea that repetitive action become second nature.

The Nazis represent the extreme example. This was planned genocide. They sat in the Wannsee Conference eating caviar and smoking cigars while they planned the extermination of six million Jews. Because of the heinous nature of the crime as well as its premeditation, the Nazis cannot be forgiven.

What about Rwanda, where there is a debate about Hutu premeditation? Yes, there was incitement, but the violence blew up when the Hutu president was killed. Many argue the genocide was spontaneous, but the historical facts suggest otherwise. The Hutu were stockpiling machetes months before.

Even if it were non-premeditated, can the Hutus be forgiven if it was a spontaneous outburst of violence? Of course not. The act is too heinous. You can't forgive mass murder or genocide. All murder is abhorrent, but genocide is the most extreme moral abomination.

Let me be more specific. The two criteria then for denying forgiveness are that the evil becomes so repetitive that it becomes an indistinguishable component of the perpetrator's character and that the sin is heinous. Otherwise, morality has no meaning.

An obvious case is Adolf Eichmann, one of the principal architects of the Holocaust, who never expressed remorse but asked for clemency. It would have been ridiculous to give it to him because he was not a German *who engaged in* murder; he was a German *mass murderer*. There was no way to purge him of what he had done because it had become an inextricable part of his character.

Still, one of his fellow Nazis, Albert Speer, remarkably, was rehabilitated. As Hitler's Armaments Minister, Speer's decisions contributed to the length of the war in which so many civilians and allied soldiers were killed along with more than six million Jews, Roma, homosexuals, and other "undesirables" who were shot, burned alive, and gassed. Yet, in three best-selling books, Speer managed to win over the Western media by contrasting himself as the "good Nazi" who was unlike the psychopaths and murderers who were "bad Nazis." While he accepted responsibility for the Nazi regime's actions, he claimed to have no direct knowledge of the Holocaust and the other unspeakable Nazi horrors. In fact, he approved the allocation of materials for the expansion of Auschwitz and visited the Mauthausen death camp and the

Gusen subcamp. After being released from twenty years in Germany's Spandau Prison, Speer became an international celebrity and made a fortune.

I am not saying redemption is impossible. In Judaism the holiest day of the year, Yom Kippur, provides the opportunity for Jews to atone for their sins and seek forgiveness from people they have wronged and from God for sins they have committed in violation of the biblical commandments.

In Christianity, Jesus died on the cross for the sins of humanity, and absolution is possible for Christian penitents who confess their mortal sins. However, the seven deadly sins—pride, lust, envy, anger, greed, gluttony and sloth—omit murder and, startingly, the worst is considered pride. This has been explained to me as a misunderstanding; that is, the Bible does not list "seven deadly sins." They are a product of Christian theology. Nevertheless, one or more of these five—pride, lust, envy, anger, and greed—are usually the motivation for murder.

Still, no sin is too big or bad to be forgiven by God. According to John 1:9, "If we confess our sins, he is faithful and just and will forgive us our sins and purify us from all unrighteousness." For us to extend forgiveness and compassion in the name of religion to people who have committed monstrous acts is to mock God, who has mercy for all, yet also demands justice for the innocent.

Elie Wiesel did not forgive the Germans, but he did not hate them either. When I asked him why he did not despise the Germans, as I referenced earlier, he said that once you allowed hatred to enter your system you couldn't control it, it overtakes you. Even after he and his wife and the Elie Wiesel Foundation for Humanity, an organization the great man had founded to promote tolerance and equality, were robbed by Bernie Madoff, Wiesel remained an optimist. He told Oprah Winfrey in an interview, "We looked at each other, and our reaction was, 'We have seen worse. Both she and I have seen worse."[152] But he also would not forgive Madoff. "To forgive, first of all, would mean that he would come on his knees and ask for forgiveness," he said. "He wouldn't do that."[153] Perhaps he would say it is justice, not hate, but Elie Wiesel had a special punishment in mind for the man who defrauded thousands of investors and lost billions of dollars:

> I would like him to be in a solitary cell with a screen, and on that screen, for at least five years of his life, every day and every night there should be pictures of his victims, one after the other after the other, always saying, "Look, look what you have done to this poor lady, look what you have done to this child, look what you have done."

I agree with Elie on the general nature of the special punishment that Madoff could have received. But I disagree with the idea that you can't control hate. I believe kosher hatred is a powerful and necessary weapon in the fight against evil, and the Hebrew Bible offers many examples where instead of forgiveness, revenge is exacted.

After being summoned by Samuel, Agag, the king of the Amalekites said, "Surely the bitterness of death is past." But Samuel said, "As your sword has made women childless, so your mother shall be childless among women." And Samuel hewed Agag in pieces before the Lord in Gilgal.

The prophetess Deborah sang:

> Most blessed of women be Jael, the wife of Heber the Kenite
>
> Of tent–dwelling women most blessed.
>
> She put her hand to the tent peg and her right hand to the workmen's mallet.
>
> She struck Sisera a blow, she crushed his head, she shattered and pierced his temple.

He sank, he fell, he lay still at her feet;

At her feet he sank, he fell;

there he sank, there he fell dead.

...So perish all your enemies, O Lord!

As with so much in the Bible, not everything is clear cut. Leviticus 19:17 explicitly forbids hatred in personal and social contexts "Thou shalt not hate thy brother in thy heart," God commands and tells the Israelites, "thou shalt surely rebuke thy neighbor, and not bear sin because of him."

The next verse explicitly forbids vengeance. "Thou shalt not take vengeance, nor bear any grudge against the children of thy people..." God then seals the couplet with possibly the most famous verse of the entire Bible: "but thou shalt love thy neighbor as thyself—I am the LORD."

From inside the Bible, we might be able to deduce the reason. The story of Joseph being sold as a slave by his brothers—a story of terrible family discord—is predicated by the assertion that "they hated him and could not speak a kind word to him (Gen. 37:4)." After he tells his brothers of his two dreams, the Bible states—again twice—that "they hated him all the more (Gen. 37:5, 8)."

Another great conflict also traces its roots to hatred. Before David's son Absalom provoked ancient Israel into civil war, we are told that he and his nemesis Amnon were filled with hate for one another.

Solomon came to power in the wake of Absalom's revolt; nevertheless, he warns, "Hatred stirs up conflicts; but love covers all transgressions." (Whether love's capacity to cover up transgressions is a completely good thing isn't entirely clear.)

The Torah even instructs that we should not react with hatred to those who hate us. "If you see the donkey of someone who hates you fallen down under its load," the Torah commands, "do not leave it there; be sure you help them with it (Ex. 23:5)."

Shortly before his death, Moses tells the Jews, "But those who hate him he will repay to their face by destruction; he will not be slow to repay to their face those who hate him." The Jews are also told, "He will not inflict on you the horrible diseases you knew in Egypt, but he will inflict them on all who hate you." God, it seems, really doesn't like those who hate an entire group of people.

It comes down to this. When we were slaves, completely overpowered by the army of Pharaoh, it is up to the Creator to exact vengeance. But where we can and must neutralize evil by our own means, like the United States fighting Nazism and Islamic terror, we must act in God's stead.

I started with a movie reference, so let me end with one.

The movie *Batman Begins* offers surprisingly deep insights—for a movie anyway—into the issues of justice, revenge, and the hatred of evil. The first half of the film focuses on Bruce Wayne's struggles with the trauma of having witnessed his parents' murder in a mugging. Consumed with a desire for vengeance, Bruce was recruited by a secret society, The League of Shadows, which hates evil—at least as they define it—and looks for places where corruption and decadence have taken root. Although the overall intentions of the League are good—their declared purpose is the eradication of every form of injustice and the liquidation of all murderers—they ultimately become the villains because they are prepared to destroy the good along with the bad to restore balance to society. One moment, the leader of the League is speaking eloquently of fighting criminals and protecting the innocent, the next he is demanding that Bruce execute a murderer who has yet to be tried. Bruce is instructed never to allow himself to feel any compassion for criminals. Compassion equals weakness, they tell him, and constitutes the principal reason the world is in chaos.

This portrayal in popular culture of how those who hate evil become evil themselves reflects a deep-seated cultural bias against the emotion of hatred.

Jews know better than most how dangerous hatred can become. Applied by dictators, tyrants, megalomaniacs, and other evil men, hatred has contributed to countless persecutions, massacres, and genocides. But hatred is not good or bad. Like a firearm, whether it is dangerous depends on who is holding the weapon and who it is being pointed at. Hatred employed by the virtuous against the wicked—kosher hatred—is righteous.

The pacifist will respond that fighting hate with hate accomplishes nothing. They'll quote the line attributed to Gandhi, "an eye for an eye only ends up making the whole world blind." This is a response to the Biblical reference where the Bible demands "an eye for an eye, a tooth for a tooth," which sounds brutal and heartless. But the Jews have never taken this verse literally. It refers to financial compensation for an eye. But the purpose of Kosher Hate is not revenge, but justice. We do not seek to breed hatred so that it might linger in our breast, but so that it might inspire us to stop murder and bloodshed.

When I lived in England, I used to hear people complain when Jewish groups identified a former Nazi concentration camp guard living comfortably in his old age in the English countryside and demand he be tried for war crimes. "What do these Jews want from this helpless old man," they would say. "The Holocaust was fifty years ago. The accused is pushing ninety. Shouldn't we feel a bit of compassion?"

But is an old murderer any less culpable than a young one? There should also be no statute of limitations in cases of unrepentant, unconscionable, and repetitive crimes such as murder, rape, terrorism, and genocide. To this end I wholeheartedly embrace the example of Simon Wiesenthal, who devoted his life to the pursuit of justice by not allowing Nazi murderers to go to their graves in peace. We do not hunt Nazis to take revenge. We have better things to do than chase nonagenarians. We track them down because God entrusted humanity with turning the jungle into a civilized society. We are obligated to demonstrate to all the world that there is no defense and no escape from accountability for genocide.

It is a travesty that so many Nazis were never caught or given the sentences they deserved. The last perpetrators to go on trial, a handful of men in their nineties, lived good lives with impunity and, due to their ages and health, will never serve prisons terms commensurate with their crimes, if they are jailed at all.

Oskar Gröning, for example, was an SS junior squad leader at Auschwitz-Birkenau, who was charged with collecting the personal property of arriving prisoners. He was found guilty of facilitating mass murder and sentenced to four years in prison. He died in 2018, at age ninety-six, before being incarcerated.

Reinhold Hanning was an SS guard at Auschwitz-Birkenau from 1942 to 1944, receiving prisoners as they were unloaded off freight cars and leading them to the gas chambers. Hanning was found guilty of 170,000 counts of being an accessory to murder and sentenced to five years in prison. Hanning died at the age of ninety-five before serving any prison time.

Bruno Dey was ninety-three when he was convicted of aiding and abetting 5,230 cases of murder while a guard at Stutthof concentration camp. He received a two-year suspended sentence in 2020.

Perhaps the case of Nazis is too far removed from the American experience. It's just those Jews with their Holocaust obsession. Americans, however, are no less determined to see evildoers brought to justice no matter how long it takes. Attorney General Jim Hood of Mississippi, for example, decided to put accused Klan leader Edgar Ray Killen on trial forty years after he killed civil rights activists Andrew Goodman, Michael Schwerner, and James Chaney. Hood was not deterred by the fact that Killen was eighty years old.

It was the prosecutor's odium for Killen that motivated him to pursue the murderer for almost forty years, finally obtaining a conviction and sending him to prison. If Hood had not detested Killen and his actions, he would have died peacefully in his home and the message would have gone out that you can get away with murder. The prosecutor was a moral and decent man. He didn't buy a shotgun and start shooting anyone in the Klan. He used the justice system but was inspired by a deep loathing for these murderers who killed innocent children and got away with it.

When Bobby Frank Cherry, the Klansman who killed four girls by an Alabama church bombing in 1963, died in prison, I expressed my satisfaction on my radio show that another evil man had perished from the earth. I did not gloat, however, because the Bible says, "Rejoice not when thine enemy falleth."

A black caller phoned in and said disgustedly, "I used to be like you Shmuley. When I was a boy growing up in the segregated South, I hated the Klan so much that I wanted to be a sniper and shoot them. But as a Christian I have worked my whole life to fight that hatred and get it out of my system."

"What do you think God would prefer?" I asked him, "That you use your energy to fight your own hatred, or that you use it to fight evil? No one would sanction you running around and indiscriminately shooting people because that is immoral and illegal. That's not hatred. That's rage."

Just imagine if after assassinating the president of the United States, Lee Harvey Oswald had escaped. Suppose he was found forty years later in upstate New York, living under an alias. Would any of us say that he's an old man and shouldn't be tried? Wouldn't we still feel hatred for the person who robbed our country of a young and dynamic leader at the height of his powers, orphaning his two young children, and demand he be brought to justice?

And what if it took us forty years to find Osama bin Laden? Would we let him go because 9/11 was a thing of the past and he was now elderly and frail? Of course, we didn't wait. We hunted him, and it was not the conservative Christian George W. Bush who found and killed him, it was the liberal, progressive icon Barack Obama. And he deserves credit for doing so.

CHAPTER 8:

KOSHER HATE AGAINST WAR CRIMINALS AND TERRORISTS

AS PRESIDENT, BARACK OBAMA killed far more terrorists and launched ten times more drone strikes than George
W. Bush, who had been vilified for identifying an "axis of
evil." One analyst calculated that Obama authorized 542
drone strikes that killed nearly 3,800 people, including more
than 500 civilians.[154] He, too, was criticized. Conor Friedersdorf wrote in *The Atlantic*, for example:

> Obama *chose* to allow the CIA, a secretive entity
> with a long history of unjust killings, to carry out
> strikes; he *chose* to keep the very fact of drone kill-
> ings classified, deliberately invoking the state-se-
> crets privilege in a way guaranteed to stymie
> oversight, public debate, and legal accountability;
> and he *chose* to permit killings outside the greater
> Afghanistan war zone, in countries with which the
> U.S. was not at war.[155]

Friedersdorf quoted Obama's response to the critics, "The
truth is that, in trying to get at terrorists who are in countries
that either are unwilling or unable to capture those terrorists
or disable them themselves, there are a lot of situations where

the use of a drone is going to result in much fewer civilian casualties and much less collateral damage than if I send in a battalion of marines."

For his part, President Trump dramatically increased the number of strikes and, mistakenly I believe, changed the rules requiring him to report the number of civilian casualties.[156]

The commitment to fight other terrorists, notably Palestinian and Lebanese groups, has been far less successful. After Palestinian terrorists stopped hijacking airplanes and threatening non-Jews, the world no longer hated them, which was best exemplified by the invitation for Yasser Arafat to speak at the United Nations General Assembly in 1974, where he appeared wearing a holster (without a gun) and was treated like a head of state. To the further disgrace of the institution, Arafat received a standing ovation and was interrupted nine times by applause from the delegates who calmly listened to him slander Zionism as "imperialist" and "racist" (excluding Israel, who walked out before the speech). Foreshadowing the Boycott, Divestment, and Sanctions (BDS) campaign that is going on today, Arafat suggested that Israel be suspended from the UN as South Africa had been the day before. He went on to use the rostrum of the "world peace organization" to threaten violence if his demands were not met: "I have come bearing an olive branch and freedom fighter's gun," he said. "Do not let the olive branch fall from my hands."[157]

From that point on, the world, including the United States, mostly looked the other way while Palestinian terrorists murdered Israelis. In fact, during the Oslo period, *after* Arafat had renounced violence, the State Department was required to report on Palestine Liberation Organization (PLO) compliance with the agreement and repeatedly whitewashed the Palestinians' continued use of terror.

It was not until Donald Trump took office more than twenty years later that the U.S. took serious action against the Palestinians for their incitement and violence. Trump cut off all aid to the Palestinians and shut the PLO's mission in Washington. Despite the hue and cry from liberals and apologists for Palestinian terror, Congress backed the president by passing the Taylor Force Act. This bill was a response to the "pay-to-slay" policy of the Palestinian Authority (PA) under which convicted terrorists in Israeli jails and the families of suicide bombers received generous stipends partially underwritten by American taxpayers.

Named after a U.S. army veteran who was murdered by a Palestinian terrorist during a study trip in Israel, the legislation, which received overwhelming bipartisan support, suspended aid to the Palestinian Authority until it met four conditions: terminating payments to terrorists, revoking laws authorizing this compensation, taking "credible steps" to end Palestinian terrorism, and "publicly condemning" and investigating such acts of violence.

Despite the desperate financial plight of the Palestinians, PA President Mahmoud Abbas not only refused to end the policy, but he also increased the stipends and repeatedly said he would continue to pay them even it cost the government its last penny.[158]

Palestinian terrorists killed Taylor Force and at least fifty-four other U.S. citizens, but most people are unaware that, other than the nearly 3,000 Americans killed by Al Qaeda on 9/11, the most Americans to die in terror attacks were killed by Iran's proxy Hezbollah.

- Hezbollah held David Dodge, acting president of the American University in Beirut, captive for a year; kidnaped and murdered Malcolm Kerr, a Lebanese-born American who was president of the American University of Beirut; abducted Jeremy Levin, Beirut bureau chief of CNN, who later escaped; held Reverend Benjamin T. Weir for sixteen months; seized diplomat William Buckley, who was never heard from again; kidnaped Frank Reed, director of the American University in Beirut, and held him forty-four months; held Joseph Cicippio, the acting comptroller at the American University in Beirut for five years; and abducted and murdered Col. William Higgins, the American chief of the United Nations Truce Supervision Organization.

- On April 18, 1983, a truck bomb exploded in front of the U.S. Embassy in Beirut, killing sixty-three employees, including the CIA's Middle East director, and wounding 120.

- On October 23, 1983, a truck loaded with a bomb crashed into the lobby of the U.S. Marines headquarters in Beirut, killing 241 soldiers and wounding eighty-one.

- On April 12, 1984, Hezbollah bombed a restaurant near a U.S. Air Force base in Torrejón, Spain, killing eighteen servicemen and wounding eighty-three people.

- On September 20, 1984, a suicide bomb attack on the U.S. Embassy in East Beirut killed twenty-three people and injured twenty-one.

- On December 4, 1984, Hezbollah terrorists hijacked a Kuwait Airways plane and murdered American passengers Charles Hegna and William Stanford.

- On June 14, 1985, Hezbollah terrorists hijacked a TWA flight and murdered Robert Stethem, a U.S. Navy diver.

Americans have good reason to direct their Kosher Hate at Hezbollah because of its murder of Americans, the threat it poses to Israel, its involvement in the Syrian war, its role in drug trafficking, and the presence of its operatives in the United States.

Hezbollah's main targets are Jews, and the genocidal organization is committed to Israel's destruction. As with the attacks on Americans, the group is prepared to travel great distances to murder Jews. In 1992, a car bomb exploded outside the Israeli embassy in Buenos Aires, killing twenty-nine people and injuring more than 250. Two years later, the Jewish community center in the city was bombed and another eighty-seven people were killed and more than one hundred were injured. The case is still being pursued but no one has been brought to justice.[159]

The war Hezbollah provoked with Israel in 2006 ended with the UN Security Council passing Resolution 1701 requiring Hezbollah to be disarmed. It also supposedly strengthened the impotent UN peacekeeping force that had been deployed in Lebanon in 1978 following the first Lebanon war, which had been precipitated by Palestinian terrorist attacks. Today, Hezbollah has an estimated 150,000 rockets, acquired mostly from Iran, pointed at Israel, along with other weapons smuggled from Syria. Hezbollah, with Iranian help, has also constructed factories to manufacture precision-guided missiles, which Israel has bombed to keep from becoming operational.

Hezbollah was strengthened thanks to Obama's naïve approach to Iran. The failure to insist that Iran stop supporting Hezbollah as a condition of the nuclear deal ensured Iranian sponsorship of terror would continue. By removing sanctions and releasing $150 billion in frozen Iranian assets, Obama provided Iran with the financial windfall to increase its support for Hezbollah and the radical Islamic Palestinian terrorists like Hamas and Palestine Islamic Jihad. None of these terror groups hide their agenda—the destruction of Israel and the murder of Jews.

While Kosher Hate toward both Hamas and Hezbollah should be a no-brainer, the Europeans have historically refused to brand either as terrorist organizations. Since both engage in social welfare activities, an artificial distinction is sometimes made between their "military" and "social" wings. It is only in the last couple of years that these distinctions have begun to be ignored.

Following Israel's disengagement from Gaza in 2005, one might have expected the Palestinians to take advantage of being free of "occupation" to focus on state building; instead, they concentrated on rocket building. Since seizing power from Fatah and the Palestinian Authority in 2007, Hamas has fired thousands of rockets into Israel. Residents in targeted areas have only fifteen seconds after hearing a warning siren to get themselves and their loved ones to a shelter. Imagine having those few instants to get a disabled child or an elderly parent to safety.

Israel has launched three major operations in response to attacks from Gaza: Operation Cast Lead (2008–2009), Operation Pillar of Defense (2012), and Operation Protective Edge (2014). Each time the Israel Defense Forces (IDF) inflicted heavy losses on Hamas and its Islamist twin, Palestine Islamic Jihad, but failed to destroy either organization or put a permanent end to the rocket fire. Israel has the capability, but not the will. One reason is that defeating the terrorists would require a massive military campaign. Think about the resources that were required to destroy the ISIS caliphate. A similar war against the Gaza terrorists would result in thousands of casualties, including many civilians used as shields by the terrorists or caught in the crossfire. Israel would have to send troops into a dense urban fighting environment where it would also suffer casualties.

Israel, being as small as its, feels each individual loss on a national scale. Israelis also share a moral code that, save for a fight for their existence, does not allow them to accept the American doctrine articulated by Colin Powell of using "decisive force."[160]

Besides the morality issue, Israel is constrained by international pressure. The minute Israel acts to defend itself, immediate media criticism comes in and every Palestinian casualty is turned into an opportunity to blame Israel for the violence. Innocent civilians are sometimes killed, but Israel, unlike terrorists, does not indiscriminately target noncombatants.

Constraints on Israeli actions illustrate the distinction between the application of Kosher Hate by large nations—the U.S., Russia, China, EU countries—and smaller countries. The more powerful the country, the less concern with international opinion and, in the case of non-democratic countries, the absence of any unease or hesitancy.

Israel has had no hesitancy to apply Kosher Hate to war criminals and terrorists. The Mossad is held responsible, though most accusations are unproven, for the deaths of many murderers. In recent years, Israel has used what it refers to as targeted killings—others consider assassinations—to eliminate terrorists. Just as 9/11 prompted the United States to begin its campaign of "targeted killings," Israel was motivated originally by the Holocaust and, later, by the massacre of eleven athletes at the 1972 Munich Olympics by the Black September terrorist group. Israel decided Nazis who escaped should pay for their crimes. The most effective way to demonstrate it was to assassinate the Black September terrorists and others directly or indirectly involved in the planning or the execution of the assault and murder of the Israeli athletes.

It may come as a surprise, but in the early years of statehood Israel did not make the search for Nazis a priority because its leaders believed it was more urgent to address immediate threats to its existence from its neighbors. This did not mean the Mossad did not search for perpetrators of the Holocaust but agents succeeded in assassinating only one

Nazi, Herbert Cukurs, who served as a General in the SS and was known as the "Butcher of Riga" for murdering 30,000 Latvian Jews. The Mossad found him in South America, lured him to Uruguay, and killed him in 1965.[161]

More famously, five years earlier, the Mossad kidnapped Adolf Eichmann, the Nazi architect of the Final Solution. He was taken from Argentina to Israel where he was tried, convicted, and executed for war crimes. Eichmann is still the only person ever sentenced to death in Israel.

The hunt for Nazis did not become a high priority until Menachem Begin became prime minister in 1977. The Mossad then drafted a list of nine prominent Nazis to pursue, including Josef Mengele, the doctor responsible for medical experiments at Auschwitz; Martin Bormann, Hitler's deputy; Heinrich Müller, the head of the Gestapo; and Alois Brunner, Adolf Eichmann's assistant. The only one on the list the Mossad came close to killing was Brunner who received letter bombs in 1961 and 1980 that wounded but did not kill him.

At least 234 terrorists have been allegedly killed by Israeli agents, including at least eight of the eleven responsible for the Munich Olympic Massacre. One other died of natural causes and the other two were assassinated, but it is not known for sure if they were killed by Israeli agents.[162]

This type of an eye-for-an-eye vengeance—what I would call, in this case, justice motivated by Kosher Hate—may still go on covertly, but there is a legal basis for targeted killings that began in 2000. This is an example of how Kosher Hate can be applied within the bounds of the law; it is not arbitrary and not conducted by vigilantes. When Begin's policy was challenged, the Israeli Supreme Court ruled in 2006 that international law permits the Israel Defense Forces (IDF) to kill Palestinian terrorists in the West Bank and Gaza Strip if the circumstances of each case meet four conditions:

- Reliable information is required before a civilian can be categorized as directly participating in hostilities.

- "A civilian taking a direct part in hostilities cannot be attacked if a less harmful means can be employed," such as detention and trial, as required by the principle of proportionality (according to which the anticipated degree of danger to soldiers' lives is also weighed versus the possibility of detaining the terrorist operative instead of harming him).

- After an attack on a civilian suspected of taking an active part in hostilities, a thorough ex post facto investigation should be carried out regarding the identity of the target and the circumstances of the attack.

- "Harm to innocent civilians caused during military attacks (collateral damage) must be proportional. That is, attacks should be carried out only if the expected harm to innocent civilians is not disproportional to the military advantage to be achieved by the attack." In certain cases, payment of compensation might be considered in the event of harm caused to innocent civilians.[163]

Then deputy chief of staff Major General Moshe Ya'alon explained the policy this way:

> There are no executions without a trial. There is no avenging someone who had carried out an attack a month ago. We are acting against those who are waging terror against us. We prefer to arrest them and have detained over 1,000. But if we can't, and the Palestinians won't, then we have no other choice but to defend ourselves.[164]

The fact that the policy could be challenged in court and adjudicated by an independent judiciary is a tribute to Israel's democracy. The leaders of other countries who I believe should be targeted for Kosher Hate do not bother with trivialities such as the law before they commit murder.

Terrorists would not have to be tracked down and killed if the countries that shelter them, such as Lebanon, Qatar, and Pakistan, arrested the murderers and extradited them to face justice in the countries where they committed their crimes.

This is another of the messages I wish to convey. Civilized nations have an obligation to root out evil in their midst. Too often, leaders of countries providing a haven to terrorists are too afraid of becoming targets themselves. The Saudis, for example, reportedly paid at least $300 million in "protection money" to Al Qaeda and the Taliban.[165] In some cases, however, the terrorists are welcomed by leaders who sympathize with their cause. For example, Turkey hosts members of Hamas and Qatar has provided a haven for leaders of Hamas and the Muslim Brotherhood.

Former Secretary of State George Shultz, who died in 2021, elaborated on the problem:

> Some states have made tacit deals with foreign terrorists, allowing them offices in their cities in return for a pledge of immunity. Some states have tolerated, subsidized, and facilitated homegrown terrorist groups with the understanding that those groups will not attempt to overthrow national leaders, creating a kind of grotesque protection racket. Some states pump out huge volumes of propaganda against other states in an effort to direct terrorists within their borders toward external targets. Some states, in a desperate search for legitimacy, have invited religions that foster terrorists to take over substantial sectors of governmental activity on condition that some functions, such as foreign affairs and defense policy, will be left alone. And some states secretly, but undeniably, support terrorism directly as a matter of state policy.[166]

I agree completely with his conclusion: "Every one of these deals between states and terrorists is an abdication of state accountability to its citizens. If these deals are not reversed, the states that make them and ultimately the international system of states will not survive. That is why the war on terrorism is of such importance."

Kosher Hate for terrorists should be universal. Only when we cease making excuses for them, refuse to accept their claims to be "freedom fighters," and stop dismissing them as "militants" can we effectively fight them.

We must be prepared to track them to the ends of the earth to bring them to justice. If that is impractical or impossible, they should be killed for their crimes before they can murder innocents again.

CHAPTER 9:

KOSHER HATE: A PRACTICAL GUIDE

IF YOU HAVE FOLLOWED ME so far and accepted that a theologically sound Kosher Hate is essential to bringing peace to humankind, we still must decide who and what is worth hating today, and how to use our righteous indignation to defeat evil.

Many questions have arisen in our journey. Should we direct our hate at individual anti-Semites, people with whom we have ideological/political disagreements, white collar criminals, rapists, pedophiles, murderers of individuals, or mass murderers? I have argued that all of these may deserve our hatred but all evils are not equal, and we do not have un-limited time and resources. Therefore, we must balance the intensity of Kosher Hate.

I've acknowledged there is always a danger of becoming consumed by hate, and ending up bitter, angry, and cynical. I see no problem with someone being obsessed, so long as they detest cruelty and wickedness and resist it.

We have become so accustomed to carnage that we are rarely moved unless a tragedy strikes close to home, as in the case of school shootings. We have reduced mass murder to a matter of statistics. I mentioned earlier how this is a problem with speaking about the six million Jewish victims of the Holocaust. Statistics are abstract; they remove the humanity and horror from the event.

Propagandists understand this. The Palestinians, for example, will often use the injury or death of a child (and sometimes the examples are contrived) to vilify Israel. This has a more powerful emotional impact. Israelis, by contrast, often focus on statistics, as in the thousands of rockets fired by Hamas terrorists into Israel. As I've mentioned in the last chapter, it is a far more effective (and accurate) way to appreciate the danger Israelis face by counting down from fifteen to convey the amount of time Israelis have to get to a shelter after hearing an incoming rocket alert. Asking people to imagine moving everyone in their family in fifteen seconds conveys the threat posed by terrorists better than a recitation of the number of rockets and mortars fired from Gaza.

We need to relate to the victims if we are to feel the necessary indignation to fight the perpetrators of evil.

As we've discussed, evil is perpetrated on both the micro and macro level. The former affects primarily an individual or small number of people, such as rape, domestic abuse, or local instances of murder. The latter refers to the victimization of an entire group or category of people on a national scale, as with genocide. Because time and resources are finite, zealous, unforgiving Kosher Hate must be reserved for the most heinous instances of evil at the macro level.

The United States has made the promotion of democracy a foreign policy goal. However, it has been pursued inconsistently. In Communist and Latin American nations, American administrations aggressively sought to impose democracy. By contrast, repressive Arab regimes are not pressured to democratize because of the fear that autocrats might be replaced by Islamists who endanger people at home and abroad.

This is one reason both Obama and Trump, as well as the Israelis, were reluctant to try to force Bashar Assad from power in Syria. As the saying goes, better the devil you know than the devil you don't.

We clearly face limitations in our ability to effect change. Therefore, Kosher Hate must utilize a variety of tools calibrated to the degree of danger, their efficacy, and a calculation of the benefits versus the costs. The principal weapons in the U.S. arsenal to fight evil are:

- Diplomacy

- Economic carrots (foreign aid) and sticks (sanctions and embargoes)

- Intelligence (covert action)

- Deterrence (requires capability and *will*)

- Military intervention (limited as in drone strikes, all-out war and invasion, or something in between)

Which evildoers rise to the threshold of meriting Kosher Hate?

For nearly half a century the United States was preoccupied with the threat posed by the Soviet Union and its proxies. After the Berlin Wall was pulled down, some believed the danger evaporated. However, as we have seen from the nefarious foreign policy of Vladimir Putin and his desire to revive the glory days of the Soviet Empire, we continue to face challenges from Russia, whether it be interference in our elections, aggression against its neighbors such as Crimea and Ukraine, destabilization efforts in Europe and the Middle East, or assassination of enemies on foreign soil.

The fear of mutually assured destruction by nuclear weapons has constrained our response to the use of deterrence and containment. Still, Ronald Reagan proved it was possible to defeat the "evil empire" by a combination of measures including signing verifiable arms control agreements, refusing to accept the inevitability of Soviet domination, containment, and demonstrating a willingness to spend whatever was necessary to gain a military edge, which forced the Soviets to play a game of catch-up they could not win.

We must hate the dictatorship of Putin as we did the Soviet Union, and the United States can be no less determined to oppose his odious regime even as war remains an untenable option. Unfortunately, first President Obama and then President Trump were outmaneuvered by Putin. President Biden, in just his third month in office, expressed Kosher Hate by labeling Putin a killer, something President Trump refused to do. But it remains to be seen whether Biden will follow through and impose sanctions on Russia—as did Trump—for Putin's continued brutality against pro-democracy advocates in Russia.

We must apply Kosher Hate to condemn nefarious activities by the Russians, impose sanctions where they can be effective, strengthen NATO, and negotiate verifiable arms agreements.

Increasingly, China is viewed as a greater threat than Russia and that country's government must also be a target of Kosher Hate. Communist China has survived and thrived, even as it limits the freedom of its people, arrests protestors and dissidents, and sends Uighur Muslims to concentration camps. What has the world done in the meantime? Where is the outrage from President Biden and other western leaders?

Some members of Congress tried to declare that China is committing genocide against the Uighurs, more than one million of whom are confined to reeducation camps where they are being forced to integrate into Chinese society and give up their Islamic heritage. The legislation was introduced late in the session, just before the election, and never came to a floor vote. The administration could use the word "genocide" without any congressional authorization and, while Robert O'Brien, Trump's national security advisor, said the Chinese action is "if not genocide, something close," it stopped short of using the word which would have likely required sanctions. Joe Biden, meanwhile, called it genocide and said he would respond more vigorously to China's human rights violations.[167]

In the case of the Uighurs, the pope has belatedly spoken out, albeit meekly. In his book, *Let Us Dream: The Path to a Better Future*, Pope Francis listed "the poor Uighurs" among the people of the world he kept in his thoughts and prayers. "I think often of persecuted peoples," Francis wrote. "The Rohingya, the poor Uighurs, the Yazidi—what ISIS did to them was truly cruel—or Christians in Egypt and Pakistan killed by bombs that went off while they prayed in church."[168]

This is not exactly the thunderous denunciation one would expect from the moral conscience of the Christian world. Shouldn't he repeat this publicly in every sermon?

Are the rabbis and imams any better? Do we hear their voices denouncing these crimes against humanity? Where are all the liberal crusaders for human rights?

A group of 130 Muslim leaders and scholars did sign an open letter in 2019 condemning China's persecution of the Uighurs and, at the end of December 2020, the chief rabbi of Great Britain, Ephraim Mirvis, wrote a scathing editorial in *The Guardian* condemning the Chinese persecution of the Uighurs. "At this very moment, an unfathomable mass atrocity is being perpetrated," he wrote and called for an investigation into what was happening and the guarantee of asylum to Uighurs who could escape.[169]

Governments remain unwilling to take any serious measures. China's persecution of the Uighurs continues unabated.

As with Russia, the United States cannot and should not go to war to try to change the Communist regime and end the suffering of the Chinese people. The chance of success is nil, and the risks of a cataclysmic nuclear war are far too great. This does not mean, however, we should not demonstrate our opposition. Now that Biden is president, he should continue Trump's strong denunciations against China's brutal treatment of pro-democracy advocates in Hong Kong and other human rights violations, imposing sanctions against all Chinese leaders who participate in them.

The people of Latin America have suffered under military juntas and dictatorships for decades. These governments have often threatened our interests by allying with our enemies (e.g., Venezuela and Iran), flooding our country with illegal drugs, and provoking mass migration. The goal of some past administrations was to undermine regimes and promote democracy by supporting the opposition, but we have had little success. One thing the United States can do is apply Kosher Hate to the war on drugs and work with Latin American countries to destroy the drug cartels, a symbol of evil if ever there was one.

Kosher Hate can bring about regime change as occurred in Iraq. Though the war was controversial, there was no doubt that Saddam was evil, that he was a mass murderer, and that he posed a threat to his people and those in neighboring countries. Unlike Russia and China, we did not have to worry about a nuclear response to our military action. We had both the capability and the duty to put an end to his reign of terror over his people and his threat to American interests.

Given that our freedom of action against a monstrous regime would be severely limited if it became a nuclear power, it is imperative that Iran be prevented from obtaining a bomb. Obama rightly said that Iran should not be allowed to have nuclear weapons and claimed that the signing of the Joint

Comprehensive Plan of Action (JCPOA) in 2015 "cuts off all of Iran's pathways to a nuclear weapon, including a covert pathway."[170] The only problem was that the administration contradicted itself and admitted this was untrue.

As the *BBC* noted, at the time the deal was signed, "experts estimated…it would take [Iran] two to three months until it had enough 90%-enriched uranium to build a nuclear weapon – the so-called 'break-out time.'"[171] But the administration also said the JCPOA would "increase its break-out time to one year or more." Obama went further and admitted that when the agreement began to expire in years 2013, 2014, and 2015, the breakout time would shrink "almost down to zero," and that was assuming Iran would not cheat on the agreement.[172]

But how would Iran ever reach breakout if the deal was supposed to cut off all pathways to a bomb? And how would we know if they were cheating? It they had secret facilities; how would we know?

Of course, as critics warned, the Iranians did not wait. They continued their covert activities; only some of which were discovered by intelligence agencies. Most dramatically, in 2018, Israeli Prime Minister Benjamin Netanyahu displayed excerpts of some 100,000 files the Mossad stole from a secret compound in Tehran detailing Iran's nuclear weapons activities.[173] The International Atomic Energy Agency (IAEA), which is supposed to know everything Iran is doing, knew nothing about it. A few months later, Netanyahu revealed the existence of a secret warehouse in Tehran where he said contained equipment and material related to Iran's nuclear weapons program. Once again, the IAEA was clueless and did not investigate it until months later, long after Iran had sanitized the area. The Iranians did not do as good a job as they thought, however, and inspectors discovered traces of uranium which supported Netanyahu's claim.[174]

The Iranians have violated the terms of the JCPOA and have taken advantage of its loopholes almost from the day it was signed. The Europeans ignored the violations because they were rushing to sign trade deals with Iran. They became furious when President Trump withdrew the United States from the JCPOA and imposed sanctions that made it difficult for any country to do business with the Iranians. The Europeans set up a mechanism to bypass the sanctions with little success, and the Trump administration repeatedly ratcheted up the pressure.

While I supported Trump's actions to prevent Iran from obtaining a bomb, they were not as successful as I and others had hoped. Now the Biden administration has signaled its desire to reinstate the JCPOA, rolling back Trump's policies on this and other regional initiatives. But if this means that Biden will relax the tough sanctions imposed on Iran for its nuclear program, human rights abuses, and genocidal threats against Israel, he will only continue the failed policies of Obama, which gave Iran a free hand to sow murder and mayhem throughout the Middle East.

It is possible, though admittedly undesirable, that the only way to stop Iran from getting a bomb is by military action. After Iraq and Afghanistan, Americans have little stomach for any large-scale military intervention, but it is possible for the United States, in cooperation with allies such as Israel, to seriously damage, if not destroy, Iran's nuclear facilities through actions short of an invasion.

Israel has no difficulty applying Kosher Hate to its enemies because, unlike the United States, its survival is at stake. Thus, Israeli officials have made it clear they will not allow Iran to get a nuclear weapon. While the United States and its allies argue over sanctions, Israel apparently took steps to sabotage Iranian facilities. In June 2020, a blast destroyed parts of a secret facility in Parchin associated with nuclear weapons research. In July, another mysterious explosion destroyed a building at the Natanz enrichment facility where Iran was developing advanced centrifuges. Several other sites were reportedly attacked either with explosives or cyberweapons.[175] Israel has also set back their nuclear program through the assassination of Iranian scientists.[176]

The U.S. and Israel have already had success using cyberwarfare to sabotage nuclear facilities. A range of options, short of all-out war are available to President Biden but they carry the risk of escalation and, Bard says, he "will have to decide whether the risks of military action against Iran outweigh the benefit of preventing it from acquiring nuclear weapons. But he will also have to consider the costs and benefits of inaction."[177]

Let me be clear. I am not calling for the United States to become the global cop. After Iraq and Afghanistan, Americans will not agree to it even if, as most Americans believe, there is no one else. Rather, I am suggesting that America lead in the realm of Kosher Hate. The president, Congress, State Department, and UN envoys must speak in clear terms about those regimes and individuals who are part of the light and those who must be stopped because they are the source of darkness. As the great sage Hillel said, "If I am not for myself, who will be for me? But if I am only for myself, who am I? If not now, when?"

Liberals like the idea of helping others if there is no cost involved (other than financial). They don't think we should get involved in others' business, assert the superiority of our values, or go to war for any reason. Many conservatives also prefer isolationism to global leadership.

Those who see a need for responding to evil abroad often oppose the United States acting unilaterally.

One of our most important tools for fighting hatred since the end of World War II has been NATO, but the collapse of the Soviet Union has rendered the alliance's mission unclear. Nevertheless, American presidents have felt compelled to obtain NATO support before acting, which caused paralysis in some cases (notably Bosnia) and in others near paralysis (reluctant allies exacerbated the Gulf crisis). NATO is further hamstrung by its rules for consensus before acting with the expansion of the alliance to include an unwieldy mix of democratic and more autocratic nations. Furthermore, the alliance has been undermined by Turkey's descent into authoritarianism, its abandonment of secularism for Islamism, and its willingness to purchase Russian weapons over U.S. objections.

The alliance has been further weakened by the refusal of our NATO allies to live up to their treaty responsibilities of spending at least 2 percent of their GDP on defense as Trump repeatedly demanded. As at the UN, the U.S. pays a disproportionate share of the budget, increasing America's burden. Trump's threats to pull out of NATO, frosty relations with European leaders, and emphasis on "America first" didn't help. Worse, Turkey's policies have become increasingly at odds with the alliance, such as with Erdogan's decision to purchase Russian anti-aircraft missiles.

Liberals and globalists protest that the United States should not be throwing its weight around and trying to impose its values on the rest of the world. International problems should be solved collectively by the world community and, if there is to be a world cop, it should be the United Nations.

Don't get me started on the UN, the home of inaction and impotent jaw-jawing. Created for the purpose of promoting world peace, its enduring failure is evident in the persistence of conflicts since its establishment. It is no surprise given that the membership includes all the most heinous regimes. "What takes place in the Security Council more closely resembles a mugging than either a political debate or an effort at problem-solving," said U.S. Ambassador to the UN Jeane Kirkpatrick.[178] When it comes to discussions regarding Israel, Israeli Ambassador Chaim Herzog commented on his feeling of being like Alice in Wonderland. Lewis Carroll "need not have done more than let Alice loose in this building. All she would have to do would be to wear a Star of David in order to hear the imperious 'Off with her head' at every turn."[179]

Much of the problem with the UN is structural. China and Russia were given a veto that allows them to prevent any serious measures from being taken by the UN to maintain order or fight evil. These are two Communist countries that are warmongers and serial abusers of human rights. In addition, a bloc of non-aligned nations and an Arab/Islamic bloc of authoritarian regimes typically work together in the General Assembly to routinely adopt resolutions backing Third World causes and insulate themselves from criticism. Though General Assembly resolutions are nonbinding, they are often given the weight of international law when they are political expressions of a near automatic majority of non-democratic regimes. Without Security Council approval, the UN cannot even try to enforce the resolutions it adopts, and even those that are affirmed by that body are routinely ignored.

The UN's failures to address human rights abuses and genocide have made it not just a failure but irrelevant. In 2004, for example, the General Assembly was unwilling even to vote on a resolution condemning genocide in Sudan. This prompted U.S. Ambassador John Danforth to say, "One wonders about the utility of the General Assembly on days like this. One wonders, if there can't be a clear and direct statement on matters of basic principle, why have this building? What are we all about?"[180]

Even worse is the farcically named Human Rights Council (HRC), whose members in 2020 include serial human rights offenders and sponsors of terrorism such as

Afghanistan, Pakistan, Qatar, Somalia, Libya, Sudan, and Venezuela. While members sit on their hands or defend terrorists and murderous regimes, they devote disproportionate attention to condemning the one democracy in the Middle East. In 2006, even Kofi Annan was embarrassed when the Council held three special sessions in the first five months of its regular sessions to condemn Israel. "There are surely other situations, besides the one in the Middle East, which would merit scrutiny by a special session [of this Council]," he said. "I would suggest that Darfur is a glaring case in point."[181]

The rot at the UN starts at the top where Secretary-Generals have led the organization's myopic and impotent approach to conflict. While the first two UN leaders were relatively benign Scandinavians, they were followed by U Thant, a former diplomat from what was then called Burma. He did take some positive actions by trying to resolve the Cuban Missile Crisis and sending a UN force to end the civil war in the Congo. He angered the United States because of his opposition to the Vietnam War and helped precipitate the 1967 Arab-Israeli war when he agreed to Egyptian President Gamal Nasser's demand to remove the UN peacekeeping force from the Sinai Peninsula.

He was followed by the former Nazi Kurt Waldheim. Imagine—the organization that arose in reaction to Hitler, led by a man who investigators later concluded had lied about his wartime activities. One historian said he believed Waldheim "played a significant role in the Wehrmacht's action, which resulted in the deportation of about 63,000 Yugoslav civilians, including 23,000 children."[182] The revelations only came out after his term as Secretary-General when he ran for president of Austria. He won that election, which tells you something about the Austrians at that time, forty years after the war. But that's another story.

Waldheim was followed by an ineffectual Peruvian and then Boutros Boutros-Ghali, a man from the despotic nation of Egypt. He was bad, but his successor Kofi Annan of Ghana was worse.

This is a man who presided over the UN during at least three genocides. He oversaw the United Nations peacekeeping forces but did not deploy them to stop the slaughter. He was meant to keep the peace, not to protect *genocidaires* as they hacked people to death with machetes.

The UN deserves our disdain for its failure to fulfill its fundamental mission. If we are to effectively oppose and challenge evil in the only terms it understands, we cannot expect the UN to make any contribution beyond serving as an enabler. With no other nation or international body willing to act, it is up to the United States, with its strong adherence to Judeo-Christian values, to defend the world against malevolent regimes and individuals.

One argument against the United States playing the role of moral cop is that we can become a bully, trying to force other nations to adopt our way of life, which some see as a form of imperialism. Beyond the philosophical issue, there is a practical one of determining priorities. With so many evildoers around the world, how can we make a difference if we are spread too thin? How can we fight tyrants on multiple continents? We already have troops in Syria, Iraq, and Afghanistan. Can we deploy more to Nigeria, Yemen, and Nicaragua? Should we?

The United States has long had the objective of maintaining the capability to fight two conventional wars at once. We're already involved to some degree in three and I've just mentioned three additional hotspots. Besides stretching our resources too thin, we also risk emboldening our most serious enemies—China and Russia—who may attempt to exploit our divided attention.

As I've described earlier in the book, some people believe war is intrinsically wrong, that evil is an illusion, or that it should be ignored, appeased, or negotiated away because fighting it would upset the inner tranquility and outer civility that is the way people should live. This also provides a way to argue against tough measures with evil regimes because it can always be viewed as a path to war.

But war may be the best option. The late cultural critic Susan Sontag saw demonstrations against the Kosovo war in Rome where protestors held banners that said, "Stop the War and Stop the Genocide." Who can disagree with the sentiment that peace is better than war? "But, she sensibly asked, "how can you stop those bent on genocide without making war?"[183]

Pacifists also argue that war cannot eradicate evil. Sontag rebutted this canard: "Is it true that war never solved anything? (Ask a black American if he or she thinks our Civil War didn't solve anything.) War is not simply a mistake, a failure to communicate. There is radical evil in the world, which is why there are just wars."[184]

War is not intrinsically wrong; it is intrinsically dangerous. Inevitably, people will die. It is also unpredictable. As George Kennan, the architect of America's containment strategy during the Cold War, said, "War has a momentum of its own...You know where you begin. You never know where you are going to end."[185] Churchill said much the same years earlier, "The statesman who yields to war fever must realize that once the signal is given, he is no longer the master of policy but the slave of unforeseeable and uncontrollable events."[186]

This is what makes going to war, when it is just and fought against a monstrous tyranny like the Nazis, an act of the greatest courage, when people choose to brave the risks and be willing to make the ultimate sacrifice in a righteous cause. Neither diplomacy nor appeasement nor disregard will rid the world of evil. Ultimately—because of its very nature—only war will destroy it.

To take the terrible decision to go to war people need to feel Kosher Hate toward evil. You are skeptical, but history has shown that we can defeat immoral and malevolent enemies when we are determined. We need leadership, the kind we have seen too infrequently in recent decades.

I am thinking of people like Churchill. When he spoke to the House of Commons for the first time as prime minister on May 13, 1940, less than a year after World War II began, he inspired the British people with one of the greatest speeches of all time, telling them, "I have nothing to offer but blood, toil, tears and sweat" and added what every leader should say when confronted with absolute evil:

> You ask, what is our policy? I can say: It is to wage war, by sea, land and air, with all our might and with all the strength that God can give us; to wage war against a monstrous tyranny, never surpassed in the dark, lamentable catalogue of human crime. That is our policy. You ask, what is our aim? I can answer in one word: It is victory, victory at all costs, victory in spite of all terror, victory, however long and hard the road may be; for without victory, there is no survival.[187]

While war may be necessary, we must be wary of efforts to find scapegoats for the decision to take such decisive action. Jews and Israel, for example, are sometimes blamed for America's policies in the Middle East.

In the case of the Iraq War, two academics, Stephen Walt and John Mearsheimer, wrote an article (later turned into the book, *The Israel Lobby and U.S. Foreign Policy*) about how the supposedly omnipotent "Israel lobby" was using its influence to push America into an unnecessary war. When asked about the notion that the Jews, Israel, and neocons were the "driving force behind the Iraq war," former Secretary of Defense Donald Rumsfeld told *The New Yorker*, "I suppose the implication of that is that the President and the Vice-President and myself and Colin Powell just fell off a turnip truck to take these jobs."[188]

Many of the same critics have subsequently argued that Jews and Israel want to drag the United States into a war with Iran when the truth is both have argued that taking tougher measures can prevent war. As in the case of Iraq, these conspiracy theorists simply ignore other actors. The only country, for example, that advocated war with Iran was not Israel but Saudi Arabia. The pro-Israel community and Israel argued that the United States had to use sanctions to strengthen its bargaining position to negotiate a deal that would be sufficiently ironclad to obviate the need for war.

The way the Obama administration handled the Iranian threat was a case study in how *not* to fight evil, beginning with the astoundingly naïve belief that easing sanctions and signing an agreement would moderate Iranian views and policies. Obama's desire to wish away the threat of radical Islam led him to ignore the Iranian belief that the world should be governed by Islam. What was and is needed is a policy that prevents Iran from obtaining a nuclear weapon that could make it immune from attack, counters its sponsorship of terror, and blocks its efforts to destabilize the region.

I do not oppose negotiations with all our enemies; diplomacy was one of the tools I mentioned to fight evil. Jaw-jawing, however, must be backed by a willingness to use lethal force. In the nuclear talks, Iran's leaders were convinced from Obama's statements and actions, as well as the vociferous opposition of liberals, pacifists, and members of the Democratic Party, that he was not going to go to war no matter what they did. Instead of using the military stick to his advantage, Obama tossed it away and gave the Iranians leverage.

Because they think in terms of centuries rather than years or even decades, they did not consider it a great sacrifice to give up some of their overt nuclear activities for a limited period in exchange for the ending of sanctions and a windfall of $150 billion.

Obama sold the deal as a way to moderate Iranian behavior, put in place a verifiable inspections regime, and block all paths to a nuclear bomb. The agreement did none of those things. Rather than pressing Obama to go to war, Israeli Prime Minister Netanyahu and other critics of the negotiations said the alternative was a better deal (which is what Trump promised but did not deliver). Obama and his supporters focused solely on the cost of war and dismissed the price to be paid by accepting an agreement full of loopholes, which did not even address Iran's sponsorship of terror, development of ballistic missiles, and destabilization of the region. The result emboldened the Iranians and increased the probability of war.

Obama violated a cardinal rule for dealing with evil men and regimes that Reagan put succinctly: "trust, but verify." By imposing that condition, Reagan could negotiate arms control agreements with the Russians. By contrast, Obama trusted the Iranians, despite their decades of duplicitous behavior, and put his faith in the IAEA to verify compliance. The examples of Iran's noncompliance and the IAEA's failures is too long to enumerate here. Suffice to say, Iran is now openly violating the agreement without any of the consequences Obama promised when he sold the deal to the American people.

There also can be no double standards in the war against evil. Sometimes it is a case of confusing the villains with those fighting them; other times, it is a matter of unfair expectations. Western democracies, for example, are held to a higher standard than authoritarian regimes. The evil of the former is exaggerated, the latter minimized. This is especially evident at the Human Rights Council where some of the world's worst serial human rights abusers sit in judgement of others.

No one, for example, bats an eye sadly when Arabs or Muslims murder their fellow Arabs and Muslims as it happens throughout the Middle East—most notably the murder of hundreds of thousands of Syrian Arabs by their "president," Bashar Assad. Think about the disinterest the world showed as hundreds of thousands of Arabs and Muslims died in the Iran-Iraq War or the more recent carnage in Syria and Yemen. On the one hand they are viewed as so barbaric that such behavior is expected. On the other, saying this is abhorrent to liberals who prefer to ignore inconvenient realities that contradict their romanticized image of humanity. Some argue it is not that any people are more barbaric than others (though Hutus cutting off the limbs of Tutsis with machetes makes one pause), but because Westerners are racist, and care less about the internecine fighting of people of color than white Europeans. Hence, they are not by moved by slaughter in the Middle East, Africa, or Asia (e.g. the genocide by Myanmar against the Muslim Rohingya).

This race-driven attitude also leads to double-standards when whites and people of color are in conflict. The most blatant international example is the case of the Arab-Israeli conflict. Though Israeli Jews are not a race and are not all white, they are held to a higher standard than those "barbaric" Arabs. As European-like, they are expected to behave accordingly. Thus, for example, if a Palestinian is killed by an Israeli soldier, justified or not, it is newsworthy, whereas Palestinians killing other Palestinians is unremarkable.

Of course democracies are rightly held to higher standards. One obstacle for democracies fighting evil is the asymmetry of the "good guys" trying to follow the "rules of war" while their enemies believe like there are no rules. This sometimes makes it difficult for democracies to defend themselves without violating international standards of decency. If they do so, it vitiates their claim to be morally superior to their enemies.

Another obstacle that democracies face in fighting evil is the notion of proportionality. This again reflects the liberal bias toward peace and fairness. We should not go to war at all, but if we do, we must try not to kill anyone except those who deserve to die, and the preference should be to capture and try the war criminals.

In World War II, the belligerents showed little concern for proportionality. You had, for example, the Allies' fire-bombing of Dresden, Berlin, and Tokyo and the United States dropping atomic bombs on Hiroshima and Nagasaki. In retrospect, many people see these as disproportionate uses of force, but they were mostly viewed as necessary, if not acceptable, measures to win the war at the time.

Israel, for example, has responded to terror attacks with sometimes large-scale military operations for air raids that have drawn criticism for being disproportionate. The question arises, "What is a proportionate response to evil?" Hezbollah and Hamas have indiscriminately targeted Israel with rockets. Should Israel respond by firing unguided missiles? If a Palestinian suicide bomber blows up a pizzeria would it be proportionate for Israel to plant a bomb in a Palestinian restaurant?

Israel is guided by a policy of restraint and goes to great lengths to avoid harming innocent civilians. This was exemplified during fighting in Gaza in 2014 when Israel would put its own soldiers at risk by dropping leaflets warning people to leave an area even though that meant giving up the element of surprise and allowing terrorists to escape. In addition, as a democracy, Israeli soldiers are held accountable for their actions and punished for abuses.

One must ask the critics, "What would the United States do if terrorists were shooting rockets into American cities from Mexico or Canada?" What would you do if your neighbor was shooting at your house? Would you say the neighbor should be ignored or would you want a SWAT team to break down the neighbor's door and restrain or kill him?

We know what the United States would do if attacked. After 9/11, we went to war in Iraq and Afghanistan. Barack Obama was famously averse to committing American troops to fight on the ground but launched more drone strikes against terrorist targets than any other president. Some might say this was a show of restraint and proportionality but the truth is, Obama's drone strikes killed numerous civilians.[189]

Still, Israel continues to be pilloried around the world for the simple act of defending itself against the Hamas terrorists, a painful notion that came to light again during the Hamas rocket attacks against Israel in May of 2021.

For the fourth time in fifteen years, Israel was essentially at war with a genocidal enemy in Hamas—a bloodthirsty death cult with a genocidal charter calling for the extermination of Jews wherever they may be found, including in the United States, Europe, and Australia. Hamas aids and abets honor killings of Palestinian women, whose only crime is having a boyfriend. They slaughter LGBTQ Palestinians. They are ruthless and brutal to the wider Palestinian population, robbing them of the international funds sent to give them a better life and using those funds instead to fire rockets at Jews to murder as many of them as they can.

You would think that the choice here between good and evil would have been stark and direct and the world would stand with Israel. But precisely the opposite occurred, as Israel was portrayed as trying to "erase" the Palestinian people.

Take the example of Mohamed Hadid, the multi-millionaire father of supermodels Bella and Gigi Hadid, all of whom are vilifying Israel with gusto to their tens of millions of followers on Instagram. He wrote on Instagram, "No one should be allowed to erase a race... you can't close your eyes... the Pope did in WW1 and WW11 and the rest of the world stood by silently...."

This is the ultimate blood libel, falsely accusing Israel—the only free society in the Middle East—of genocide. Hadid shockingly compared the Holocaust of six million Jews to Israel fighting back against Hamas rockets intent on murdering children. It takes incredible audacity to accuse the Jews of pursuing a genocide against the Palestinians, and this anti-Semitic blood libel about the Jewish people should be rejected by all people who value truth and human rights.

Instead, the blood libel continued to spread.

Mohamed's daughters, Bella and Gigi, joined by the singer Dua Lipa (purportedly dating their brother), have become an unholy trinity of Hamas terror-splaining It-girls engaged in the outright demonization of Israel and the Jewish people.

Speaking to their nearly one hundred million followers on social media, they vilified the Jewish State with an all-consuming hatred.

They accused Israel—a nation built in large part by Holocaust survivors—of ethnic cleansing, even as millions of Jews in Israel descend from refugees savagely forced out of every Arab land. They condemned Israel for the military checkpoints that were erected only after 700 innocent Israeli Jews and Arabs were blown to bits by suicide bombers on buses and cafés, many of them sent by Hamas. They called Israel an apartheid state, even as it is the only country in world history to airlift Africans into freedom and sets the standard for multi-racial and multi-cultural coexistence, with millions of Christians, Muslims, and Jews living side by side as doctors, teachers, and soldiers.

If Bella, Gigi, and Dua cared about Palestinians, they would have condemned Hamas and demand it stop its use of Palestinian children as human shields, cease its murders of LGBTQ Palestinians, and reverse their denial of the Palestinian people's right to elections after fourteen autocratic years. But those demands didn't fit into a campaign that's solely about hating and defaming Jews.

Worst of all, in defending the Hamas terrorists, Bella, Gigi, and Dua make themselves apologists for the genocidal aspirations of Hamas, whose charter calls for the murder of Jews "wherever they are found." Hamas seeks nothing less than a second Holocaust: 1,800 shrapnel-packed rockets should be more than enough to prove they mean it.

Americans are used to seeing shallow celebrities peddling scams like FYRE festival, as Bella and Gigi infamously did, or embarrassing themselves with their political ignorance. But serving as apologists for genocidal terrorists takes celebrity abasement to a whole new level.

But that's my whole point. The Jewish state is the only nation on earth of whom it is acceptable to falsely malign as genocidal murderers, even as Israel is the easily the most righteous nation in the entire Middle East and one of the most humane on Earth.

Why is this happening? It's easy to simply blame anti-Semitism, and no doubt that is a big part of it. But the truth is that Jews have never believed in the importance of public relations and getting the truth of our message out. While Hamas arguably has hundreds of celebrity social media influencers with hundreds of thousands of followers who peddle their lies, Israel has virtually none.

Witness where we are now, where even Gal Gadot, the world's most famous Israeli actor, will write on Instagram of how her family is under attack and suffering but will still not come out with a full-fledged defense of Israel as a righteous democracy fighting a terrorist tyranny.

And then there is the fact that for four years the Trump administration personalities were so effective at defending Israel—from Mike Pence to Mike Pompeo to David Friedman to Nikki Haley to Jared Kushner to Ivanka Trump to Jason Greenblatt and more—that the Jewish community got lazy about doing it ourselves. Now that they are not in office, Israel is being vilified in the media with few to defend her.

But the United States is often vilified in the same way, whenever it fights terrorists. As a superpower it does not hesitate to apply the "Powell Doctrine," articulated by General Colin Powell, which holds that "America should enter fights with every bit of force available or not at all." To give one example of an American response to evil, the U.S. launched twenty-three cruise missiles at Iraq's intelligence headquarters following an attempt to assassinate President Bush. A civilian neighborhood was accidentally hit; nevertheless, Powell said the attack was an "appropriate, proportional" response.[190]

While I acknowledge a range of tools to fight evil, only war can ultimately eliminate it. I don't take any satisfaction in saying this because all war is hell and to be avoided if possible—but not at any cost.

Amazingly, the Jewish cry for morality in the ancient world was misrepresented by Judaism's opponents as a cynical attempt to dominate the planet. Likewise, America's honest effort to bring democracy to the world's most troubled areas is speciously interpreted as an attempt to assert American hegemony.

The world has not been totally oblivious to genocide even though its inaction makes it appear so. In 1948, The Convention on the Prevention and Punishment of the Crime of Genocide was adopted by the UN General Assembly to establish genocide as a crime under international law.[191]

The decision to declare genocide a crime was an outgrowth of World War II and meant to outlaw and, ideally prevent, anything like the Holocaust from happening again. To win the support of the Soviet Union and the Communist bloc, however, the convention had to exclude from the definition of genocide actions that would have incriminated *them*, such as the killing of members of a social class, dissidents, or political or ideological groups. The expectation was that "persons charged with genocide" would "be tried by a competent tribunal of the State in the territory of which the act was committed."

No one was charged under the convention, however, for fifty years. It was not until 1998 that the International Criminal Tribunal for Rwanda found Jean-Paul Akayesu, the former mayor of a small town in Rwanda, guilty of nine counts of genocide.

Ideally, an impartial court could mete out justice to *genocidaires*. However, the institution created to do so, the International Criminal Court (ICC), has been a failure and increasingly politicized. As with most international politics, it is typically only the weakest parties that can be held accountable. Europeans, Communists, dictators, Israelis, and Americans do not recognize the jurisdiction of the ICC. Western democracies justifiably argue that they have independent courts to judge the actions of their citizens; authoritarians simply reject any external judgement of their behavior.

In 2020, the United States went so far as to impose sanctions on ICC officials "directly engaged in investigating U.S. personnel or allied personnel against their state's consent, and against others who materially support such officials' activities."[192] The executive order (13928) was prompted by ICC investigations into alleged crimes committed by U.S. personnel in Afghanistan, which President Trump said threatened "to infringe upon the sovereignty of the United States and impede the critical national security and foreign policy work of United States Government and allied officials, and thereby threaten the national security and foreign policy of the United States."[193] President Biden reiterated the U.S. objection to ICC claims of jurisdiction over the United States and its allies, but revoked the order and the sanctions it had imposed on ICC personnel.[194]

Israel, like the United States, never joined the ICC and likewise denies the court has any jurisdiction over the actions of its citizens.[195] Nevertheless, the Palestinians have attempted to use the ICC as a weapon against Israel. Rather than investigate the true war criminals, Hamas, Hezbollah, Palestinian Islamic Jihad (PIJ), and other terrorists who have committed such war crimes as using civilians as shields, the prosecutor has focused her attention on Israel's military response to the violence directed at its citizens, inverting its role from prosecutor of evildoers to enabler.

When a country or individual satisfies the criteria in the UN's Genocide Convention, the crime is clear cut. In places like the Middle East, however, it is not so easy to tell the good guys from the bad guys, and even those the United States considers "good" may have their own evil tendencies. As Paul Pillar, a nonresident fellow at the Quincy Institute and at the Center for Security Studies at Georgetown University, observed, "the region is a tangle of cross-cutting rivalries and conflicts—of Sunnis against Shia, Arabs against Israelis, Arabs against Iranians, fundamentalists against secularists, and monarchies against republics.[196]

Some of the "good guys" we partner with in the Middle East are not so good and often act against our interests. The U.S. is allied, for example, with serial human rights abusers such as Saudi Arabia and Egypt. We sell billions of dollars' worth of arms to these countries but they vote against us most of the time at the UN and often take other positions that conflict with our own as in the Saudi opposition to the Israel-Egyptian peace treaty and refusal to join the Abraham Accords (the normalization agreement between Israel, Bahrain, and the United Arab Emirates).[197]

Some on the far left have their own conception of evil, which is no less Manichean than the conservatives. They divide the world into colonizer and colonized, capitalist and proletarian, Communist and capitalist as Gitlin describes in chapter one. Though typically opponents of war, they are advocates of violent revolution when it suits their purposes; that is, they are in favor of eradicating what *they view* as evil. Frantz Fanon, a guru for the Manichean left argued, "[T]he colonist turns the colonized into a kind of quintessence of evil," which produces "the Manicheanism of colonialism."[198] He believed no conciliation was possible between the two and that violence, which he called a "cleansing force," was needed to liberate the colonized.[199]

Thus, right and left agree that war is necessary to defeat evil; but they have very different ideas of who the malevolent party is.

As a rabbi and a human being, I do not want to see war. Still, it may sometimes be necessary.

The best way to avert war, or to minimize the cost, is to recognize danger and do something about it before it grows unmanageable. Evil is like a fire. If we smell smoke or see a flame, we must act immediately to put it out; waiting until it becomes a conflagration results in disaster.

CHAPTER 10:

WHY WE CAN AND MUST DEFEAT EVIL

THE ANCIENT DREAM OF A messianic world and a utopian society bereft of war, death, and corruption is not achievable without Kosher Hate. It may seem paradoxical but unless we despise evil and fight it with all our might, we will never purge the world of the cancer of hatred. It is not true that you don't fight fire with fire. The Saddams, Kim Jong-uns and Assads of this world can only be defeated with fire.

This admission does not spell the death of optimism. It simply changes it.

I used to be a conventional optimist, a believer in the perfectibility of mankind, right in line with Judaism's most important teaching—*tikkun olam*–to repair the world. Once achieved, the world will no longer suffer from contention, disease, and drought.

The founding fathers of the United States also wished to build a utopia. As I've described early on in the text, they believed, however, that any perfect society was first predicated on a belief in right and wrong, as articulated in the Ten Commandments. It was for this reason that they enshrined their values not in dogma, but in a system of law that we call the Constitution.

While this utopian belief might strike some as unrealistic, as recently as the early nineties it was easy to be buoyant about the world's future. It was a time of relative peace and prosperity. The dreaded Soviet Union crumbled without a shot being fired, democracy was spreading around the world, stock markets seemingly had no ceiling, new technologies such as the internet were changing the world, the Oslo Accords promised an end to the Israeli-Palestinian conflict, the Good Friday Agreement ended thirty years of violence in Northern Ireland, Nelson Mandela was released from prison and elected president of South Africa, and humankind seemed to be pulling together. The Christian dualistic vision of the world, which subdivided existence into two antithetical parts—heaven and earth, body and soul, ambition and conscience, and ultimately good and evil—had had its day. Hatred had no place for there was nothing to hate. Monism, the mystical belief that everything has an underlying divine nature and that there is a latent unity behind all creation, was in ascendance.

I found secular substantiation for my messianic optimism in Francis Fukuyama's epoch-defining book, *The End of History and the Last Man*. Like a prophet stepping out of the ancient Hebrew bible, Fukuyama made a convincing case that utopia was nigh. The spread of liberal democracy had ushered in an era of prosperity and peace. Evil had been vanquished. Tyrannical and dictatorial regimes were collapsing because of their inner hollowness.

Pessimists of the world be damned! We were living in an age when you could have it all. Even God and Mammon seemed compatible, as the materialistic citizens of the United States embarked upon a spiritual journey with New Age gurus like Deepak Chopra and self-help stylists like John Gray leading the way. Along with our fancy cars and expensive vacations, we wanted God in our lives—as well as deeper, more intimate relationships. And it was all happening. Much of what Isaiah and Jeremiah prophesied about a world of material plenty and spiritual renewal was coming to fruition before our very eyes.

Of course, it was largely an illusion. The 1990s were also the time of the Oklahoma City bombing, the Columbine High School shooting, riots in Los Angeles, the Waco siege, and the Monica Lewinsky scandal. And that was just in the United States. Beyond our shores, Saddam invaded Kuwait, precipitating the Gulf War, a civil war in the Congo led to the overthrow of Zairian dictator Mobutu Sese Seko, Russia went to war against Chechnya, the Taliban seized control of Afghanistan, Al Qaeda bombed the U.S. embassies in Kenya and Tanzania, Iran-backed Hezbollah terrorists blew up the AMIA Jewish community center in Buenos Aires, ongoing Palestinian terrorism sabotaged the Oslo Accords, a Jew assassinated Israeli Prime Minister Yitzhak Rabin, the Bosnian genocide took the lives of approximately 100,000 people, and the Rwandan genocide killed as many as one million.

The illusion was completely shattered at the turn of the twenty-first century with the suicide attacks of September 11. The idea that we were approaching the fairy tale ending of "peace in our time" had about as much credibility as when Neville Chamberlain tried to pacify Hitler. Fukuyama's professor at Harvard, Samuel Huntington, had argued in his far more prescient classic, *The Clash of Civilizations and the Remaking of World Order*, that violent conflicts between cultures that base their traditions on religious faith and dogma were increasingly likely. This time it was the teacher's vision of apocalypse that eclipsed his student's dream of utopia. The need for a doctrine of Kosher Hate became more urgent than ever.

My fading optimism for the world's moral maturity was dealt another crushing blow as I watched great democracies like France and Germany attempt to keep the world's foremost assassin, Saddam Hussein, in power. They later signed an agreement with the mullahs in Iran that allowed them to continue their pursuit of a nuclear weapon to advance their own economic interests.

Of course, as Alexander Pope said, "hope springs eternal in the human breast."

In 2010, the "Arab Spring" began with protests in Tunisia and spread across the region, inspiring hope for the democratization of the Middle East and the downfall of autocrats. That too proved to be a mirage.

False hope was created mainly by the media and those with little knowledge of the region. The best example was Egypt where large-scale demonstrations were mistakenly expected to bring about democracy. We were told how it was being driven by young people mobilizing using modern technology. In the interest of pushing Egypt toward the freedom protestors demanded, the Obama administration forced President Hosni Mubarak from office. As with most of Obama's policies in the Middle East, he had good intentions but received bad advice and the consequences were disastrous.

Anyone knowledgeable about Egypt knew that all those young people in the streets were not organized in any way that would give them power in a democratic government. The one group that was prepared for an election was the Muslim Brotherhood terror organization, which for decades had sought to overthrow the Egyptian government and been suppressed as a result. There was no chance this group would adopt the freedoms expected of a democracy and when, as expected, the organization won the election held to replace Mubarak, the new president Mohamed Morsi immediately began to take measures to move the country in the direction of an authoritarian Islamic state.

By throwing Mubarak, a thirty-year ally of the United States, under the bus, Obama further undermined the prospects for democracy. I understood Obama's intent and applauded his call for democracy in Egypt. But what it led to, aside from the Muslim Brotherhood gaining power, was Arab leaders, particularly in the Gulf states, who also were allies of the United States now fearing that the president would support unseating them as well. Within two years, the authoritarians had suppressed dissent in what became the "Arab Winter" and General Abdel Fattah el-Sisi seized power in Egypt and jailed Morsi and other members of the Muslim Brotherhood. Ten years after the Arab Spring began, the only country that had democratized was the place where it started, Tunisia.

As events increased my pessimism, I was forced to accept, for now, the dualistic belief in light and darkness and the need to intensify our moral capacity for hate. It seemed that the world was indeed divided into combatant forces of good and evil that would be permanently in conflict. The monist vision of everything stemming from God and humanity ultimately achieving a singular purpose of compassion and goodness seemed dreamy and elusive.

To be sure, I am still at heart a Messianist, but I believe the violation of human rights that has characterized human existence from ancient times to the present must be fought with every fiber of our being. Hatred, as the strongest weapon in the heart's armory, is the only force potent enough to make the world safe for decency and democracy.

But how do we mobilize the masses and convince our leaders of the need for Kosher Hate, laser-focused on the world's most malevolent regimes?

Today, I see the United States divided into six principal groups.

The first are hedonists and materialists—those for whom America is an opportunity for indulgence—who have little or no interest in any larger American mission to the world. They want to enjoy life. They neither hurt nor harm anyone. They are focused mostly on themselves.

The second are the New Age spiritualists who think more about their inner selves, pretend evil does not exist, and believe that even the most depraved human beings have some good in them.

The third are the liberal religionists, both Christian and Jewish, who believe in right and wrong, but are careful never to use the terminology because they believe only God can judge and that love and understanding can conquer evil.

The fourth are social conservatives who think more in terms of what they can do for their country, have an interest in foreign policy, and domestically focus on family value issues.

The fifth are social liberals who, in terms of foreign policy, often see America as a source of evil and are cynical about foreign entanglements. They live for a career that they enjoy and think more about what their country should do for them. Ironically enough, some from the America First crowd join them in this assessment. America should be focusing all its energy and resources first and foremost at home.

Finally, there are a growing number of religious Christians and Orthodox Jews, dismissed as reactionary and unsophisticated, who favor creating a world rooted in Judeo-Christian ethics.

The surprising development is that the last group, traditionally the most powerless, has grown increasingly influential from the time of Jerry Falwell's Moral Majority in the 1980s to the mobilization of evangelicals in the twenty-first century. Presidents Carter, Reagan, Bush (Sr. and Jr.), and Obama used Christian values as at least partial basis for policymaking. Carter was especially concerned with the promotion of human rights while the Republican presidents were more interested in fighting tyranny.

The year 2020 was a presidential election year in the United States. On the Democratic side there was a lot of support for "progressives" who too often cannot distinguish good from evil, focus on blaming their government and capitalism for social ills, and offer excuses for immorality and criminality. Their standard bearer was Bernie Sanders who, like many on the far left, is either oblivious to the history and context of Middle East politics or simply chooses to ignore facts that conflict with a worldview that sees Israel as an evil occupier. Sanders was outspokenly critical of Benjamin Netanyahu but had no criticism for President Mahmoud Abbas, now serving the fourteenth year of his four-year term. He defended Rep. Ilhan Omar's anti-Semitic remarks and could not manage to unequivocally oppose the anti-Semitic BDS movement that seeks Israel's destruction. It was particularly despicable for Sanders to repeatedly use his own Jewish heritage as a shield for his numerous attacks on Israel.

My old friend Senator Cory Booker also sought the presidency. When asked whether he would meet Louis Farrakhan, the Nation of Islam leader, Booker said, "I don't feel the need to do that, but I'm not one of these people that says I wouldn't sit down with anybody to hear what they have to say."[200]

How disappointing. The correct answer was, "Of course I would not meet with Louis Farrakhan, who has called Jews 'termites,' 'satanic,' and referred to Hitler as 'a very great man.'" But Cory did not say this. Instead, he left the door open to meeting a man who employs Nazi terminology about Jews. The one thing you do with termites is exterminate them. Pretty scary, coming from an American pastor.

A moral revulsion against evil was missing from many of the presidential candidates. Tulsi Gabbard of Hawaii, whom I also consider a friend, made the colossal mistake of meeting with Bashar Assad, even after he used poison gas against Arab children.

There were some appalling examples on the right as well. The Republicans have their share of problematic candidates and officials whose hate was and is misplaced and, in some cases, despicable. For example, Republicans have tolerated racists in Congress such as Jesse Helms, Strom Thurmond, and more recently Steve King (even as Democrats lionized the late Robert Byrd, a former Klansman and the longest serving member of the Senate).

Republican Roy Moore ran for the Senate in Georgia with President Trump's endorsement. He was accused by multiple women of sexual misconduct, which he denied, but still lost the race.

Trump also endorsed Republican Laura Loomer who won her primary for a Florida House seat. Loomer is a self-described "proud Islamophobe" who endorses the QAnon conspiracy theories, some of which are anti-Semitic. Trump said of this evil group, which is deserving of Kosher Hate, "I don't know much about the movement other than I understand they like me very much, which I appreciate."[201] President Trump, who was an unprecedented friend of Israel and the American Jewish community, was nevertheless culpable in failing to clearly condemn fringe groups like the Proud Boys and the white supremacists who rioted in Charlottesville. I will forever remain grateful to Trump for all he did for the Jewish state. But someone must have told him not to condemn these white supremacists otherwise risk losing their support, leading to an outsized moral failure of leadership.

Since the election of representatives Rashida Tlaib and Ilhan Omar to Congress, the Democratic Party has been normalizing anti-Semitism. Rather than unequivocally censuring Omar's anti-Semitic comments, the House passed an omnibus resolution that condemned "anti-Semitism, Islamophobia, racism and other forms of bigotry" without mentioning her or her remarks.[202] Neither changed their views, continuing, for example, to support the BDS movement calling for Israel's destruction. Nevertheless, House Speaker Nancy Pelosi endorsed both in their reelection campaigns.[203]

Politicians too often exploit evil for their own self-interest. Typically, voters are encouraged to vote against the other person rather than for a particular candidate. Optimistic, goal-oriented campaigns are less common than negative ones that play on the fears and hatreds of Americans (it works in other countries as well). Hence, you have the use of dog whistles and divisive ads such as the Willie Horton commercial used by President George H.W. Bush in the 1988 campaign. Before the 2018 midterm elections, the Republican Party broadcasted what CNN called, "the most racially charged national political ad in 30 years" (i.e., since Horton) in which Democrats are accused "of plotting to help people they depict as Central American invaders overrun the nation with cop killers."[204]

Why do candidates run racist and other negative ads? Because they work. Politicians have found that it is often better to focus on making their opponent look bad than themselves look good. The result, as in the 2016 election, is that the winner is not the most popular, but the least unpopular.

Generally, anger and hate are stronger motivators for voters. Love does not jolt people to act. Love is agreeable and nice, so you stay home in your cocoon and enjoy peace and quiet within your personal castle.

No one understood this better than Hitler who mobilized an entire country to hate "the other," the inferior, and the supposedly dangerous. He convinced the German people and later, many of those Germany occupied, that Jews, homosexuals, Roma, the disabled, Communists and others who were not of Aryan stock were parasites on society. The image of these people infesting the nations was as powerful as it was disturbing. We see echoes of this in American campaigns that demonize immigrants.

Americans also often look inwards for scapegoats for their predicament. Unless we are at war, foreign policy related issues typically rank far below bread-and-butter issues such as jobs and health care.

One of the biggest obstacles to Kosher Hate in the United States is that too many politicians on both sides are confused as to who our friends and enemies are and, like Obama and Trump, treat the latter better than the former.

Sometimes the problem operates in reverse, that is, people fighting evil are cowed or afraid to speak out for fear of being accused of bigotry. A top State Department official, for example, gave a speech in which he said Islamic fundamentalism would not replace communism as the next "ism" the United States would confront. Obama had the term "radical Islam" scrubbed from his administration's lexicon.[205]

The State Department official was totally wrong. Islamism did become the next great threat to the Western world. It was brought home to Americans on 9/11, which had both a positive and negative impact on the fight against evil. On the positive side, the attacks brought into sharp relief the determination of our enemies and their belief in a global jihad. On the negative side, it also created an overreaction among those who would not distinguish between ordinary Muslims and extremists. The bigotry directed against innocent Muslims allowed apologists for the radicals to accuse anyone who raised the alarm about the danger of "Islamophobia."

This was an interesting development that reflected efforts by Israel's detractors (as radical Islam targeted Israel) to take what they believed was a page out of the Jewish playbook. They believe that Jews have effectively silenced critics by accusing them of anti-Semitism, ignoring the fact that Jews distinguish between legitimate criticism and Jew-hatred. Israel's critics use the word "Islamophobia" to stifle discussion of the threat of radical Islam without making any distinction between bigots and truth-tellers. Ironically, the word was coined by Iranian fundamentalists to silence *Muslims*.

"The aim of this word was to declare Islam inviolate. Whoever crosses this border is deemed a racist," French philosopher Pascal Bruckner explained. "The term 'Islamophobia' serves a number of functions: it denies the reality of an Islamic offensive in Europe all the better to justify it; it attacks secularism by equating it with fundamentalism. Above all, however, it wants to silence all those Muslims who question the Koran, who demand equality of the sexes, who claim the right to renounce religion, and who want to practice their faith freely and without submitting to the dictates of the bearded and doctrinaire."[206]

Obama was particularly sensitive to references to Islam and preferred the phrase "violent extremism."

He went so far as to defend radical Islam by comparing it to Christianity, telling the audience at the 2015 National Prayer Breakfast that "during the Crusades and the Inquisition, people committed terrible deeds in the name of Christ. In our home country, slavery and Jim Crow all too often was justified in the name of Christ."[207]

Years earlier, Bernard Lewis, the doyen of Middle East historians debunked this analogy:

> I would not wish to defend the behavior of the Crusaders, which was in many respects atrocious. But let us have a little sense of proportion. We are now expected to believe that the Crusades were an unwarranted act of aggression against a peaceful Muslim world. Hardly. The first papal call for a crusade occurred in 846 C.E., when an Arab expedition from Sicily sailed up the Tiber and sacked St. Peter's in Rome. A synod in France issued an appeal to Christian sovereigns to rally against "the enemies of Christ," and the Pope, Leo IV, offered a heavenly reward to those who died fighting the Muslims. A century and a half and many battles later, in 1096, the Crusaders actually arrived in the Middle East. The Crusades were a late, limited, and unsuccess-

ful imitation of the jihad – an attempt to recover by holy war what had been lost by holy war. It failed, and it was not followed up.[208]

So, what are we to do about evil in the world? How do we overcome indifference?

I say "we" because this cannot be solely an American responsibility. The United States does not have the resources to perform the duty of world cop. All freedom-loving nations should be willing to work together to eradicate evil. This may require compromises at times, as in World War II, when the United States allied with Russia. Stalin was a murderous tyrant, but we could not defeat the greater evil of Nazism without his help. As the sole superpower today, the United States is in a stronger position to build coalitions without compromising its principals but that has still not been our history. To vanquish Saddam Hussein, for example, President Bush was willing to ally with other unsavory Middle East regimes.

Israel is in a very different position because of its isolation in the world. This has led the government to sometimes associate with disreputable leaders such as Hungarian president Viktor Orban because Hungary, unlike Western European countries, has sided with Israel.

One instance where both Israel and the United States have sacrificed principle to realpolitik is in the reluctance to acknowledge the Armenian genocide. Both have been willing to ignore history for the sake of maintaining relations with Turkey. This is also an example of an unnecessary compromise with evil. Turkey's Erdogan has become increasingly autocratic with Islamist tendencies that threaten both U.S. and Israeli interests.

Blessedly, during the course of the writing of this book, on April 24, 2021, President Joe Biden finally reversed the American refusal to acknowledge the Armenian genocide.

He said, "Each year on this day, we remember the lives of all those who died in the Ottoman-era Armenian genocide and recommit ourselves to preventing such an atrocity from ever again occurring. Beginning on April 24, 1915, with the arrest of Armenian intellectuals and community leaders in Constantinople by Ottoman authorities, one and a half million Armenians were deported, massacred, or marched to their deaths in a campaign of extermination. We honor the victims of the Meds Yeghern so that the horrors of what happened are never lost to history. And we remember so that we remain ever-vigilant against the corrosive influence of hate in all its forms."[209]

This was an extremely moral position to take. The United States finally erased its moral sin of failing to recognize the Armenian Genocide. It took President Joe Biden to finally rise to the occasion of standing up to Turkish tyrant Recep Tayyip Erdogan and declare that America's soul is not for sale.

Over the past decade the United States has often held up Turkey as the model of a moderate, democratic ally in the Muslim world, serving as a bridge between America and illiberal autocracies in the Middle East.[210] President Barack Obama used to publicly showcase a warm working relationship with President Erdogan even as he dismantled Turkish democracy and media freedoms.

Today, that idealism has been washed away by Erdogan's authoritarian rule, persecution of his political opponents, support of terrorism, and anti-Semitism.

Of course, it's not uncommon for our nation to hold its nose when dealing with thuggish autocrats in the face of pressing global crises. But in denying the Armenian Genocide, America was selling its moral soul to hold on to a man whose increasing tyranny is antithetical to all American values.

In recent history, Turkey has pulled every lever of influence at its disposal to prevent formal acknowledgment by the United States that Ottoman Turkey slaughtered 1.5 million Christian-minority Armenians under the cover of a world war and its aftermath. America's concession to this morally bankrupt stipulation for good relations set a gut-wrenching precedent of turning a blind eye to genocide.

Consider the words of Adolf Hitler to Nazi officers in August 1939, a week before the invasion of Poland: "Go, kill without mercy... who, after all, speaks today of the annihilation of the Armenians?"

Evil doesn't happen in a vacuum but, rather, incubates amid the silence of bystanders. As Edmund Burke famously said, "The only thing necessary for the triumph of evil is for good men to do nothing."

The Armenian Genocide was Hitler's proof-of-concept for his belief that the world has a short memory and would be largely indifferent to unspeakable horrors.

Once examined thoroughly, the connections between the Nazis and the Young Turks are troubling. Hitler's confidants learned from Turkey's genocidal playbook. As Hitler strategized his rise to power in the early 1920s, his lead political adviser was Max Erwin von Scheubner-Richter, a young German consular office in Erzurum during World War I, a region of Ottoman Turkey densely populated with Armenians.

Scheubner-Richter saw the galvanizing, nationalistic effect of blaming a well-educated, affluent religious minority for a nation's woes. He witnessed the strategy of rounding up dissident intellectuals and political leaders first and the use of starvation as a means for mass slaughter.

Although Scheubner-Richter died literally marching arm in arm with Hitler in the Beer Hall Putsch of November 1923, he was so influential to Hitler's thinking that the latter dedicated the first part of *Mein Kampf* to him and later singled him out as the only "irreplaceable loss" of the Putsch.

It wasn't only Nazi elites that took notes from Turkey. Turkey's ethnic cleansing in World War I was well known and admired by Nazi ideologues. In 1923, journalist Hans Trobst wrote in the Nazi newspaper *Heimatland*, "These bloodsuckers and parasites, Greeks and Armenians, had been eradicated by the Turks." This chilling praise of genocide foretold atrocities to come.

Turkey's approach to its own genocide has been the precise opposite of Germany's efforts at atonement and reconciliation. In recent years, Turkey charged scholars and journalists with crimes for "insulting Turkishness" by speaking of genocide. In a chilling and terrifying example of blaming the victim, high school textbooks in Turkey today refer to the "Armenian matter" (the word "genocide" is never used) and describe it as being the result of provocation by Armenians.

Insinuations of genocide are said to be a lie used in an attempt to harm and break up Turkey.

The "Armenian matter" isn't the only area where Erdogan has displayed detachment from reality. He aggressively contests the claim that atrocities in Darfur were genocide, yet he libeled Israel as being guilty of an attempted "genocide" during its air campaign against Hamas in 2014 and called Zionism a "crime against humanity" in 2013. In July of last year he disgraced himself further with the stomach-turning charge that Israel's "barbarism has surpassed even Hitler's."

This wretched anti-Semitic fervor continued with Turkey welcoming the relocation of Hamas's so-called West Bank and Jerusalem headquarters to Istanbul in 2015, even while the genocidal Hamas charter calls for the murder of Jews wherever they may be found. And rather than demonstrating even a hint of sympathy after the bloody Paris terrorist attacks took the lives of four Jews guilty only of buying bread for the Sabbath, Turkish Prime Minister Ahmet Davutoglu equated Prime Minister Benjamin Netanyahu to the terrorists who carried out the attacks.

Until this past Saturday, when Biden—who also courageously labeled Erdogan an autocrat—reversed course and recognized the Armenian Genocide, the United States was refusing to challenge a country that not only denies its own guilt in genocide but aids and abets organizations committed to the repetition of this most horrific of all human sins.

In standing up for truth and justice, Biden has deeply shamed his predecessor Obama, who had campaigned extensively in the Armenian-American community with his promises to recognize the genocide, which he ultimately refused to do. The Obama White House demonstrated its own faulty moral compass by both ignoring the intensifying anti-Semitism of its NATO "ally" and by refusing to acknowledge the Armenian Genocide.

While Obama supported formal recognition of the Armenian Genocide as a senator and made promises to Armenian-Americans to recognize the genocide while seeking their votes in 2008, he failed to live up to this promise over the eight years of his presidency; and while Donald Trump—Israel's great friend—did not promise to recognize the genocide, his White House could and should have done so. It was embarrassing to think that America seemed to cower at the thought of an autocrat's displeasure.

I cannot begin to imagine the pain of the Armenian community of having to suffer—especially in 2015 at the centenary of the Armenian genocide—the final indignity: that after the murder of 1.5 million innocent victims, the world refused to acknowledge their deaths; that after being robbed of their lives, the victims were robbed of their memory.

When we dishonor the lives of the Armenians killed, we embolden those who would commit unspeakable evil, much in the way Hitler was emboldened by the world's indifference to this dress rehearsal for the Holocaust.

Obama could have used the 100th anniversary of the genocide in 2015 as an opportunity to finally place the United States on the right side of history and morality and make it clear to Turkey that its choices have consequences. Sadly, he chose to do precisely the opposite. After intense lobbying by the Armenian-American community, to whom he made a campaign promise in 2008 that "as president I will recognize the Armenian Genocide," the White House announced three days before the centenary that the president would break his promise for the sixth year running.

Now, to his eternal credit, Biden has righted the wrong of the president under whom he served—and, indeed, of all his predecessors since the Second World War, when the term "genocide" was established after the Holocaust—and removed the stain of denial from the United States.

Erdogan is only one really bad actor. The list of evildoers we need to resist is a long one. As we discussed earlier, the tactics must be calibrated to both the degree of the threat and the capacity to achieve a decisive outcome. Kosher Hate is not omnipotent. We don't have God's power so our limited might must be deployed judiciously against the worst offenders that we can defeat without unnecessary loss of life. So, let me divide the world accordingly.

Under the category of evil regimes that we have a limited capacity to fight, I would include North Korea, Russia, China, and Iran. The principal impediment to defeating each is their nuclear capability. No American president is going to risk a confrontation that could escalate to a nuclear war.

Kim Jong-un presides over a Stalinist-style dictatorship that has starved to death hundreds of thousands of its own citizens. He is lionized as a deity even as he reached a level of sickening evil that saw him use an anti-aircraft gun to murder his own uncle in a public spectacle.[211]

Though mutually assured destruction is not a threat in the case of North Korea, we still have limited options for eliminating the evil Kim dynasty. North Korea does have nuclear weapons and has been trying to develop an intercontinental ballistic missile (ICBM) that could reach the United States with a nuclear warhead. The more immediate concern is that any military action against North Korea would trigger what is widely seen as a devastating attack on South Korea and our troops stationed there.

Because of Kim Jong-un's unpredictability and fanaticism, North Korea may be the most dangerous regime on the planet. Obama had warned Donald Trump that Kim could succeed in building an ICBM with a nuclear warhead that could reach the United States. In 2017, before agreeing to a summit, Trump exhibited Kosher Hate when he threatened to unleash "fire and fury" on North Korea, which led to concerns that we were on the brink of nuclear war.[212] Still, I was proud of our president for standing up to the tyrant.

Bizarrely, however, Trump abruptly changed tactics when he agreed to meet Kim in February 2019, hoping to seduce the monstrous dictator with words. He agreed to a historic meeting with Kim without preconditions, breaking with the policy of his predecessor and bestowing legitimacy on the person he had derisively referred to as "Little Rocket Man."[213] Defense Secretary James Mattis thought Trump's mocking was "unproductive, childish and dangerous."[214] Nevertheless, Trump's confidence in his deal-making skills convinced him he could succeed where others had failed in convincing Kim to accept denuclearization. Trump deserves immense credit for never removing the sanctions against North Korea after Kim refused to denuclearize, even as such action could have created a false peace that might conceivably have yielded Trump a Nobel Peace Prize. Still, Trump had little chance of success, because Kim believes his survival depends on his possession of nuclear weapons—he already has twenty to sixty—and the protection they give him against a U.S. attack.[215]

Former National Security Adviser John Bolton wrote in his recent memoir of the Trump administration that the president was "prepared to sign a substance-free communique, have a press conference to declare victory," and then leave the first summit.[216] That would have been terrible. The meeting would have given this evil man the legitimization he craved with the United States getting nothing in return. This would have rendered him even more dangerous.

Still, I think this is too unfair to President Trump. Yes, he met with the brutal tyrant from North Korea, and yes, he said nice things about him. But no, he never gave him any concessions, save halting some American-South Korean military exercises, which for Trump was probably about America not being "ripped off" for other nation's military expenses, than anything else. Trump never lifted any sanctions. Still, I would have been much more comfortable with Trump not giving any legitimacy to Kim Jong Un. But when it comes to possible nuclear war, we have to extend ourselves in negotiation, so long as we never make any material concessions, as President Obama did with the 2015 Iran deal.

I know that others felt differently.

"They were never offering to disarm," according to Jeffrey Lewis, a nonproliferation expert at the Middlebury Institute of International Studies at Monterey. "What they were offering to do was to give Trump good news stories for his political campaign, in exchange for sanctions relief."[217]

Nevertheless, Trump declared that Americans can "sleep well at night" because "there is no longer a Nuclear Threat from North Korea," intimating that North Korea was prepared to give up its nuclear weapons.[218] Trump spoke of Kim as if they were engaged more in courtship than nuclear diplomacy. On the first night of the summit with Kim, for example, he said, "Our relationship is a very special relationship." At a rally in West Virginia, he gushed that Kim "wrote me beautiful letters" and "we fell in love."[219]

His praise of the dictator made me very uncomfortable and it got worse when we learned the president exchanged at least twenty-five "love letters" with Kim. On June 12, 2019, for example, Trump wrote: "You and I have a unique style and a special friendship." He added, "Being with you was truly amazing," adding, "Only you and I, working together, can resolve the issues between our two countries and end nearly 70 years of hostility, bringing an era of prosperity to the Korean Peninsula that will exceed all our greatest expectations—and you will be the one to lead. It will be historic!"[220]

Discussing the letters in his book *Rage*, Bob Woodward said CIA analysts "marveled at the skill someone brought to finding the exact mixture of flattery while appealing to Trump's sense of grandiosity and being center stage in history."[221] Hence, it is not surprising the North Koreans "think they've got Trump's number" in the words of Susan Thornton, who served as acting assistant secretary of state for East Asia and the Pacific under Trump (other advisers said the same about Russia's Vladimir Putin).[222]

One can imagine that if Roosevelt had swapped flattering letters with Hitler and announced they fell in love, the American public would have thought the president had lost his mind. Still, Trump never made any concessions to North Korea and held the line on economic sanctions. Trump uncomfortably flattered evil, but never appeased Kim in the way Chamberlain did, sacrificing Czechoslovakia in the fanciful hope that Hitler would be pacified. Trump canceled joint

U.S. and South Korean military exercises but maintained sanctions that crippled North Korea's economy. North Korea did release five Americans Kim had jailed. One, Otto Warmbier, a college student imprisoned for more than a year, was returned in a vegetative state believed to be the result of torture and died six days later.

Disappointingly, Trump said he believed Kim's claim that North Korea was not responsible for his death. Reminiscent of when he stood next to Vladimir Putin and said he believed the Russian over his own intelligence agencies regarding Russian interference in the 2016 election, Trump said of Kim, "He tells me that he didn't know about it and I will take him at his word." Warmbier's parents excoriated the president for making excuses for "Kim and his evil regime." Senator Sherrod Brown said: "North Korea murdered Otto Warmbier and the president of the United States has a responsibility to make sure they face the consequences. Anything short of that is unacceptable."[223]

Following the public uproar over his comments Trump said, "Of course I hold North Korea responsible for Otto's mistreatment and death," adding: "I love Otto and think of him often!" But he did nothing to punish North Korea for his murder.

I respect President Trump for attempting to cajole and persuade Kim to give up his nuclear weapons. But I respect him even more for never removing sanctions in the naïve belief that Kim would ever do so. But Trump was wrong to speak so warmly about a killer like Kim or write "love letters" to the Korean dictator. If ever a man deserved to be the target of Kosher Hate it is Kim Jong-un, a leader (like his father Kim Jong-il) who starves his people, puts disobedient citizens in concentration camps, and executes his domestic enemies.

Hatred of evil doesn't mean we never engage the perpetrators; it means that we seek to repulse, stop, and neutralize their actions. Unfortunately, in this case, Trump's engagement failed to achieve those goals as Kim retained his weapons and advanced his ballistic missile program. God willing, sanctions may yet have the effect of bringing down the regime or at least forcing Kim to choose between survival and continued belligerence.

Trump sent a powerful message, for which he deserves enormous praise, when he ordered an air strike to punish President Hafez al-Assad for gassing his own citizens. He should also be universally commended for approving the killing of arch-terrorist, Qassem Soleimani, a major general in the Islamic Revolutionary Guard Corps who help direct Iran's proxy wars in Iraq, Syria, Lebanon, and Yemen.

On the other hand, he failed to follow through in the application of Kosher Hate when, at the last minute, he called off a strike in June 2019 to retaliate against Iran for shooting down a U.S. surveillance drone. At the beginning of 2020, Trump threatened to unhesitatingly unleash a disproportionate response with "brand new beautiful" weapons if Iran attacked U.S. forces, but did nothing when Iran fired ballistic missiles at two U.S. bases in Iraq.[224] His unwillingness to follow through on his threats was a serious error, reminiscent of Obama's failure to enforce his "red line" in Syria, which emboldens Iran and makes regional allies question America's resolve.

What do we do about an increasingly aggressive Russia? Former U.S. Ambassador to Moscow Michael McFaul summarized who we are dealing with:

> Vladimir Putin is evil. Over the past 20 years, Russia's current leader has constructed a ruthless dictatorship.[225] He has shut down independent media and civil society organizations, and he has arrested crit-

ics and business leaders who dare to challenge his unconstrained powers. Abroad, Putin has annexed Ukrainian territory, sent troops to Syria to prop up one the most brutal dictators of our time, violated American sovereignty in 2016 to try to influence the outcome of our presidential election, and is interfering again in our election now. At home and abroad, Putin's regime and its proxies have repeatedly killed, or tried to kill, its critics.

Under President Trump, the U.S. imposed sanctions on Russia, but the president was unwilling to publicly criticize him during his entire term in office. Critics suggested, without proof, that the Russians had information to blackmail him or that he colluded with them to win reelection. This was pure slander as it was never substantiated. But rather than condemning Russia's aggression in Crimea, for which Russia was expelled from the G7, Trump wanted to reinvite Putin to the group's next meeting over the opposition of the other members. He stood next to the autocrat and said he believed Putin's denial of interfering in the 2016 election over his own intelligence services. This was a serious mistake. After stories surfaced that Russia was paying bounties for Taliban fighters to kill American troops, he dismissed them as "fake news" and ignored advice to publicly warn Putin of severe consequences if Russia did any such thing. He failed to act in the other cases cited by McFaul who was writing just after Putin poisoned one of his critics without any response from the president. In addition, McFaul said past leaders stood up for American values when meeting with Soviet and Russian leaders by meeting with dissidents. To his knowledge, he said, "Trump has never praised, let alone met with, activists or opposition leaders in Russia, Ukraine or Belarus."[226]

It pains me to agree with McFaul when he wrote, "In an earlier period in American history, our government and people would have stood united on the side of good in this fight against evil. There was no partisan divide when it came to standing up for heroes and standing against villains. Yes, U.S. presidents sometimes had to negotiate with dictators to advance American national interests. And yes, there have often been cases in which we failed to defend those who were doing the right thing. But even when we were not doing enough to embrace good and stand up to evil, previous U.S. presidents knew they were in the wrong."

Given that we are not prepared to use force against Russia, we are limited in our response largely to economic sanctions, public denunciation, and containment. We long have had troops stationed in Germany and talked about deploying missiles in Poland as a deterrent to Russian aggression. Trump, however, ordered the withdrawal of soldiers from Germany over congressional objections. I understand that he felt American taxpayers were being ripped off by all these troop deployments to defend others, but maintaining a strong presence in Europe as a deterrent to Russia remains essential and I would hope and expect President Biden to reverse the decision.

Thus far President Biden has shown strength in his posture toward Iran by refusing to remove sanctions to bring them to the table, a precondition the Iranians are demanding. Nevertheless, his administration's comments about wanting to revive the disastrously flawed JCPOA are concerning. Biden's foreign policy should be guided by the philosophy of Kosher Hate and vehemently oppose Iranian genocidal intent against Israel. He should make it clear he will never negotiate with the regime until they repudiate completely their calls for a second holocaust.

Likewise, Biden has it in his power to make the promotion of human rights and democracy—in Turkey, China, and North Korea—a central plank of his administration. Biden has already made the mistake of rejoining the United Nations Human Rights Commission, correctly abandoned by Trump, without first demanding their reform. Showing Kosher Hate to regimes who persecute their citizens and slaughter pro-democracy advocates is critical to turning around the UN from a protector of dictatorships into a forum for freedom.

China is another difficult case as we are not prepared to risk a nuclear war over the evils of that Communist regime. We cannot be silent, however, when we know the Chinese have put hundreds of thousands of Uighur Muslims in concentration camps. I wish we could do more to stop them, but we are not completely impotent. Why, for example, don't we place restrictions on the importation of Chinese goods? I believe the president should say that we are prepared to pay a bit more for our iPhones, our bedsheets, and our sneakers in response to China's human rights abuses. It may sound obvious, but we need to find other places to manufacture and purchase consumer goods that do not abuse their workers or other citizens.

Given the limited military options, besides various sanctions, we must focus on reaching nuclear arms agreements to reduce the arsenals in Russia, China, India, and Pakistan. Negotiations must be based on the Reagan doctrine: "trust, but verify." We must also do everything in our power to prevent other nations from joining the nuclear club. That means not only Iran but other Middle East states that have been looking for a nuclear option.[227]

Our top priority regarding nuclear weapons must be preventing Iran from getting the bomb. Iran is one of the greatest threats to world peace and I believe they will not hesitate to use a nuclear weapon against Israel if they acquire one. Once they have the bomb, we will have far more limited options and little leverage to prevent Iran from destabilizing the region further and advancing its goal of spreading its brand of radical Islam.

For the United States, Iran is dangerous but not an existential threat, so it is difficult to justify the cost in American blood and money of going to war. The Iranians have threatened to wipe Israel off the map, however, and would have the capability to do so should it acquire nuclear weapons. That is why Israel has made clear that it is prepared to do whatever is necessary to stop Iran from getting the bomb. It set precedents by destroying nuclear facilities in Iraq and Syria before the genocidal maniacs in those countries could produce one.

The United States still has good reason to take every measure short of war to sabotage Iran's nuclear program. To be successful, however, the threat of force must be credible, unlike under the Obama administration, which Iran never believed had the will to use force. President Trump took several positive steps—including pulling out of the nuclear deal, undertaking a "maximum pressure" campaign of sanctions that crippled the Iranian economy, and engaging in cyberwarfare. Unfortunately Europe, China, and Russia did not cooperate and worked assiduously to provide the Iranian regime a lifeline. China's $25 billion deal in 2020 threatened to undermine much of what Trump accomplished with sanctions.

Obama's failure to support the "green revolution" in Iran allowed it to be crushed in 2009. Trump failed to take advantage of the disaffection of the public as the economy collapsed due to his "maximum pressure" campaign, which saw the Iranian Riyal lose 80 percent of its value. Worse, Iran's effort to build a bomb accelerated under Trump as the Iranians continued their covert activities and began openly violating the terms of the nuclear agreement.

The Iranian case illustrates the limits to U.S. power and the need for cooperation from allies. Iran was only able to flout the JCPOA because Europe, Russia, and China refused to enforce the agreement by imposing "snapback sanctions" which Obama had promised as a way to win support for the deal in Congress.

We do have the capability, however, to have a greater impact on other countries, such as Syria. Bashar Assad is a sponsor of terrorism and drug trafficking who has murdered his own people with chemical weapons, killed tens of thousands more to hold onto power, and created a refugee crisis that threatens the stability of its neighbors. President Obama warned Assad against using chemical weapons and then did nothing after Assad did, which emboldened the dictator to continue his murderous campaign against civilians. President Trump made the same threat and carried it out, but only once and, worse, withdrew American troops from Syria. The leave allowed not only the slaughter of Syrians to continue but opened the door for Turkey to enter the war and wipe out our Kurdish allies who Erdogan considers terrorists.

To prevent Iran from establishing a foothold in Syria and smuggling weapons to Hezbollah, Israel has not hesitated to act, launching hundreds of attacks on convoys, weapons depots, and Iranian bases. It should not have to act alone as the Western nations all have an interest in preventing Iran from establishing a land bridge to Lebanon, providing support to Hezbollah terrorists, establishing bases from which to threaten Israel and the Gulf states, and destabilizing the region. Failing to act has undermined our strategic interests and allowed a humanitarian catastrophe.

What is holding us back? It is not difficult to make the case for hating Bashar Assad, but Obama and Trump wanted to withdraw America from the Middle East. The vacuum created by our isolationism inevitably is filled by our enemies.

In response to 9/11, we first fought in Iraq and then Afghanistan to defend ourselves against terrorism based on the belief it is better to fight terrorists there than here in America. However the Taliban, who protected the leaders of Al Qaeda, have survived against the mighty U.S. military in what is now our longest war. *New York Times* South Asia correspondent

Mujib Mashal noted, "The insurgency came to embrace a system of terrorism planning and attacks that kept the Afghan government under withering pressure, and to expand an illicit funding engine built on crime and drugs despite its roots in austere Islamic ideology" while changing "little of their harsh founding ideology." He added, "the second decade of the insurgency, the Taliban have been defined by the ruthlessness of their violence."[228]

To his credit, despite a desire to withdraw from the Middle East, Obama raised the number of U.S. troops in Afghanistan to near 100,000. Still, the Taliban have persisted. "The Taliban keep replacing their dead and wounded and delivering brutal violence," reports Mashal.

Trump also hoped to bring U.S. troops home from Afghanistan and reduced the force to about 12,000. After more than a year of negotiations, the U.S. reached an agreement with the Taliban in February 2020, laying out a timetable for American troops to withdraw from Afghanistan. The cost has been enormous—$2 trillion and the lives of more than 3,500 American and coalition troops from about forty nations, and tens of thousands of Afghans. Mashal compared the result to Vietnam. "In both," he observed, "a superpower bet heavily on brute strength and the lives of its young, then walked away with seemingly little to show." He said the deal is a result of "a dawning sense of futility, perhaps best demonstrated in the American acceptance of relatively small concessions from Taliban in the agreement, that has driven efforts of successive administrations to find a way out."[229]

The deal may yet fall apart, troops remain, and it is true the U.S. did not accomplish the goals of bringing democracy and the protection of human rights to the country. But America did not suffer further attacks on its shores from Al Qaeda. Though the Taliban refused to use the word "terrorist" to describe Al Qaeda in the agreement, the group committed to preventing future attacks, which was the principal objective of the war. Only time will tell if they will honor their promise.

Again, our response should be calibrated. We do not have to invade every country that is a threat to us or its own people. The United States, ideally working with allies, has a variety of tools—sanctions, cyberwarfare, special operations, drones, cruise missiles, and more, with the use of troops most often a last resort. We have also learned from experience it is important to convince the American people of the necessity of acting against evil. As I noted earlier, the public is skeptical of the justification for the use of force after the experiences in Vietnam and Iraq.

The wars in Iraq should have taught us several lessons. Unlike many Americans, I still believe we did the right thing by responding to Iraq's invasion of Kuwait and, subsequently, by ousting Saddam from power. Had George H. W. Bush killed Saddam, he might have risked the breakup of the coalition he built, but it also would have preempted the need to return to Iraq ten years later.

We also learned that winning the war is not enough if you do not have a postwar plan. In the Iraqi case, we strengthened Iran and created a vacuum filled by ISIS. We also learned the merit of the Powell Doctrine of using overwhelming force. The emphasis placed on Saddam having WMDs and then the failure to find any, illustrated the importance of government credibility. The lies told to the public during Vietnam created a level of distrust that was an impediment to supporting subsequent wars, which then was exacerbated by the Gulf War.

President Bush was criticized for adopting a preemptive war doctrine, but I believe that is exactly what we need to fight an evil leader who is about to commit genocide, or mass atrocities and human rights violations, or has done so already. Once the killing begins, it is still necessary to act, but historically our interventions have been too little and too late.

The Bible offers some guidance when God speaks to Abraham about the intention to destroy Sodom and Gomorrah. Abraham repeatedly implores God not to destroy the cities; first, if fifty righteous people can be found, then forty-five, and he continues to reduce the number down to ten. Each time God agrees he will spare the cities. When it is clear that not even ten righteous people remain, however, God destroys the cities because the outcry against these sinful places could not be ignored. When the outcry becomes so great that it cannot be ignored, as in Rwanda, Bosnia, or Saddam's Iraq we cannot look the other way; we must act.

There is a high cost to failure. Besides the lives lost in what many people see as needless wars, we are gun shy about using force when we should, as in the case of Obama failing to respond to Syria's use of chemical weapons. Worse, when Assad did it again after Obama drew a "red line," U.S. credibility in the region was shot.

We should have removed Assad. I know many people, including some in Israel, prefer the devil they know to the one who might replace him, but could there be someone worse than this mass murderer?

The resistance to war will not be easily overcome in the future. George W. Bush should have made the case that there comes a time when aggressors are so evil good people cannot look the other way. Saddam killed more people than almost anyone in the last half century and should have been removed for that reason alone. While we can't remove every dictator, we can make an example of the worst murderers. We have learned the hard way it is impossible to impose democracy, but we can at least create the possibility by eliminating some of the obstacles. If we are successful, it is rewarding for us and for those we helped. Remember how excited the Iraqi people were when they held the first democratic election after the war? People were proudly showing the blue ink on their fingers from casting their votes for the first time in their lives.

All parties to a conflict are not equal. They may indeed love their children, as Sting put it in his song, but that does not mean some are not prepared to sacrifice their lives for a misguided cause. How else do you explain the willingness of mothers to allow their children to be used by Islamists as human bombs? Think about the carnage that could have been prevented if the mothers of the 9/11 bombers loved their children enough to stop them from joining Al Qaeda. Instead of marching to the border fence with Israel to throw Molotov cocktails and shoot at soldiers, what if Palestinian mothers marched by the thousands in Gaza's cities to protest Hamas recruiting their children and the cynical leaders willing to use them as cannon fodder?

To reiterate, Kosher Hate is not an extremist ideology. It does not say to go to war as a first resort. To the contrary, no one wants to see soldiers die. Yes, there can be a high cost to resorting to violence, but we must always weight it against the potentially greater price of inaction.

I have always wished that goodness could triumph through the strength of its own virtue and would not necessitate violence to be victorious. But if this is the only way for innocence and righteousness to prevail, then I will happily cast aside my fear of a permanently dualistic world and work to build a more lasting Godly kingdom on this earth in which evil is finally defeated.

Until now, no country, not even the United States, could be trusted to prevent genocide. Even as presidents have championed democracy, we have too often failed to act or to intercede in time to save lives. We have limited resources and cannot intervene everywhere though we have long had a military doctrine of being able to fight two and a half wars (two major and one limited) simultaneously, with the focus on Russia and China.

We must be cognizant that deploying troops to one area of the world means they are not available if needed to fight our most dangerous foes. But America should not have to be the lonely world cop. If so many other countries, especially in Europe, were not so feckless, we could depend on them to join the fight. We have a structure for keeping autocrats in check—NATO—but its mission must be redefined to contribute to the global battle against evil. Surely, the thirty member states have the resources to police the world.

The United States cannot be deterred by global criticism, moral ambiguity, or isolationism from using its God-given blessings to make the world more just, democratic, and free. America, along with its allies, liberated Europe from Hitler, stopped Japanese imperialism, rolled back North Korean aggression, and ended the Cold War. America continues to preach the values of Sinai and the Ten Commandments more than any other nation.

Let me reiterate that no one, including me, wants war but we should treat evil like the cancer it is. Nobody wants surgery, but sometimes radiation and chemotherapy are not enough to stop it from spreading. At some point the patient must decide whether to continue to fight and undergo surgery, or to succumb. We do not have a choice. We cannot surrender to evil.

Former ambassador McFaul got it right when he wrote:

> American indifference to evil has consequences. It emboldens the villains and weakens the heroes. But sometimes presidents must say and do things—for example, to impose sanctions on Alexander Lukashenko for stealing an election in Belarus, to criticize Putin for aiding the Taliban, to signal solidarity with Navalny [the poisoned Russian dissident] and offer assistance as European leaders have—not because these actions might be effective, but because they are right. In a world divided by good and evil, it's time for America to get back on the right side.[230]

Hollywood can do what our leaders cannot: make us hate villains. Whether it's war movies, superhero franchises, or horror flicks, we are usually riveted to our seats waiting for the hero to exact vengeance or bring the criminal to justice. The minute we leave the theater, however, we forget about the evil in our world.

We cannot depend on our leaders to do the right thing. Generals are, paradoxically, reluctant to go to war. Less surprisingly, politicians too often base their decisions of how to confront evil on how they believe it will affect their chances for reelection. Except for the attacks on Pearl Harbor and 9/11, the American public has not been sufficiently roused by the perpetrators of evil to pressure their representatives to act. Therefore, education is vital, because if the public is not conditioned to believe the necessity of fighting evil it will be too easy for policymakers to ignore or minimize the danger.

We do our youth no favors by teaching them phony universalistic ideas, like all people have the same attitudes toward humanity. Teachers cannot be afraid to express fact-based opinions that distinguish, for example, between terrorists and freedom fighters. They should not contort themselves to avoid defining and identifying evil. Educators, politicians, and faith leaders must all reiterate over and over the values we hold dear and vilify those who would abuse or take them away.

More than ever before, the world's future depends on a return to religious morality with its strict emphasis on loving goodness and hating evil. Yes, I subscribe to the mystical idea that everything is of God and that divine sparks inhabit every part of creation. Grotesque evil must be combated, however, before goodness and innocence perish. Religion is no longer a way for the narcissistic personality to cleanse itself after a life of material indulgence and workaholism. Rather, it is a social necessity to guide our kosher hatred without which the diseases plaguing our society will never heal.

To paraphrase John F. Kennedy, we must choose Kosher Hate not because it is easy but because it is hard, because it is an emotion we are willing to accept, and because it is necessary to eradicate evil.

Is my prescription feasible? To answer, I quote Nelson Mandela, "It always seems impossible until it's done."[231]

Let me end where I began, with Edmund Burke's warning that all it takes for evil to succeed is for good people to do nothing. Kosher Hate ensures that we will not be indifferent to suffering, human rights abuses, and genocide. Hatred is a powerful emotion that can motivate us to act. I also know that it is temporary. Once democracy and freedom spread throughout the world, and human rights are respected by all, we can finally build a world whose foundation is love.

ENDNOTES

1   Natan Sharansky, "Antisemitism in 3-D," *Forward*, January 21, 2005, https://forward.com/opinion/4184/antisemitism-in-3-d/.

2   UN Watch, https://unwatch.org/.

3   "WHO Meeting Deviates From COVID-19 to Single Out Israel As Violator of Health Rights," UN Watch, May 26, 2021, https://unwatch.org/who-meeting-deviates-from-covid-19-to-single-out-israel-as-violator-of-health-rights-2/.

4   Nicole Chavez, Brynn Gingras and Kristina Sgueglia, "Anti-Semitic attacks are being reported in US cities as tensions flare over the Israeli-Palestinian conflict," CNN, May 21, 2021, https://www.cnn.com/2021/05/21/us/anti-semitic-attacks-new-york-los-angeles/index.html.

5   Tobias Buck, "Anti-Semitism prompts 40% of European Jews to consider emigration," *Financial Times*, December 10, 2018, https://www.ft.com/content/a8f26a56-fc62-11e8-aebf-99e208d3e521.

6   "2021 Survey on Jewish Americans' Experiences with Antisemitism," ADL, March 31, 2021, https://www.adl.org/blog/2021-survey-on-jewish-americans-experiences-with-antisemitism.

7   The White House, December 11, 2019, https://www.whitehouse.gov/presidential-actions/executive-order-combating-anti-semitism/.

8   "QAnon," ADL, accessed June 6, 2021, https://www.adl.org/qanon.

9   "Understanding QAnon's Connection to American Politics, Religion, and Media Consumption," PRRI, May 27, 2021, https://www.prri.org/research/qanon-conspiracy-american-politics-report/.

10 Hannah Sparks, "With an estimated 30M followers, QAnon as popular as some religions: poll," *New York Post*, (May 28, 2021) https://nypost.com/2021/05/28/with-30m-followers-qanon-as-popular-as-some-religions-poll/.

11 Ilhan Omar (@IlhanMN), May 10, 2021, accessed June 6, 2021, https://twitter.com/IlhanMN/status/1391841207588999168.

12 Jacob Magid, "Democratic leadership slams AIPAC for attack ad targeting Ilhan Omar," *Times of Israel*, May 20, 2021, https://www.timesofisrael.com/liveblog_entry/democratic-leadership-slams-aipac-for-attack-ad-targeting-ilhan-omar/.

13 Mitchell Bard, "Intersectionality and Israel," Jewish Virtual Library, accessed June 6, 2021, https://www.jewishvirtuallibrary.org/intersectionality-and-israel.

14 Ziva Dahl, "'Intersectionality' and the Bizarre World of Hating Israel," *Observer*, March 15, 2016, https://observer.com/2016/03/intersectionality-and-the-bizarre-world-of-hating-israel/.

15 Emma Green, "Why Do Black Activists Care About Palestine?" *The Atlantic*, August 18, 2016, https://www.theatlantic.com/politics/archive/2016/08/why-did-black-american-activists-start-caring-about-palestine/496088/.

16 Samuel Chamberlain, "BLM co-founder called in 2015 to 'end imperialist project' of Israel," *New York Post*, May 30, 2021, https://nypost.com/2021/05/30/blm-co-founder-called-to-end-imperialist-project-of-israel/.

17 Black Lives Matter (@Blklivesmatter), "Black Lives Matter Stands," Twitter, May 17, 2021, 8:52 a.m., https://twitter.com/Blklivesmatter/status/1394289672101064704.

18 BDS Movement (@BDSmovement), "Thank You," Twitter, May 18, 2021, 4:00 a.m., https://twitter.com/BDSmovement/status/1394578742920552453.

19 John-Paul Pagano, "The Women's March Has a Farrakhan Problem," *The Atlantic*, March 8, 2018, https://www.theatlantic.com/politics/archive/2018/03/womens-march/555122/.

20 James Kirchick, "Dykes Vs. Kikes," *Tablet*, June 26, 2017, https://www.tabletmag.com/sections/news/articles/dykes-vs-kikes.

21 Aiden Pink, "DC Dyke March Bans Jewish Pride Flag," *Forward*, June 6, 2019, https://forward.com/fast-forward/425533/dc-dyke-march-bans-jewish-pride-flag/.

22 Farah Stockman, "Women's March Roiled by Accusations of Anti-Semitism," *New York Time*s, (December 23, 2018) https://www.nytimes.com/2018/12/23/us/womens-march-anti-semitism.html; Stockman, "Three Leaders of Women's March Group Step Down After Controversies," *New York Times*, September 16, 2019, https://www.nytimes.com/2019/09/16/us/womens-march-anti-semitism.html.

23 "Preliminary ADL Data Reveals Uptick in Antisemitic Incidents Linked to Recent Mideast Violence," ADL, May 20, 2021, https://www.adl.org/news/press-releases/preliminary-adl-data-reveals-uptick-in-antisemitic-incidents-linked-to-recent.

24 "Global Public Opinion in the Bush Years (2001-2008)," Pew Research Center, December 18, 2008, https://www.pewresearch.org/global/2008/12/18/global-public-opinion-in-the-bush-years-2001-2008/.

25 Lydia Saad, "U.S. Conservatism Down Since Start of 2020," Gallup, July 27, 2020, https://news.gallup.com/poll/316094/conservatism-down-start-2020.aspx.

26 "Views about religion in American society," Pew Research Center, March 12, 2020, https://www.pewforum.org/2020/03/12/views-about-religion-in-american-society/.

27 Todd Gitlin, "Frantz Fanon Is the Manichaean Prophet of Today's Middle East," *Tablet*, December 8, 2014, https://www.tabletmag.com/sections/israel-middle-east/articles/frantz-fanon-me.

28 Philip Gourevitch, *We Wish to Inform You That Tomorrow We Will Be Killed With Our Families*, (New York: Farrar, Straus & Giroux, 1998).

29 Jim Geraghty, "Susan Rice, April 1994: 'If we use the word 'genocide' and are seen as doing nothing, what will be the effect on the November [congressional] election?'" *National Review*, June 18, 2008, https://www.nationalreview.com/the-campaign-spot/susan-rice-april-1994-if-we-use-word-genocide-and-are-seen-doing-nothing-what/.

30 John Darnton, "Revisiting Rwanda's Horrors With an Ex-National Security Adviser," *New York Times*, December 20, 2004, https://www.nytimes.com/2004/12/20/movies/revisiting-rwandas-horrors-with-an-exnational-security-adviser.html.

31 Ivo H. Daalder, "Decision to Intervene: How the War in Bosnia Ended," Brookings, December 1, 1998, https://www.brookings.edu/articles/decision-to-intervene-how-the-war-in-bosnia-ended/.

32 President Bill Clinton, address to the nation, Washington, D.C., March 24, 1999.

33 Tony Blair: "'We must act - to save thousands of innocent men, women and children,'" *The Guardian*, March 23, 1999, https://www.theguardian.com/world/1999/mar/23/balkans.tonyblair.

34 David Clark, "Kosovo was a just war, not an imperialist dress rehearsal," *The Guardian*, April 15, 2009, https://www.theguardian.com/commentisfree/2009/apr/16/clark-kosovo-war-crimes.

35 Ibid.

36 Charles Krauthammer, "The Consequences Of Clinton's 'Little Kosovo War,'" *Chicago Tribune*, April 5, 1999, https://www.chicagotribune.com/news/ct-xpm-1999-04-05-9904050119-story.html.

37 Susan Sontag, "Why Are We in Kosovo?" *New York Times*, May 2, 1999, https://www.nytimes.com/1999/05/02/magazine/why-are-we-in-kosovo.html.

38 "Martin Niemoeller: The Failure to Speak Up Against the Nazis," Jewish Virtual Li-

brary, accessed May 27, 2021, https://www.jewishvirtuallibrary.org/martin-niemoeller-the-failure-to-speak-up-against-the-nazis.

39 Sontag, *New York Times*, May 2, 1999, https://archive.nytimes.com/www.nytimes.com/books/00/03/12/specials/sontag-kosovo.html.

40 David Konstan, *The Emotions of the Ancient Greeks: Studies in Aristotle and Classical Literature* (Toronto: University of Toronto Press, 2007).

41 "Former President Bush: 'I hate Saddam,'" CNN, September 18, 2002, https://www.cnn.com/2002/ALLPOLITICS/09/18/elder.bush.saddam/.

42 Hannah Arendt, "Eichmann in Jerusalem," *The New Yorker*, February 9, 1963.

43 Jude Sheerin, "Matthew Shepard: The murder that changed America," BBC News, October 26, 2018, https://www.bbc.com/news/world-us-canada-45968606.

44 Mary Anne Weaver, "The Short, Violent Life of Abu Musab al-Zarqawi,' *The Atlantic*, July/August 2006, https://www.theatlantic.com/magazine/archive/2006/07/the-short-violent-life-of-abu-musab-al-zarqawi/304983/.

45 Jeff Robinson, "Does Jesus Really Want Me to Hate My Family?" TGC, March 8, 2018, https://www.thegospelcoalition.org/article/does-jesus-want-hate-family/.

46 "What did Christ mean when He said, 'If anyone comes to Me and does not hate his father and mother, wife and children, brothers and sisters, yes, and his own life also, he cannot be My disciple'?" The Restored Church of God, accessed December 23, 2020, https://rcg.org/questions/p102.a.html.

47 Jen Wilkin, *In His Image*, (Wheaton: Crossway, 2018).

48 "Ask A Priest: Should We Not Love Evil People?" RC Spirituality, accessed December 23, 2020, https://rcspirituality.org/ask_a_priest/ask-a-priest-should-we-not-love-evil-people/.

49 "Do Christians Love Their Enemies Even Now?" United States Conference of Catholic Bishops, 2011, https://www.usccb.org/resources/do-christians-love-their-enemies-even-now.

50 Ibid.

51 Thomas Gumbleton, "Jesus shows us there is a special way of overcoming evil and violence," *National Catholic Reporter*, April 2, 2015, https://www.ncronline.org/blogs/peace-pulpit/jesus-shows-us-there-special-way-overcoming-evil-and-violence.

52 Bob Herbert, "The Lost Voice of Protest," *New York Times*, January 18, 2007, https://www.nytimes.com/2007/01/18/opinion/18herbert.html.

53 Mitchell G. Bard, *Forgotten Victims: The Abandonment of Americans in Hitler's Camps*, (Boulder: Westview Press, 1994).

54 "Marcionites," Catholic Online, accessed May 27, 2021, https://www.catholic.org/encyclopedia/view.php?id=7526.

55 Philip Schaff, "St. Augustine: Sermon on the Mount; Harmony of the Gospels; Homilies on the Gospels," *Christian Classics Ethereal Library*, accessed May 27, 2021, https://www.ccel.org/ccel/schaff/npnf106.v.ii.i.html.

56 Saint Augustine, *The Confessions*, (Oxford: Oxford University Press, 2009).

57 Philip Schaff, "St. Augustine's City of God and Christian Doctrine," *Christian Classics Ethereal Library*, accessed May 27, 2021, https://www.ccel.org/ccel/schaff/npnf102.iv.XIV.6.html.

58 Meir Y. Soloveichik, "The Virtue Of Hate," First Things, February 2003, https://www.firstthings.com/article/2003/02/the-virtue-of-hate.

59 "Pius XII," *New World Encyclopedia*, accessed May 27, 2021.

60 Martin Gilbert, *The Second World War: A Complete History*, (New York: Henry Holt And Co., 1992), 40, https://www.amazon.com/exec/obidos/ISBN=0805017887/theamericanisraeA/.

61 Israel Gutman, ed., Encyclopedia of the Holocaust, vol. 3. (New York: Macmillan, 1995), 1137, https://www.amazon.com/exec/obidos/ISBN=0028645278/theamericanisraeA/.

62 "Pope Pius XII and the Vatican Archives," Inside the Vatican, accessed September 22,

2020.

[63] Raul Hilberg, *The Destruction of the European Jews*. (New York: Holmes & Meier, 1985), 315.

[64] William R Perl, *The Holocaust Conspiracy: An International Policy of Genocide*, (New York: Shapolsky Publishers, 1989), 200.

[65] Paul Kengor, "The Fall Of Communism And John Paul II's Push," *Catholic Digest*, November 7, 2019, http://www.catholicdigest.com/news/nationworld/the-fall-of-communism-and-john-paul-iis-push/.

[66] John Barnes and Helen Whitney, "John Paul II and the Fall of Communism," *Frontline*, https://www.pbs.org/wgbh/pages/frontline/shows/pope/communism/.

[67] "Pope sends condolences to Palestinian people upon death of Yasser Arafat," Catholic News Agency, November 11, 2004, https://www.catholicnewsagency.com/news/pope_sends_condolences_to_palestinian_people_upon_death_of_yasser_arafat.

[68] "Vatican reiterates desire for two independent and reconciled states in Holy Land," Catholic News Agency, November 11, 2004, https://www.catholicnewsagency.com/news/vatican_reiterates_desire_for_two_independent_and_reconciled_states_in_holy_land.

[69] James Martin, "Vatican Statement on Death of Osama Bin Laden," *America*, May 2, 2011, https://www.americamagazine.org/content/all-things/vatican-statement-death-osama-bin-laden.

[70] Michelle Boorstein and Sarah Pulliam Bailey, "Still saintly? Vatican's new report on McCarrick may complicate the legacy of Pope John Paul II," *Washington Post*, November 11, 2020, https://www.washingtonpost.com/religion/2020/11/11/pope-john-paul-saint-mccarrick-report-legacy-francis/.

[71] "Pope appeals to London attackers, terrorists to stop," *The Catholic News & Herald*, July 22, 2005, https://issuu.com/catholicnewsherald/docs/cnh_issue_07_22_05.

[72] Ibid.

[73] William Safire, "ON LANGUAGE; No Shades of Gray," *New York Times*, June 12, 1988, https://www.nytimes.com/1988/06/12/magazine/on-language-no-shades-of-gray.html.

[74] Scott Manning, "Churchill's Earliest Warning About Hitler," Historian on the Warpath, March 8, 2011, https://scottmanning.com/content/churchills-earliest-warning-about-hitler/#footnote_5_198.

[75] Thomas Sowell, "A Churchill for Our Times," *National Review*, March 17, 2015, https://www.nationalreview.com/2015/03/churchill-our-times-thomas-sowell/.

[76] Scott Manning, "'Friendship with Germany' by Winston Churchill (Sep 17, 1937)," Historian on the Warpath, July 26, 2008, https://scottmanning.com/content/friendship-with-germany-by-winston-churchill-sep-17-1937/.

[77] "Meeting Hitler, 1932," The Churchill Project, March 5, 2015, https://winstonchurchill.hillsdale.edu/meeting-hitler-1932/.

[78] Scott Manning, "'Friendship with Germany' by Winston Churchill, Sep 17, 1937," Historian on the Warpath, July 26, 2008, https://scottmanning.com/content/friendship-with-germany-by-winston-churchill-sep-17-1937/.

[79] Winston S. Churchill, "Friendship with Germany," *Evening Standard*, September 17, 1937, https://scottmanning.com/content/friendship-with-germany-by-winston-churchill-sep-17-1937/.

[80] Ibid.

[81] Patrick J. Buchanan, *Churchill, Hitler, and the "Unnecessary War"* (New York: Crown Publishing Group, 2008), 174.

[82] Sir Winston S. Churchill, *Never Give In!* (London: A&C Black, 2013), 102–103.

[83] "Gathering Storm," National Churchill Museum, https://www.nationalchurchillmuseum.org/winston-churchill-and-the-gathering-storm.html.

[84] Richard M. Langworth, "Who tried to silence Churchill's 1930s Warnings about Nazi Germany?" The Churchill Project, June 5, 2018, https://winstonchurchill.hillsdale.edu/

churchills-1930s-warnings-nazi-germany/.

85 Thomas Sowell, "A Churchill for Our Times," *National Review*, March 17, 2015, https://www.nationalreview.com/2015/03/churchill-our-times-thomas-sowell/.

86 Jennifer Szalai, "In 'Appeasement,' How Peace With the Nazis Was Always an Illusion," *New York Times*, June 4, 2019, https://www.nytimes.com/2019/06/04/books/review-appeasement-chamberlain-hitler-churchill-tim-bouverie.html.

87 "Neville Chamberlain's "Peace For Our Time" speech," EuroDocs, September 30, 1938, https://eudocs.lib.byu.edu/index.php/Neville_Chamberlain's_%22Peace_For_Our_Time%22_speech.

88 "Gathering Storm," National Churchill Museum, https://www.nationalchurchillmuseum.org/winston-churchill-and-the-gathering-storm.html.

89 Ibid.

90 David T. Pyne, "How Nazi Germany Could Have Won the War in The West (Get Churchill to Make Peace?)," *The National Interest*, October 20, 2019, https://nationalinterest.org/blog/buzz/how-nazi-germany-could-have-won-war-west-get-churchill-make-peace-89691.

91 Von Klaus Wiegrefe, "How Winston Churchill Stopped the Nazis," *Spiegel International*, August 20, 2010, https://www.spiegel.de/international/europe/the-man-who-saved-europe-how-winston-churchill-stopped-the-nazis-a-712259.html.

92 See, for example, Mortimer B. Zuckerman, "Obama's Unforgivable Betrayal," *U.S. News & World Report*, April 17, 2015, https://www.usnews.com/opinion/articles/2015/04/17/obamas-iran-nuclear-deal-is-an-unforgivable-betrayal-of-israel; Charles Krauthammer, "The Worst Agreement in U.S. Diplomatic History," *National Review*, July 3, 2015, https://www.nationalreview.com/2015/07/iran-nuclear-deal-obama-sanctions-inspections-capitulates/.

93 Seung Min Kim And Burgess Everett, "Senate Dems block GOP measure to kill Iran deal," *Politico*, September 10, 2015, https://www.politico.com/story/2015/09/iran-deal-senate-dems-block-gop-measure-to-kill-213506; Erin Kelly, "Democrats block Senate vote to reject Iran nuclear deal for second time," *USA Today*, September 15, 2015, https://www.usatoday.com/story/news/2015/09/15/democrats-block-senate-vote-reject-iran-nuclear-deal-second-time/72317408/.

94 Mitchell Bard, "Israeli-Palestinian Peace Plans," Jewish Virtual Library, June 2006, accessed May 29, 2021, https://www.jewishvirtuallibrary.org/israeli-palestinian-peace-plans.

95 "Momentous Step Toward Mideast Peace: Knesset Approves Camp David Accords by Vote of 84-19 and 17 Abs," *JTA*, September 29, 1978, https://www.jta.org/1978/09/29/archive/momentous-step-toward-mideast-peace-knesset-approves-camp-david-accords-by-vote-of-84-19-and-17-abs.

96 Daniel Pipes, "If only America would let Israel win," *Jerusalem Post*, April 4, 2006, https://www.jpost.com/opinion/if-only-america-would-let-israel-win.

97 "Israel Victory Project," Middle East Forum, accessed December 19, 2020, https://www.meforum.org/israel-victory-project/.

98 Mitchell Bard, "There Was Never a Two-State Solution, It's Time to Move On," *Times of Israel*, January 17, 2017, https://blogs.timesofisrael.com/there-was-never-a-two-state-solution-its-time-to-move-on/.

99 Peter Baker, "How Obama Came to Plan for 'Surge' in Afghanistan," *New York Times*, December 5, 2009, https://www.nytimes.com/2009/12/06/world/asia/06reconstruct.html.

100 Mahatma Gandhi, *The Essential Gandhi: An Anthology of His Writings on His Life, Work, and Ideas*, (New York: Vintage Spiritual Classics, 1962), 181.

101 Mahatma Gandhi, Mind of Mahatma Gandhi, (India: Navajivan Trust, 1960) https://www.mkgandhi.org/momgandhi/chap28.htm.

102 Mahatma Gandhi, "The Jews," *Harijan*, November 26, 1938, http://circle.org/jsource/gandhi-on-nazism-and-the-jews/.

103 Ibid.

104 Ibid.

105 Martin Buber, "Open Letter to Gandhi Regarding Palestine," February 24, 1939, Jewish Virtual Library, accessed December 20, 2020, https://www.jewishvirtuallibrary.org/letter-from-martin-buber-to-gandhi.

106 Mahatma Gandhi, "No Apology," *Harijan*, February 5, 1939, https://www.jewishvirtuallibrary.org/quot-no-apology-quot-by-gandhi-gebruary-1939.

107 "Mohandas Gandhi's letter to Adolf Hitler, 1939," *The Guardian*, October 12, 2013, https://www.theguardian.com/culture/interactive/2013/oct/12/mohandas-gandhi-adolf-hitler-letter.

108 Aron Heller, "Unearthed Gandhi WWII letter wishes Jews 'era of peace,'" *AP*, September 24, 2019, https://apnews.com/article/f40d8c2c7d8d4ffeadd576ded89acc0c.

109 Mahatma Gandhi, "To Every Briton," *Harijan*, July 6, 1940, https://www.jewishvirtuallibrary.org/quot-no-apology-quot-by-gandhi-gebruary-1939.

110 Alex Ivanov, *Gandhi*, (New Word City, 2017).

111 Mahatma Gandhi, "Some Questions Answered," *Harijan*, December 17, 1938, http://circle.org/jsource/gandhi-on-nazism-and-the-jews/.

112 Harrison Jacobs, "Gandhi's 1940 letter to Adolf Hitler: Seek peace or someone will 'beat you with your own weapon,'" *Business Insider*, April 2, 2015, https://www.businessinsider.com/gandhis-1940-letter-to-adolf-hitler-2015-4.

113 Louis Fischer, *The Life of Mahatma Gandhi* (New York: Collier Books, 1950), quoted in Aron Heller, "Unearthed Gandhi WWII letter wishes Jews 'era of peace,'" *AP*, September 24 2019, https://abcnews.go.com/International/wireStory/unearthed-gandhi-wwii-letter-wishes-jews-era-peace-65821500.

114 Sarah Honig, "Impelled by filial piety?" *Jerusalem Post*, April 30, 2010, https://www.jpost.com/opinion/columnists/another-tack-impelled-by-filial-piety.

115 "The Tank Man," Frontline, April 11, 2006, https://www.pbs.org/wgbh/pages/frontline/tankman/etc/transcript.html.

116 Jeffrey T. Richelson and Michael L. Evans, Eds., "Tiananmen Square, 1989: The Declassified History," The National Security Archive, June 1, 1999, https://nsarchive2.gwu.edu/NSAEBB/NSAEBB16/#f8.

117 John L. Esposito and Dalia Mogahed, *Who Speaks for Islam? What a Billion Muslims Really Think*, (New York: Gallup Press, 2007).

118 Bard, *The Arab Lobby*, 295.

119 Robert Satloff, "Just Like Us! Really?" *Weekly Standard*, May 12, 2008, https://www.washingtoninstitute.org/policy-analysis/just-us-really.

120 Daniella Diaz, "Obama: Why I won't say 'Islamic terrorism,'" CNN, September 29, 2016, https://www.cnn.com/2016/09/28/politics/obama-radical-islamic-terrorism-cnn-town-hall/index.html.

121 "Remarks by President Trump in Joint Address to Congress," U.S. Embassy in Uruguay, February 28, 2017, https://www.whitehouse.gov/briefings-statements/remarks-president-trump-joint-address-congress/.

122 Eldad J. Pardo, "Review of Selected Saudi Textbooks 2020-21," IMPACT-se, December 2020, file:C://Users/MITCHELL/OneDrive/Wp60/JVL WP/Review of Selected Saudi Textbooks 2020-21 - Final.pdf.

123 "Saudi will seek nuclear arms if Iran gets them – report," *Reuters*, June 29, 2011, https://www.reuters.com/article/uk-saudi-iran-nuclear/saudi-will-seek-nuclear-arms-if-iran-gets-them-report-idUKTRE75S83X20110629.

124 Mitchell Bard, "Saudi Arabia's anti-Semitism is biggest obstacle to normalizing relations with Israel," *Fox News*, December 22, 2020, https://www.foxnews.com/opinion/saudi-arabia-israel-anti-semitism-mitchell-bard.

125 "Suspect in Paris knife attack confesses to stabbings," France 24, September 26, 2020, https://www.france24.com/en/20200926-suspect-in-paris-knife-attack-was-un-

kown-for-radicalisation.

[126] "France's Macron asks Muslim leaders to back 'republican values' charter," *BBC News*, November 19, 2020, https://www.bbc.com/news/world-europe-55001167.

[127] Bernard Lewis, *The Multiple Identities of the Middle East* (New York: Schocken Books, 1998), 121–122, https://www.amazon.com/exec/obidos/ISBN=0805211187/theamericanisraeA/.

[128] Mitchell Bard, *Myths and Facts: A Guide to the Arab-Israeli Conflict* (Chevy Chase: AICE, 2017), 331–332.

[129] Howard Kurtz, "Commentators Are Quick to Beat Their Pens into Swords," *Washington Post*, September 13, 2001, https://www.washingtonpost.com/archive/lifestyle/2001/09/13/commentators-are-quick-to-beat-their-pens-into-swords/cb4afb99-4125-418a-96d0-0a361603c400/.

[130] Raymond Ibrahim, "Why Muslims Think of Islam as a 'Religion of Peace,'" *American Thinker*, May 11, 2020, https://www.americanthinker.com/articles/2020/05/how_and_why_muslims_delude_themselves_about_islam.html.

[131] "Charles Lindbergh urges Congress to negotiate with Hitler," History, January 23, 1941, https://www.history.com/this-day-in-history/lindbergh-to-congress-negotiate-with-hitler.

[132] Lior Zaltzman, "The real history behind HBO's 'The Plot Against America,'" *JTA*, March 20, 2020, https://www.jta.org/2020/03/20/culture/true-story-the-plot-against-america-hbo-show.

[133] Susan Dunn, "The Debate Behind U.S. Intervention in World War II," *The Atlantic*, July 8, 2013, https://www.theatlantic.com/national/archive/2013/07/the-debate-behind-us-intervention-in-world-war-ii/277572/.

[134] Meir Y. Soloveichik, "The Virtue Of Hate," First Things, February 2003, https://www.firstthings.com/article/2003/02/the-virtue-of-hate.

[135] Ibid.

[136] Andrea Stone, "Proxy Baptism Seekers Eyed Holocaust Survivor Elie Wiesel For Posthumous Mormon Rite," *HuffPost*, February 14, 2020, https://www.huffpost.com/entry/proxy-baptism-elie-wiesel_n_1274271.

[137] Maurice S. Friedman, *Martin Buber's Life and Work*, vol. 1–3, (Detroit: Wayne State University Press, 1988), 278.

[138] Maurice S. Friedman, *Martin Buber: The Life of Dialogue*, (London: Routledge, 2003).

[139] Lisa Leff, "Peace mom's son remembered," *AP*, August 13, 2015, http://archive.decaturdaily.com/decaturdaily/news/050813/casey.shtml.

[140] Ibid.

[141] Richard W. Stevenson, "Mother Takes Protest to Bush's Ranch," *New York Times*, August 7, 2005.

[142] Sheila Samples, "The Revolution is NOW...," Countercurrents.org, August 11, 2005, https://countercurrents.org/us-samples110805.htm.

[143] "Crime Against Humanity," Cornell Law School, https://www.law.cornell.edu/wex/crime_against_humanity; "Crime Against Humanity," Trial International, https://trialinternational.org/topics-post/crimes-against-humanity/; Richard Vernon, "Crime Against Humanity," Encyclopædia Britannica, June 2, 2017, https://www.britannica.com/topic/crime-against-humanity.

[144] "U.S. Sisters Recall 7/7 Bombings," *AP*, July 22, 2005, https://www.foxnews.com/story/u-s-sisters-recall-7-7-bombings.

[145] Simon Wiesenthal, *The Sunflower*, (New York: Schocken Books, 1998), 97.

[146] "The Sunflower (book)," Wikipedia, https://en.wikipedia.org/wiki/The_Sunflower_(book).

[147] Simon Wiesenthal, *The Sunflower*, (New York: Schocken Books, 1998), 267–268.

[148] Meir Y. Soloveichik, "The Virtue Of Hate," First Things, February 2003, https://www.firstthings.com/article/2003/02/the-virtue-of-hate.

149 Ibid.

150 Debra Nussbaum Cohen, "The Nazi Victim Who Forgave Her Perpetrators," My Jewish Learning, accessed December 21, 2020, https://www.myjewishlearning.com/article/the-nazi-victim-who-forgave-her-perpetrators/.

151 *The Sunflower*, 98.

152 Julie Shapiro, "How Elie Wiesel Responded to Losing His Life Savings to Bernie Madoff," *Time*, July 2, 2016, https://time.com/4392286/elie-wiesel-dead-bernie-madoff/.

153 "Elie Wiesel says he can't forgive Bernie Madoff," CNN, February 27, 2009, http://www.cnn.com/2009/CRIME/02/27/wiesel.madoff/index.html.

154 Bethania Palma, "Did President Obama Order More Than 500 Drone Strikes?" Snopes, January 6, 2020, https://www.snopes.com/fact-check/obama-drone-strikes/.

155 Conor Friedersdorf, "Obama's Weak Defense of His Record on Drone Killings," *The Atlantic*, December 23, 2016, https://www.theatlantic.com/politics/archive/2016/12/president-obamas-weak-defense-of-his-record-on-drone-strikes/511454/.

156 S. E. Cupp, "Under Donald Trump, drone strikes far exceed Obama's numbers," *Chicago Sun Times*, May 8, 2019, https://chicago.suntimes.com/news/2019/5/8/18619206/under-donald-trump-drone-strikes-far-exceed-obama-s-numbers.

157 Paul Hofmann, "Dramatic Session," *New York Times*, November 14, 1974, https://www.nytimes.com/1974/11/14/archives/dramatic-session-plo-head-says-he-bears-olive-branch-and-guerrilla.html.

158 See, for example, "Abbas vows to continue paying terrorist salaries, even if just 'one penny is left,' Palestinian Media Watch, January 28, 2020, https://palwatch.org/page/17465.

159 Mitchell Bard, "Bombings in Argentina," Jewish Virtual Library, accessed December 26, 2020, https://www.jewishvirtuallibrary.org/terrorist-bombings-in-argentina.

160 "Powell's Doctrine, in Powell's Words," *Washington Post*, October 7, 2001, https://www.washingtonpost.com/archive/opinions/2001/10/07/powells-doctrine-in-powells-words/e8fd25c5-a97f-4550-8cbd-0588eb4a9d8e/.

161 Mitchell Bard, "The Mossad Hunt For Nazis," Jewish Virtual Library, accessed December 26, 2020, https://www.jewishvirtuallibrary.org/the-mossad-hunt-for-nazis.

162 "Targeted Killings of Terrorists," Jewish Virtual Library; "Munich Olympic Massacre: Background & Overview," Jewish Virtual Library accessed December 21, 2020, https://www.jewishvirtuallibrary.org/background-and-overview-munich-olympic-massacer.

163 "Israel Supreme Court decision on targeting terrorist operatives," Israel Ministry of Foreign Affairs, accessed December 26, 2020, https://mfa.gov.il/mfa/aboutisrael/state/law/pages/israel supreme court decision on targeting terrorist operatives 20-dec-2006.aspx.

164 *Jerusalem Post*, August 10, 2001.

165 Dore Gold, *Hatred's Kingdom*, (Washington, D.C.: Regnery, 2003), 181; Seymour M. "King's Ransom," *The New Yorker*, October 22, 2001, https://www.newyorker.com/magazine/2001/10/22/kings-ransom.

166 George P. Shultz, "What Must Be Done," Hoover Institution, April 30, 2002, https://www.hoover.org/research/what-must-be-done.

167 Shaun Tandon, "US senators seek to declare China 'genocide' against Uighurs," *Digital Journal*, October 27, 2020, http://www.digitaljournal.com/news/world/us-senators-seek-to-declare-china-genocide-against-uighurs/article/580209#ixzz6hBB6X5Io.

168 Gaia Pianigiani, "Pope Calls Uighurs 'Persecuted,' Prompting Pushback From China," *New York Times*, November 24, 2020, https://www.nytimes.com/2020/11/24/world/europe/pope-francis-uighurs-persecuted.html.

169 Aysha Khan, "US Muslim leaders call on China to end persecution of Uighurs," Religion News Service, February 8, 2019, https://religionnews.com/2019/02/08/us-muslim-leaders-call-on-china-to-end-persecution-of-uighurs/; Ephraim Mirvis, "As chief rabbi,

I can no longer remain silent about the plight of the Uighurs," *The Guardian*, December 15, 2020, https://www.theguardian.com/commentisfree/2020/dec/15/chief-rabbi-silent-plight-uighurs-atrocity-china.

[170] K.P. Vijayalakshmi, "What to expect from Biden's walk back to JCPOA with Iran," *Sunday Guardian*, April 10, 2021.

[171] "Iran nuclear deal: Key details," *BBC News*, June 11, 2019, https://www.bbc.com/news/world-middle-east-33521655.

[172] Josh Lederman, "Obama says Iran could easily get a nuke 13 years after proposed deal," *AP*, April 7, 2015, https://www.businessinsider.com/obama-says-iran-could-cut-nuke-time-to-near-zero-in-13-years-2015-4.

[173] "Netanyahu Claims Iran Nuclear Deal Based on Lies," *Haaretz*, April 30, 2018, https://www.haaretz.com/israel-news/full-text-netanyahu-s-reveals-iran-s-atomic-archive-in-speech-1.6045556.

[174] David Albright, Olli Heinonen, Frank Pabian, and Andrea Stricker, "Revealed: Emptying of the Iranian 'Atomic Warehouse' at Turquz Abad," Institute for Science and International Security, November 29, 2018, https://isis-online.org/isis-reports/detail/revealed-emptying-of-the-iranian-atomic-warehouse-at-turquz-abad/#ref9; Laurence Norman, "Iran's Enriched Uranium Stockpile Is 12 Times Nuclear Accord's Cap, U.N. Agency Says," *Wall Street Journal*, November 11, 2020, https://www.wsj.com/articles/irans-enriched-uranium-stockpile-is-more-than-10-times-nuclear-accords-cap-u-n-agency-says-11605120768.

[175] Arie Egozi, "Cyber Strike By Foreign Force Caused Iran Explosion: Israeli Experts," *Breaking Defense*, July 2, 2020, https://breakingdefense.com/2020/07/cyber-strike-by-foreign-force-causes-iran-explosion-israeli-experts/; "Israeli Analysts Say Incident At Nuclear Facility A Message To Iran," Radio Farda, July 5, 2020, https://en.radiofarda.com/a/israeli-analysts-say-incident-at-nuclear-facility-a-message-to-iran/30708367.html; Farnaz Fassihi, Richard Pérez-Peña and Ronen Bergman, "Iran Admits Serious Damage to Natanz Nuclear Site, Setting Back Program," *New York Times*, July 5, 2020, https://www.nytimes.com/2020/07/05/world/middleeast/iran-Natanz-nuclear-damage.html.

[176] Aresu Eqbali and Sune Engel Rasmussen, "Iran Vows to Avenge Slain Nuclear Scientist, Says It Won't Be Lured Into Conflict," *Wall Street Journal*, November 28, 2020, https://www.wsj.com/articles/iran-vows-to-avenge-killed-nuclear-scientist-but-says-it-wont-be-lured-to-conflict-11606584350?mod=world_major_2_pos1; Max Boot, "Targeted killings won't end the Iranian nuclear program — but could make a deal more likely," *Washington Post*, November 28, 2020, https://www.washingtonpost.com/opinions/2020/11/28/fakhrizadehs-killing-wont-end-iranian-nuclear-program-could-make-deal-more-likely/.

[177] Mitchell Bard, "Stopping Iran from getting nukes requires military force — here's what Biden can do," *Fox News*, December 11, 2020, https://www.foxnews.com/opinion/iran-nuclear-force-biden-mitchell-bard.

[178] Cal Thomas, "For secretary of state: John Bolton," *AP*, December 5, 2016, https://apnews.com/article/ea87977ad3064e00a9c7177c6e8958b8.

[179] "The Question of Palestine," United Nations, March 19, 1976, https://www.un.org/unispal/document/auto-insert-181580/.

[180] Warren Hoge, "Danforth Faults U.N. Assembly on Sudan Ruling," *New York Times*, November 24, 2004, https://www.nytimes.com/2004/11/24/world/africa/danforth-faults-un-assembly-on-sudan-ruling.html.

[181] "Secretary-General's message to the Third Session of the Human Rights Council," United Nations, November 29, 2006, https://www.un.org/sg/en/content/sg/statement/2006-11-29/secretary-generals-message-third-session-human-rights-council.

[182] "Panel Finds 'No Proof' Waldheim Committed War Crimes, but Says He Lied About His War Record," *JTA*, February 9, 1988, https://www.jta.org/1988/02/09/archive/

panel-finds-no-proof-waldheim-committed-war-crimes-but-says-he-lied-about-his-war-record.

[183] Susan Sontag, "Why Are We in Kosovo?" *New York Times*, May 2, 1999, https://www.nytimes.com/1999/05/02/magazine/why-are-we-in-kosovo.html.

[184] Ibid.

[185] Richard Norton-Taylor, "Jaw-jaw is better than war-war," *The Guardian*, September 15, 2015, https://www.theguardian.com/news/defence-and-security-blog/2015/sep/10/jaw-jaw-is-better-than-war-war.

[186] Winston Churchill, *Great Contemporaries: Churchill Reflects on FDR, Hitler, Kipling, Chaplin, Balfour, and Other Giants of His Age*, (New York: Rosetta Books, 2016).

[187] Winston Churchill, "Blood, Toil, Tears and Sweat," International Churchill Society, May 13, 1940, https://winstonchurchill.org/resources/speeches/1940-the-finest-hour/blood-toil-tears-and-sweat-2/.

[188] Jeffrey Goldberg, "A Little Learning," *The New Yorker*, May 9, 2005, https://www.newyorker.com/magazine/2005/05/09/a-little-learning-2.

[189] Micah Zenko, "Obama's Final Drone Strike Data," *Council on Foreign Relations*, January 20, 2017, https://www.cfr.org/blog/obamas-final-drone-strike-data.

[190] Colin Powell, *My American Journey*, (New York: Random House, 1995), 434; Interview with Colin Powell, CNN, June 27, 1993.

[191] "Convention on the Prevention and Punishment of the Crime of Genocide," UN, December 9, 1948, https://www.un.org/en/genocideprevention/documents/atrocity-crimes/Doc.1_Convention on the Prevention and Punishment of the Crime of Genocide.pdf.

[192] "Executive Order on Blocking Property Of Certain Persons Associated With The International Criminal Court," The White House, June 11, 2020.

[193] Donald J. Trump, "Executive Order 13928-Blocking Property of Certain Persons Associated With the International Criminal Court," *Federal Register*, vol. 85, no. 115, June 15, 2020, https://home.treasury.gov/system/files/126/13928.pdf.

[194] "Executive Order on the Termination of Emergency With Respect to the International Criminal Court," The White House, April 1, 2021, https://www.whitehouse.gov/briefing-room/presidential-actions/2021/04/01/executive-order-on-the-termination-of-emergency-with-respect-to-the-international-criminal-court/.

[195] "The International Criminal Court's Lack Of Jurisdiction Over The So-called 'Situation In Palestine.' Office of the Attorney General, State of Israel, December 20, 2019, https://www.jewishvirtuallibrary.org/jsource/UN/ICC_no_jurisdiction.pdf.

[196] Paul Pillar, "Moving Beyond Good and Evil in the Middle East," *The New Republic*, July 20, 2020, https://newrepublic.com/article/158570/moving-beyond-good-evil-middle-east.

[197] "United Nations: Voting Coincidence with the United States," Jewish Virtual Library, accessed May 30, 2021, https://www.jewishvirtuallibrary.org/united-nations-member-states-voting-records.

[198] Adam Kirsch, "Interpreter of Malice," *Foreign Policy*, March 8, 2016, https://foreignpolicy.com/2016/03/08/interpreter-of-malice-refugees-colonization-political-violence/.

[199] Adam Shatz, "The Doctor Prescribed Violence," *New York Times*, September 2, 2001, https://www.nytimes.com/2001/09/02/books/the-doctor-prescribed-violence.html.

[200] Ronn Blitzer, "Booker opens door to meeting with Farrakhan after blasting Biden for 'hurtful' comments on bigots," *Fox News*, June 25, 2019, https://www.foxnews.com/politics/booker-farrakhan-after-blasting-biden-for-hurtful-comments.

[201] Philip Bump, "'They like me very much': Why Trump's QAnon comments are dangerous," *Washington Post*, August 19, 2020, https://www.washingtonpost.com/politics/2020/08/19/trump-gives-more-oxygen-dangerous-qanon-movement-they-like-me-very-much/.

[202] U.S. House of Representatives, H.Res.183, 116th Congress, Congress.gov, March 7, 2019, https://www.congress.gov/bill/116th-congress/house-resolution/183/text.

[203] Ron Kampeas, "Ilhan Omar snags Pelosi endorsement, but falls behind in fundraising,"

JTA, July 15, 2020, https://www.timesofisrael.com/ilhan-omar-snags-pelosi-endorse-ment-but-falls-behind-in-fundraising/; Rachael Bade and David Weigel, "Pelosi endors-es Rep. Tlaib in primary fight, moves to help members of the 'Squad,'" *Washington Post*, July 29, 2020, https://www.washingtonpost.com/powerpost/pelosi-endorses-rep-tlaib-in-primary-fight-moves-to-help-members-of-the-squad/2020/07/29/028b5692-d1c6-11ea-9038-af089b63ac21_story.html.

204 Stephen Collinson, "Trump shocks with racist new ad days before midterms," CNN, November 1, 2018, https://www.cnn.com/2018/10/31/politics/donald-trump-immigra-tion-paul-ryan-midterms/index.html.

205 David Frum, "Why Obama Won't Talk About Islamic Terrorism," *The Atlantic*, February 16, 2015, https://www.theatlantic.com/politics/archive/2015/02/why-obama-wont-talk-about-islamic-terrorism/385539/; Bill Gertz, "Orlando Attack Is a Failure of Obama's 'Politically Correct' Policy, Analysts Say," *Washington Free Beacon*, June 14, 2016, https://freebeacon.com/national-security/orlando-attack-failure-obamas-political-ly-correct-policy-analysts-say/.

206 Pascal Bruckner, "The invention of Islamophobia," signandsight.com, March 1, 2011, http://www.signandsight.com/features/2123.html.

207 James Taranto, "Obama's Crusades," *Wall Street Journal*, February 6, 2015, https://www.wsj.com/articles/obamas-crusades-1423256805.

208 The 2007 Irving Kristol Lecture by Bernard Lewis, AEI, March 7, 2007, https://www.aei.org/research-products/speech/the-2007-irving-kristol-lecture-by-bernard-lewis/.

209 Reuters, "Joe Biden recognizes 1915 massacres as Armenian Genocide," *The Jerusa-lem Post*, April 24, 2021, https://www.jpost.com/breaking-news/biden-says-1915-mas-sacres-of-armenians-constitute-genocide-666227.

210 Seth J. Frantzman, "Biden ends decades of US appeasement of Turkey, recognizes genocide – analysis," *The Jerusalem Post*, April 25, 2021, https://www.jpost.com/inter-national/biden-ends-decades-of-us-appeasement-of-turkey-recognizes-genocide-analy-sis-666243.

211 Choe Sang-Hun, "In Hail of Bullets and Fire, North Korea Killed Official Who Wanted Reform," *New York Times*, March 12, 2016, https://www.nytimes.com/2016/03/13/world/asia/north-korea-executions-jang-song-thaek.html.

212 Peter Baker and Choe Sang-Hun, "Trump Threatens 'Fire and Fury' Against North Korea if It Endangers U.S.," *New York Times*, August 8, 2017, https://www.nytimes.com/2017/08/08/world/asia/north-korea-un-sanctions-nuclear-missile-united-nations.html.

213 Meghan Keneally, "From 'fire and fury' to 'rocket man,' the various barbs traded between Trump and Kim Jong Un," *ABC News*, June 12, 2018, https://abcnews.go.com/International/fire-fury-rocket-man-barbs-traded-trump-kim/story?id=53634996.

214 Jamie Gangel and Jeremy Herb, "'A magical force': New Trump-Kim letters provide window into their 'special friendship,'" CNN, September 9, 2020, https://www.cnn.com/2020/09/09/politics/kim-jong-un-trump-letters-rage-book/index.html.

215 Michael E. O'Hanlon, "What Donald Trump should have done with North Korea – and what the next president should do," Brookings Institution, September 3, 2020, https://www.brookings.edu/blog/order-from-chaos/2020/09/03/what-donald-trump-should-have-done-with-north-korea-and-what-the-next-president-should-do/.

216 Noah Bierman, "North Korea was Trump's chief foreign policy boast, but things got worse on his watch," *Los Angeles Times*, August 24, 2020, https://www.latimes.com/politics/story/2020-08-24/north-korea-trump-foreign-policy.

217 Ken Dilanian, "From 'beautiful letters' to 'a dark nightmare': How Trump's North Korea gamble went bust," *NBC News*, June 13, 2020, https://www.nbcnews.com/news/north-korea/beautiful-letters-dark-nightmare-how-trump-s-north-korea-gam-ble-n1230866.

218 Ibid.

[219] "Trump-Kim Summit: Leaders Have Dinner in Vietnam," *New York Times*, February 26, 2019; Roberta Rampton, ""We fell in love:' Trump swoons over letters from North Korea's Kim," *Reuters*, September 30, 2018.

[220] Jamie Gangel and Jeremy Herb, "'A magical force': New Trump-Kim letters provide window into their 'special friendship,'" CNN, September 9, 2020, https://www.cnn.com/2020/09/09/politics/kim-jong-un-trump-letters-rage-book/index.html.

[221] Bob Woodward, *Rage*, (New York: Simon & Schuster, 2020), 181.

[222] Noah Bierman, "North Korea was Trump's chief foreign policy boast, but things got worse on his watch," *Los Angeles Times*, August 24, 2020, https://www.latimes.com/politics/story/2020-08-24/north-korea-trump-foreign-policy.

[223] Julie Bosman and Kevin Williams, "Trump Faces Fury After Saying He Believes North Korean Leader on Student's Death," *New York Times*, March 1, 2019, https://www.nytimes.com/2019/03/01/us/trump-otto-warmbier-north-korea.html.

[224] Philip Rucker, Ashley Parker and Josh Dawsey, "After days of dire threats, Trump's tone shifts in the wake of Iran's retaliation," *Washington Post*, January 7, 2020, https://www.washingtonpost.com/politics/after-days-of-dire-threats-trumps-tone-shifts-in-the-wake-of-irans-retaliation/2020/01/07/2a2ac35a-31c0-11ea-9313-6cba89b1b9fb_story.html.

[225] Michael McFaul, "A Russian dissident is fighting for his life. Where is the U.S.?" *Washington Post*, August 20, 2020, https://www.washingtonpost.com/opinions/a-russian-dissident-is-fighting-for-his-life-where-is-the-us/2020/08/20/2acf79ca-e31f-11ea-8181-606e603bb1c4_story.html.

[226] Ibid.

[227] "Nuclear Proliferation in the Middle East," Jewish Virtual Library, accessed December 23, 2020, https://www.jewishvirtuallibrary.org/nuclear-proliferation-in-the-middle-east.

[228] Mujib Mashal, "How the Taliban Outlasted a Superpower: Tenacity and Carnage," *New York Times*, May 26, 2020, https://www.nytimes.com/2020/05/26/world/asia/taliban-afghanistan-war.html.

[229] Mujib Mashal, "Taliban and U.S. Strike Deal to Withdraw American Troops From Afghanistan," *New York Times*, February 29, 2020, https://www.nytimes.com/2020/02/29/world/asia/us-taliban-deal.html.

[230] Michael McFaul, "A Russian dissident is fighting for his life. Where is the U.S.?" *Washington Post*, August 20, 2020, https://www.washingtonpost.com/opinions/a-russian-dissident-is-fighting-for-his-life-where-is-the-us/2020/08/20/2acf79ca-e31f-11ea-8181-606e603bb1c4_story.html.

[231] Jessica Durando, "15 of Nelson Mandela's best quotes," *USA Today*, December 5, 2013, https://www.usatoday.com/story/news/nation-now/2013/12/05/nelson-mandela-quotes/3775255/.

ACKNOWLEDGMENTS

I want to first and foremost thank my dear friend and partner in much of what I write on politics, values, and human rights, Mitchell Bard, a great scholar and deeply good and moral man. Mitchell was instrumental in much of the facts presented here as it pertains to genocides, the holocaust, and global geopolitics and edited and helped me formulate the manuscript for this book. I am so grateful to him for our ongoing collaboration and the incisive ideas and commentary he brings to my work.

I also want to thank my son Mendy, a brilliant young scholar and historian, who did a great deal of the research for this book and edited it in its early stages. It is a special privilege for a father to have a son who is so vastly knowledgeable and who is so lovingly dedicated to his father's ideals and work. Mendy, as you know, I always call you "Golden Son," and you radiate brilliance and goodness always.

The World Values Network, which I head, is funded by many individuals who love righteousness and hate evil. I thank them all for their ongoing support.

Adam Bellow, the head of the Wicked Son imprint, is a fundamentally good and brilliant man, an expert publisher, and a dear friend. Thank you, Adam, for believing in my ideas and work.

My children and grandchildren are the loves of my life, my inspiration, and my guiding lights. I thank them for making me a better person each and every day.

My mother, Eleanor Paul, always instilled within me a deep moral outlook on life, even as she raised five children alone as a single mother. I love you Mom. You're my hero.

My wife Debbie is my soulmate and partner in all my work. Coming from a Holocaust survivor family, she understands how important it is to hate evil and fight for justice. She inspires me to do the same every day of my life.

May 2021.

ABOUT THE AUTHOR

Rabbi Shmuley Boteach is one of the world's most respected voices on values and spirituality. An international bestselling author of thirty-three books and founder of the World Values Network, he also hosted *The Rabbi Shmuley Show* on the Oprah and Friends Radio Network and the award-winning *Shalom in the Home* on TLC. He won the *London Times* "Preacher of the Year Award" at the millennium and the American Jewish Press Association's Highest Award for Excellence in Commentary. Rabbi Shmuley lives with his Australian wife Debbie in Englewood, New Jersey. They are the parents of nine children.